UNDERSTANDING SWAPS

WILEY FINANCE EDITIONS

UNDERSTANDING SWAPS

John F. Marshall
St. John's University, New York
Kenneth R. Kapner
Hongkong and Shanghai
Banking Corporation, Limited

John Wiley & Sons, Inc.

New York • Chichester • Brisbane • Toronto • Singapore

This book is dedicated to those persons, beginning with Harry M. Markowitz and Merton H. Miller, whose work transformed finance from a descriptive discipline to an analytical science.

This text is printed on acid-free paper.
Copyright © 1993 by John Wiley & Sons, Inc.

Portions of this book have been previously published under the titles *Understanding Swaps,* South-Western, 1989, and *The Swaps Market, Second Edition,* Kolb Publishing, 1993.

This publication is designed to provide accurate and authoritative information in regard to the subject matter covered. It is sold with the understanding that the publisher is not engaged in rendering legal, accounting, or other professional services. If legal advice or other expert assistance is required, the services of a competent professional person should be sought. FROM A DECLARATION OF PRINCIPLES JOINTLY ADOPTED BY A COMMITTEE OF THE AMERICAN BAR ASSOCIATION AND A COMMITTEE OF PUBLISHERS.

Library of Congress Cataloging-in-Publication Data:

Marshall, John F. (John Francis), 1952–
    Understanding swaps / John F. Marshall, Kenneth R. Kapner.
        p.   cm. — (Wiley finance editions)
    Includes bibliographical references and index.
    ISBN 0-471-30827-7
    I. Swaps (Finance) I. Kapner, Kenneth R.   II. Title.
III. Series.
    HG6024.A3M373   1994
332.4′5—dc20   93-23846

Printed in the United States of America

10 9 8 7 6 5 4

Foreword

The swaps markets emerged in the late 1970s with the introduction of the first currency swaps. These products were a relatively simple modification of preexisting structures called back-to-back loans which had been developed as a means to circumvent controls on capital flows. Although a rather modest alteration of the earlier back-to-back loan structure, by eliminating principal risk, the swap structure was significantly superior and led to a flood of innovative financial products that, collectively, constitute the over-the-counter derivative products markets.

Currency swaps were followed almost immediately by interest rate swaps. Some years later, the concept was extended to develop commodity swaps and, still later, equity swaps. Most recently, innovative thinkers have suggested even more novel extensions of the basic swap model to hedge risks ranging from insurance to business cycles.

Swaps have emerged as a powerful tool to reduce financing costs, to hedge price risks, to better manage seasonal cash flows, to synthesize other instruments, to take advantage of all variety of market imperfections, and much more. The market has exploded in size and, today, the collective notional principals of all swap products is measured in trillions of dollars.

Despite the phenomenal growth of the swaps markets, the uses and potential of the swaps product has only just begun to be understood by potential users. Universities are only now beginning to focus attention on these activities and to incorporate discussion of them in their curricula. Unfortunately, for those of us who have already finished our university study, clearly written and comprehensive information is still hard to come by. In this book, Jack Marshall and Ken Kapner, both well known for their many articles and earlier books on swaps and related derivatives, have provided a very comprehensive primer on the swaps markets.

One needs no previous experience with swaps or other derivatives to understand and to follow this book. The authors begin by placing swaps in a historical context, discussing the foundation principles on which the business rests, and examining the players. They then provide a nice generic swap structure before moving on to a discussion of specific types of swaps. This is followed by discussion of interest rate swaps, currency swaps, commodity swaps and equity swaps. They describe how swaps can be combined with cash market positions and with other derivatives to engineer very sophisticated, but very workable, solutions to complex problems. The authors then explore swap pricing arithmetic and the management of a swap portfolio. Finally, Jack and Ken take a unique look forward at macroeconomic swaps—a product that may, arguably, be the next major development in the derivatives markets.

The authors' experience in the swaps markets—as theorists, as practitioners, and as innovators of new swaps products—is clearly evident in this book. It is well written, well organized, and pedagogically complete. The authors have included end-of-chapter questions for those readers who might like to test their knowledge (solutions are at the end of the book).

Take the time to work through the examples that the authors provide. Draw the boxes, the arrows, and the cash flows. If you do, you will see that seemingly complex swap structures can be easily understood by decomposing them into their elemental components.

Joseph P. Bauman
Chairman
International Swaps and Derivatives Association
(*ISDA*)

Preface

No other markets have ever grown or evolved as rapidly as have the swaps markets. This is a testament to the efficacy and flexibility of the instrument, the resourcefulness and the professionalism of the new breed of financial engineer, and the increased appreciation by financial managers of the importance of risk management in a volatile interest rate, exchange rate, commodity price, and equity return environment. The swaps markets have proven very adaptable. The original swap products, now known as "plain vanilla" swaps, have given way to hundreds of variants designed to serve very special purposes. Swaps are now used by industrial corporations, financial corporations, thrifts, banks, insurance companies, world organizations, and sovereign governments. They are used to reduce the cost of capital, manage risks, exploit economies of scale, arbitrage the world's capital markets, enter new markets, and to create synthetic instruments. New users, new uses, and new swap variants emerge almost daily. Clearly, it is difficult to overstate the importance of the swaps markets to modern finance.

More than any other modern markets, the swaps markets are dependent upon the existence and liquidity of other markets. These other markets include the market for corporate debt, the market for U.S. Treasury debt, the futures and options markets, the cash markets, and the forward markets. It is not surprising then that the explosive growth in swap volume has been accompanied by enormous growth in trading volumes in these other markets. Today, if one wants to understand these other markets, one cannot ignore the impact of the swaps market—both as substitutes for other instruments and as complements to them.

This is our fourth book on swaps and our second for the professional market (as opposed to the academic market). Our first book for the professional market was published in 1990 by the New York Institute of Finance and is called *The Swaps Handbook: Swaps and Related Risk Management Instruments*. That book was well received by the swaps trade. With its annual supplements, *The Swaps Handbook* has grown to about 1,350 pages—far longer and with much more detail than that required by a beginner. With this book, we hope to make the swaps markets and the swaps products more accessible to a wider audience. Nevertheless, when you have finished with this "primer" you might want to consider delving into *The Swaps Handbook*.

Much has changed since we wrote our first book on swaps in 1987: Swap pricing has become much more rigorous, swap spreads have narrowed considerably, commodity swaps were granted safe harbor by the CFTC, equity swaps were introduced, and regulation governing the markets has intensified. Also, microhedging by swap dealers has given way to macrohedging, mark–to–market accounting has become standard practice, and dealers have come to rely on derived zero coupon swap yield curves as their primary tool for repricing and hedging their swap books. Financial engineers outside the swaps trade have become considerably more sophisticated and knowledgeable. They have learned to use swaps effectively and to combine swaps with 1. other swaps, 2. other derivative instruments, and 3. nonderivative instruments. The result of all this engineering is a well–understood ability to solve complex problems simply and efficiently. This book reflects these developments.

While swap structures are complex, they are founded on relatively simple concepts. The complexity can actually be broken down into a series of elemental components. How these individual components are combined determines the end product. By building up from the bottom, we believe that the swap product can be made understandable—even to a novice.

The reader of this book is expected to have a reasonable grounding in financial theory. In particular, the reader should be familiar with present value arithmetic and standard statistical concepts associated with measuring risk and return in an uncertain world.

We do not want to leave the mistaken impression that swaps are easy. They are not. This is not a book to be read lightly. If the book is to serve the purpose for which it is intended, the reader must work his or her way through it. Take paper and pen and run through each example we use. Try out each computation before proceeding. Take the time to work some of the end–of–chapter problems and answer the questions. (We have provided solutions at the end of the text.) For those interested in additional literature on any specific topic covered in this text, we have provided a Reference and Suggested Reading section at the close of each chapter. To help the reader pick up the vernacular of the trade, we have bold-faced important terms the first time they appear or when they are first defined. (A glossary is provided at the end for easy reference.)

In writing this book, we have benefited more than we can possibly say from both industry practitioners and academic reviewers who have commented on various drafts of the manuscript. These include Ravi Mehra of Banco Santander, Steve Katz of Marine Midland Bank, and Craig Messenger of Shearson Lehman, Inc. Our special thanks go to Bob Schwartz of Mitsubishi Capital Market Services, Inc. Bob's readings of the several drafts of the manuscript and his detailed comments and suggestions proved invaluable. Additionally, much of the content of this text is built on, or derived from, various collaborative works with other coauthors. In all cases, our coauthors allowed us to adapt our earlier joint works to this text format. We would like to take this moment to offer them our special thanks. More pointedly, we wish to share credit for the chapters involved. So we say thank you to Vipul K. Bansal of St. John's University (Chapters 2, 6, 7, 9), James L. Bicksler of Rutgers University (Chapter 7), Andrew H. Chen of Southern Methodist University (Chapter 7), M. E. Ellis of St. John's University (Chapter 7), Anthony F. Herbst of the University of Texas (Chapter 9), Eric H. Sorensen of Salomon Brothers, Inc. (Chapter 5), Alan L. Tucker of Temple University (Chapters 5, 9), and Robert P. Yuyuenyongwatana of St. John's University (Chapter 9 and solutions to end-of-chapter questions). We are also indebted to the International Swaps and Derivatives Association, which accommodated all our requests for information, and to its officers and directors, some of whom read and commented upon portions of the manuscript. Finally, we would like to thank several persons who have asked to remain anonymous. Their comments were no less valuable. Any errors that may remain are, of course, entirely our own.

Much of the analytical work in this text was facilitated by the software package *A-Pack: An Analytical Package for Business*, published by MicroApplications (516-821-9355). This DOS-based package is inexpensive and loaded with easy-to-use analytical tools. We suggest the reader consider it (under $300).

As a final note, the authors invite the reader to consider joining the International Association of Financial Engineers. The Association is a nonprofit professional membership association that seeks to network persons interested in the practice or study of financial engineering. The Association publishes a quarterly journal, *The Journal of Financial Engineering*, sponsors regional dinner meetings and periodic conferences, funds research, operates a placement service, and is building publication and data libraries to assist researchers. Persons interested in membership should contact the Association's office at: the International Association of Financial Engineers, St. John's University, Jamaica, New York 11439 (phone: 718–990–6161, extension 7381).

Jack Marshall   Ken Kapner
Graduate School of Business   The Hongkong and Shanghai
St. John's University, New York   Banking Corporation, Limited

About the Authors

John F. Marshall is Professor of Finance in the Graduate School of Business at St. John's University, New York, where he teaches courses in investment finance, corporate finance, and derivative products. He holds the M.B.A., M.A., and Ph.D. degrees. Dr. Marshall is also Senior Partner with Marshall & Associates, a consulting firm that provides trust services, training programs, and financial engineering expertise. Dr. Marshall is also the Executive Director of the International Association of Financial Engineers. He has written extensively on futures, options, and swaps as risk management tools, and on financial engineering more generally. His publications include thirteen books and dozens of articles and book chapters. He developed a number of widely used swap variants and he participated in the development of the macroeconomic swap concept.

Kenneth R. Kapner is Treasury Training Manager for The Hongkong and Shanghai Banking Corporation Limited. He is responsible for training treasury managers in support of the bank's global operations. Prior to this position, Mr. Kapner was Vice President for Domestic Treasury for the same firm. He holds an M.B.A. degree. Mr. Kapner has extensive trading experience in both the foreign exchange and money markets and was, for many years, a frequent user of the swap product for hedging his bank's positions. He has written extensively on the subject of swap finance and lectures regularly on swap structures and swap uses. He is coauthor of *The Swaps Handbook* and co-editor of the *Swaps Handbook Supplements.* Mr. Kapner serves on the advisory board of the International Association of Financial Engineers.

Comments should be addressed to the authors in care of:

John F. Marshall, Ph.D.
Graduate School of Business
St. John's University, New York
Jamaica, NY 11439
(516) 689-2768 (voice)
(516) 689-3527 (fax)

Contents

1

An Overview and Brief History of the Swaps Markets

1.1 OVERVIEW

No other market in financial history has grown as rapidly or evolved as quickly as have the swaps markets. From their initial inception in 1979, notional principal outstandings have grown from virtually nothing to over five trillion dollars. Annual growth rates have exceeded 30 percent every year and have often exceeded 100 percent. This is a testament to the efficacy and flexibility of the instruments, the resourcefulness and the professionalism of the new breed of financial engineer, and the increased appreciation by financial managers of the importance of financial risk management in a volatile interest rate, exchange rate, commodity–price, and equity–return environment. Swaps are one of the most important classes of what have come to be known as **derivative instruments**.[1] Other classes of derivative instruments include futures, listed options, forwards, OTC options, and hybrid securities.

Swaps are now used by industrial corporations, financial corporations, thrifts, banks, insurance companies, pension funds, world organizations, and sovereign governments. They compete with other risk management

1

tools (such as futures, forwards, and options) but, at the same time, they complement these other instruments. In addition to their value as risk management tools, swaps are also very useful for reducing the cost of finance, for smoothing seasonal cash flows, for arbitraging the yield curve, for creating synthetic instruments, for entering new markets, and for exploiting economies of scale, to name just a few.

In this book, we will look at the four basic types of swaps: interest rate swaps, currency swaps, commodity swaps, and equity swaps. We will examine the most basic form of each type. The basic forms are called **plain vanilla** or **generic** swaps. We will also look at some of the many variants of the plain vanilla forms and at the uses for each. We will also look at how swaps are priced, how markets are made by swap dealers and brokers, and how swap dealers manage their swap portfolios, called **swap books**. We will also see how complex financial structures can be built by using a number of different swaps (and related instruments) as building blocks. Finally, we will look at a potentially important new variety of swaps, called macroeconomic swaps, that are just now being introduced.

This book is divided into nine chapters. The remainder of this chapter examines the origins of the swaps markets, makes some observations about the size of the markets, introduces some of the most important uses for swaps, and introduces the players. Chapter 2 provides a generalized swaps model. This is a simple model that accurately describes the plain vanilla form of any swap whether it be an interest rate, a currency, a commodity, an equity, or a macroeconomic swap. If you understand this generalized form, you are already a long way toward understanding all swaps. Chapters 3 and 4 examine interest rate swaps and currency swaps, respectively. We examine the specifics of their structure, their uses, and a number of variant forms. Chapter 5 does the same for commodity and equity swaps—the most recent forms to be introduced. Chapter 6 demonstrates how elaborate structures are built to solve complex problems by combining swaps and by combining swaps with other instruments. Chapter 7 considers the pricing of swaps with the focus on the pricing of interest rate swaps. Chapter 8 examines a number of important considerations for swap dealers and focuses attention on the management of a swap portfolio. The closing chapter, Chapter 9, introduces a new and potentially important form of swap that has an altogether different purpose from swaps that came before. These are **macroeconomic** swaps, which were first proposed in 1991 by one of the authors of this book.

As we go through this book, you will see that each time an important term is introduced, it is highlighted and defined. Once terms have been defined, we will use them in subsequent discussion. Most readers will already have some background in other derivative products, particularly futures and options. For this reason, we were tempted to dispense with any discussion of these latter instruments. However, because it is difficult to fully appreciate swaps without some grounding in futures and options, we have placed a short section on futures and a short section on options at the end of this chapter.

1.2 THE SWAP PRODUCT DEFINED

A definition would be a useful place to begin. A **swap** is a contractual agreement evidenced by a single document in which two parties, called **counterparties**, agree to make periodic payments to each other. Contained in the swap agreement is a specification of the currencies to be exchanged (which may or may not be the same), the rate of interest applicable to each (which may be fixed or floating), the timetable by which the payments are to be made, and any other provisions bearing on the relationship between the parties.

The most common type of swap is a **fixed–for–floating** rate swap. In this type of swap, the first counterparty agrees to make fixed–rate payments to the second counterparty. In return, the second counterparty agrees to make floating–rate payments to the first counterparty. These two payments are called the **legs** or **sides** of the swap. The fixed rate is called the **swap coupon**. The payments are calculated on the basis of hypothetical quantities of underlying assets called **notionals.**[2] When the notionals take the form of sums of money, they are called **notional principals**. Notional principals are ordinarily not exchanged. Further, if the counterparties' payments to each other are to be made at the same time and in the same currency, then only the **interest differential** between the two counterparties' respective payments needs to be exchanged. Some variants of this basic structure include zero coupon–for–fixed and floating–for–floating swaps. A simple schematic of the cash flows between swap counterparties is depicted in Figure 1.1.

Swap contracts are tailor–made to meet the needs of the individual counterparties. As such, they are created with the aid of swap specialists who serve either or both the roles of broker and market maker. As tailor–

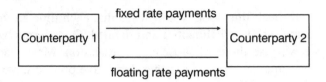

FIGURE 1.1   Interest Flows on a Rate Swap

made contracts, swaps trade in an **over–the–counter** (OTC) type environment, as opposed to the organized exchanges on which highly standardized contracts like futures and listed options trade.

1.3 THE ORIGINS OF THE SWAPS MARKETS

An **exchange rate** (foreign exchange rate) is the number of units of one currency that can be purchased for one unit of another currency. These rates became extremely volatile in the early 1970s following the collapse of the **Bretton Woods Agreement**.[3] The dramatic increase in exchange rate volatility created an ideal environment for a swaplike instrument that could be used by multinationals to hedge long–term foreign exchange exposures. Nevertheless, the first swaps were created for an altogether different purpose and only later were the cost–reducing and risk–management uses of these instruments recognized.

Swaps were a natural extension of **parallel** and **back–to–back loans** that originated in the United Kingdom as a means of circumventing foreign–exchange controls, which were intended to prevent an outflow of British capital.[4] Throughout the 1970s, the British Government imposed taxes on foreign–exchange transactions involving its own currency. The intent was to make the outflow of capital more expensive in the belief that this would encourage domestic investment by making foreign investment less attractive. The parallel loan became a widely accepted vehicle by which these taxes could be avoided. The back–to–back loan was a simple modification of the parallel loan and the currency swap was a simple extension of the back–to–back loan.

Back–to–back loans involve two corporations domiciled in two different countries. One firm agrees to borrow funds in its domestic market and then to lend those borrowed funds to the other firm. The second firm, in return, borrows funds in its domestic market and then lends those funds to the first firm. By this simple arrangement, each firm is able to access the capital markets in the foreign country without any exchanges of currencies in the foreign exchange (FOREX) markets. Parallel loans work similarly, but involve four firms.

There are two problems with back–to–back and parallel loans that limit their usefulness as financing tools. First, a party with a use for this type of financing must locate another party having mirror image financing requirements—called **matched needs**. These requirements include the loan principal, the type of interest to be applied (fixed or floating), the frequency of the coupon payments, and the term of the loan. The **search costs** associated with finding such a party can be considerable—assuming it is even possible. Second, both the parallel and back–to–back loans are actually two loans involving two separate loan agreements that exist independently of one another. Thus, if the first firm defaults on its obligations to the second, the second firm is not relieved of its obligations to the first. To avoid this problem, a separate agreement, defining **rights of set–off**, must be drafted. If this agreement is not registered, the outcome described above can still occur. On the other hand, registration itself can cause problems.[5]

The cash flows of the early currency swaps were identical to those associated with back–to–back loans. For this reason, these early currency swaps were often called **exchanges of borrowings**. However, unlike the two loan agreements that characterize the back–to–back and parallel loans, the swap involves a single agreement. The agreement details all cash flows and provides for the release of the first counterparty from its obligations to the second if the second counterparty should default on its obligations to the first. Thus, swaps provide the solution to the rights of set–off problem. Importantly, the release of a counterparty from its obligations following the default of the other counterparty does not prevent the nondefaulting counterparty from seeking damages from the defaulting counterparty.

The other problem associated with back–to–back and parallel loans—finding a party with matched financing requirements—was solved through the intervention of swap brokers and market makers who saw the potential of this new financing technique. We will discuss these players shortly.

The first currency swap is believed to have been written in London in 1979. However, the landmark currency swap, which brought the developing currency swap market from labor pains to actual birth, involved the World Bank and IBM as counterparties.[6] The swap was put together by Salomon Brothers, and it allowed the World Bank to obtain Swiss francs and deutschemarks to finance its operations in Switzerland and West Germany without having to tap the Swiss and West German capital markets directly. The stature of the parties involved gave long–term credibility to currency swaps. Although swaps originated from an effort to circumvent foreign–exchange controls, it wasn't long before the cost-reducing benefits of swap finance and the risk–management uses for swaps were recognized. The market grew rapidly thereafter.

It was a short step from currency swaps to interest rate swaps. After all, if swaps could be used to convert one type of currency obligation to another at the applicable interest rate on each currency, then why couldn't a similar type of contract be used to convert one type of borrowing (fixed rate) to another (floating rate)? The first interest rate swap is believed to have been put together in London in 1981.[7] The interest rate swap product was introduced in the United States shortly thereafter when, in 1982, the Student Loan Marketing Association (Sallie Mae) executed a fixed–for–floating interest rate swap.[8]

The swap concept was extended in 1986 when The Chase Manhattan Bank introduced the commodity swap. Immediately after the introduction of commodity swaps, however, the Commodity Futures Trading Commission (CFTC) questioned the contracts' legality. The result was to shift commodity swap activity overseas but, even so, commodity swap activity remained minimal. In 1989 the CFTC reversed itself and granted the contracts safe harbor. Commodity swap activity grew rapidly thereafter. Also in 1989, Bankers Trust introduced the first reported equity swap. It was an immediate success for its originator and was soon copied. Transactional volumes and outstanding notionals in equity swaps continue to grow rapidly.

Figure 1.2 depicts the combined outstanding notionals for interest rate and currency swaps in all currencies after conversion to their U.S. dollar equivalents. The currency swap notionals have been divided by two to avoid double counting. The values for 1981 through 1986 are our own composites developed from various sources.[9] The values for 1987 through 1991 were provided by the International Swap Dealers Association (ISDA). Figures 1.3 and 1.4 depict notional transactional volumes for interest rate swaps and currency swaps, respectively, for the years 1987 through 1991. Again, data for 1987 through 1991 were provided by the ISDA.

**Notional
Principal**

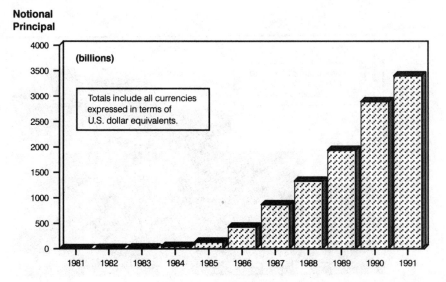

FIGURE 1.2 Combined Notionals Outstanding Interest Rate and Currency Swaps (Source: 1981–1986 Authors' estimates; 1987–1991 International Swap Dealers Association)

**Notional
Principal**

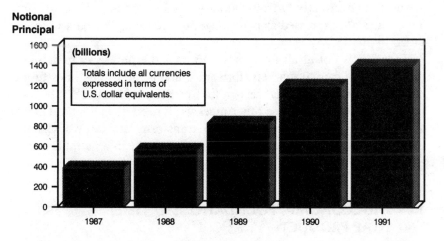

FIGURE 1.3 Interest Rate Swaps Notional Principal Year–by–Year Transactional Volumes (Source: International Swap Dealers Association)

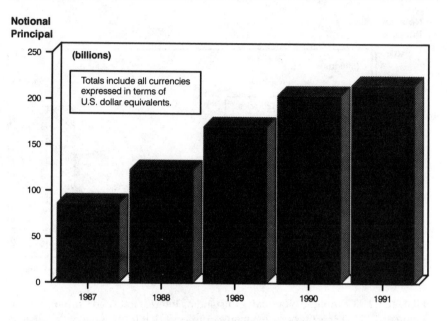

FIGURE 1.4 Currency Swaps Notional Principal Year–by–Year Transactional Volumes (Source: International Swap Dealers Association)

Figures 1.5 and 1.6 provide recent comparative values for the currency composition of the transactional notionals for interest rate and currency swaps and cover activity from January 1, 1991, through June 30, 1991. The values are expressed as percentages of the total. The data were provided by the ISDA.

Today, it is not at all uncommon to hear the phrase **swap driven** in discussions of capital markets, forward markets, and sometimes futures markets. This is an explicit recognition of the profound effect the swap products have had on these other markets. Indeed, the advent of swaps, as much as anything else, helped to transform the world's segmented capital markets into a single, truly integrated, international capital market.

1.4   THE ECONOMIC FOUNDATIONS OF THE SWAP PRODUCT

The viability of swap finance rests on a number of important economic principles. The two most often cited of these are the principle of com-

Percent of Global Total

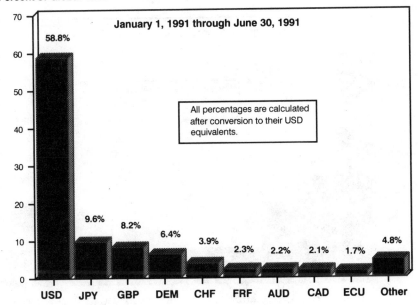

FIGURE 1.5 Composition of Transactional Volumes for Interest Rates Swaps *(by currency)* (Source: International Swap Dealers Association)

parative advantage and the principle of offsetting risks. The **principle of comparative advantage** was long ago identified as the theoretical underpinning of international trade.[10] This principle is most easily illustrated in the context of a world having only two economic goods.

Consider two countries, which we will call X and Y. Each has 100 inhabitants and each produces only two goods: wine and cheese. Let's consider each country's annual production possibilities. Suppose that, given their productive endowments, the inhabitants of country X can produce 400 bottles of wine *or* 200 pounds of cheese *or* any combination of the two goods that reflects the 2:1 trade–off of wine for cheese. At the same time, given their productive endowments, the inhabitants of country Y can produce 1,200 bottles of wine *or* 300 pounds of cheese *or* any combination of the two goods that reflects the 4:1 trade–off of wine for cheese. Finally, suppose that the inhabitants of each country find that their utility is maximized when they consume wine and cheese in equal proportions.[11] In the absence of trade, the collective utility of the inhab-

Percent of Global Total

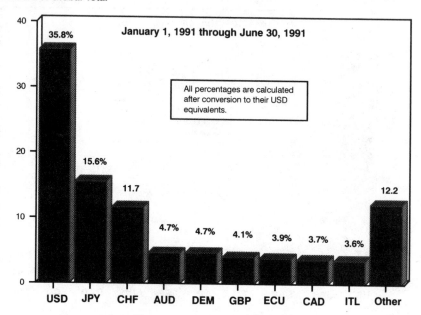

FIGURE 1.6 Composition of Transaction Volumes for Currency Swaps *(by currency)* (Source: International Swap Dealers Association)

itants of country X is maximized when the inhabitants of X produce and consume 133 bottles of wine and 133 pounds of cheese. Similarly, the collective utility of the inhabitants of country Y is maximized when the inhabitants of country Y produce and consume 240 bottles of wine and 240 pounds of cheese. It is clear that the inhabitants of country Y enjoy a higher standard of living than do the inhabitants of country X, since both countries have the same number of inhabitants. We also observe that country Y has an absolute advantage in the production of both wine and cheese. That is, if both X and Y produce just wine, Y can produce more wine per inhabitant. If both X and Y produce just cheese, Y can also produce more cheese per inhabitant.

Although Y enjoys an **absolute advantage** in both wine and cheese production, X nevertheless has a **comparative advantage** in the production of cheese. Country Y, on the other hand, has a comparative advantage in the production of wine. The comparative advantage that X holds in cheese production stems from X's 2:1 trade–off of wine for cheese. By giving up two bottles of wine, X can obtain an additional pound of cheese. If Y gives up two bottles of wine, it will only obtain an additional one-half pound of cheese. It is in this comparative sense that X holds an advantage in cheese production.

Whenever there are comparative advantages, there is a *possibility* that both countries can benefit from trade. To see this, suppose that each country concentrates more of its productive resources on producing that good in which it holds a comparative advantage and that all trade between X and Y takes the form of simple barter. For simplicity, we will assume the barter exchange rate is 3 for 1. That is, three bottles of wine can be exchanged for one pound of cheese. It is easily shown that the optimal strategy to maximize the collective utility of the two countries' inhabitants is for X to produce 0 bottles of wine and 200 pounds of cheese while Y produces 400 bottles of wine and 200 pounds of cheese. Country X would then trade 50 pounds of its cheese for 150 bottles of country Y's wine. After this transaction, the inhabitants of country X have 150 bottles of wine and 150 pounds of cheese while the inhabitants of country Y have 250 bottles of wine and 250 pounds of cheese.

Notice that both countries' inhabitants enjoy improved living standards as a consequence of trade. In this specific case, the inhabitants of country X gained proportionately more than did the inhabitants of country Y. But *both* did gain. The extent of each country's gains from trade will depend on the barter exchange rate and the degree of comparative advantage that each enjoys.

It is clear that when comparative advantages exist, there can be benefits to all parties from trade. Whether actual benefits can be realized will depend on the exchange rate and the **transaction costs**. These are of paramount importance, both for simple barter and for the viability of the swaps market. For purposes of the example, we implicitly assumed that wine and cheese could be costlessly traded. That is, there were no commissions to pay agents for arranging the barter trade and there were no transportation costs associated with moving wine and cheese between X and Y. To the extent that execution costs exist, the gains from trade will be diminished.

While swaps can and will occur even in the absence of comparative borrowing advantages, we can easily demonstrate that swaps are, in fact, often motivated by a desire to exploit comparative advantages. Let's work through a complete example using a currency swap to see how this might work.

Suppose that a British firm decides to borrow dollars in the United States to finance its operations in the United States. As a foreign entity in the United States, the British firm's credit is not as good as it might otherwise be and it is forced to pay 12 percent for dollars. In its own country, it can borrow pounds for 9 percent. At the same time, an American firm decides to borrow pounds in England to finance its operations in England. Again, as a foreign entity in England, the American firm's credit is not as good as it might otherwise be and it is forced to pay 11 percent for pounds. In its own country, it can borrow dollars for 10 percent. We may summarize as follows:

	Company	
Country	British Firm	American Firm
England	9.0%	11.0%
United States	12.0%	10.0%

It is clear that the British firm has a comparative borrowing advantage in England and that the American firm has a comparative borrowing advantage in the United States. The swap looks to exploit these comparative advantages. In the swap, the British firm will borrow in its domestic market at 9 percent and lend the funds obtained to the American firm at the same 9 percent rate. At the same time and as part of the same agreement, the American firm will borrow in its domestic market at 10 percent and lend the funds obtained to the British firm at the same 10 percent rate. Thus, the British firm obtains dollars at 10 percent for a net savings of 2 percent and the American firm obtains pounds at 9 percent for a net savings of 2 percent. Both counterparties to the swap have enjoyed a gain by exploiting their respective comparative advantages. Of course, the British firm did not have to lend to the American firm at the British firm's cost. Nor did the American firm have to lend to the British firm at the American firm's cost. The gains from the swap could just as easily have been split unevenly. In either case, if there are gains to be realized, the swap is viable.

In banking circles, interest rates are most often quoted in terms of basis points. A **basis point** is $\frac{1}{100}$ of 1 percent (0.01%). Thus, 2 percent is 200 basis points. We will often use this convention in our discussion of interest rates, interest rate spreads, and interest rate differentials.

The second important principle on which swap finance rests is the **principle of offsetting risks**. Swaps are often used to hedge interest rate risk, exchange rate risk, commodity price risk, and equity return risk. **Interest rate risk** is the risk that interest rates will deviate from their expected values; **exchange rate risk** is the risk that exchange rates will deviate from their expected values; **commodity price risk** is the risk that commodity prices will deviate from their expected values; and **equity return risk** is the risk that equity returns (including both the change in the market value of the equity portfolio and any dividends generated) will deviate from their expected values.

A **hedge** is a position that is taken for the purpose of reducing the risk associated with another position. This risk reduction is accomplished by taking a position having a risk that is opposite that of the original position. The result is that the two risks are offsetting. Thus, hedging involves the principle of offsetting risks.

1.5 SWAP FACILITATORS

One of the problems with swaps that we noted earlier is the difficulty of finding a potential counterparty with matching needs. This problem is resolved by swap dealers, working for investment banks, commercial banks, and merchant banks, who take one side of the transaction themselves—this is called **positioning the swap** or **booking the swap**. (The positioning of swaps is also called **warehousing** swaps.) That is, the swap dealer becomes a counterparty to the swap. For its services as a dealer, the swap dealer earns a **pay–receive spread**. Pay–receive spreads are also known as **bid–ask spreads**. The pay–receive spread is the difference between the swap coupon the dealer pays and the swap coupon the dealer receives.

The problem of finding a suitable counterparty can also be solved by employing a swap broker. Brokers match counterparties without themselves becoming counterparties to swaps. They do this in exchange for commissions. Since most swap activity involves swap dealers, we will concentrate on the role of the dealer throughout this book. Both swap brokers and swap dealers facilitate swap activity by making it easier to match end users' needs. In the two sections that follow, we take a closer look at these two types of facilitators.

1.5.1 Brokers

Financial institutions first became involved in swaps in the role of swap brokers. The function of the swap broker is to find counterparties with matched needs. The **swap broker** performs the search to locate parties with matched needs and then negotiates with each on behalf of the other. During the search process and during the early stages of negotiation, the swap broker ensures the anonymity of the potential counterparties. Should the negotiations break off, neither party is at risk of having its financial condition divulged by the other. When acting in the role of a broker, the financial institution providing the service assumes no risk, since it is not taking a position in the swap. Its role is limited to that of agent.

When the swap technique was first developed, the potential gains from swaps were often considerable. The combined benefits to the swap counterparties sometimes amounted to 100 basis points or more. In such an environment, the brokers who arranged swap transactions could command significant fees. But, as the swaps market attracted an ever growing number of participants, much of the potential cost–saving gains from swap finance were arbitraged away. This did not diminish the risk–management uses of swaps but it did create a need for a more efficient and streamlined swap product. Financial institutions soon created such a product. In the process, they discovered their own potential as market makers by assuming the role of counterparties and acting as swap dealers.

1.5.2 Dealers

The trick to streamlining the swap process and standardizing the swap product is for the bank to transform itself from a broker into a dealer or market maker. The **swap dealer** stands ready to match any client's currency or interest rate requirements by offering itself as the counterparty to the swap. Assuming that the dealer does not wish to bear exchange rate risk or interest rate risk, it must be able to lay off the risks in other swaps so that the dealer–pays–fixed–rate side of the swap book is balanced with the dealer–receives–fixed–rate side of the swap book.[12] Alternatively, the dealer could lay off the risk associated with the swap in some standardized form of debt or its equivalent. We focus, for the moment, on the latter.

The broadest debt market in the world is the market for U.S. Treasury securities. The market for Treasury debt is made by U.S. Government securities dealers. These dealers make a market in short–term T–bills, intermediate–term T–notes, and long–term T–bonds. Because of the breadth and the immense volume of trading activity, this market is very liquid and the **bid–ask spread** is typically very narrow. Further, at any given time, there is a near continuum of Treasury maturities ranging from a few days to 30 years.[13] It is not surprising that the Treasury market was the market of choice for laying off the dealer's interest rate risk. It also explains why swap dealers price their products as a spread over Treasuries of similar average life. (The relationship between average life and maturity is discussed in Chapter 3.)

Consider a simple example involving a swap–dealer bank and an interest rate swap. Each morning, the bank's swap staff prepares an **indicative swap pricing schedule**. This schedule specifies the prices at which the dealer bank will enter into swaps for that day. Examine the pricing schedule in Figure 1.7, which provides quotes for the fixed-rate side of five-year swaps. These rates are interpreted as follows: The dealer will pay its counterparty **LIBOR flat** (LIBOR is the London Interbank Offered Rate, and flat means without a premium or discount) in exchange for the counterparty paying the dealer the five–year T–note rate plus 80 basis points. If the counterparty wants to receive the fixed rate rather than pay the fixed rate, the dealer will pay the counterparty the five–year T–note rate plus 72 basis points in exchange for the counterparty paying the dealer LIBOR flat. The dealer makes its profit from the bid–ask spread, which is easily seen to be 8 basis points. In addition, the dealer *might* charge the client a front–end fee.[14]

Assume the current five–year T–note rate is 9.15 percent. The dealer will receive 9.95 percent or pay 9.87 percent against LIBOR. Suppose

Maturity	Bank Receives	Bank Pays
5 years	TN rate + 80 bps sa	TN rate + 72 bps sa

All quotes are against six–month LIBOR flat and assume bullet transactions. **Bullet transaction** means that the principal, either real or notional, is nonamortizing. These are sometimes called bullets.

bps denotes basis points, **sa** denotes semiannual. Other notations we will be using in this book include **pa**, which denotes percent annual, **qr**, which denotes quarterly rate, and **mr**, which denotes monthly rate.

FIGURE 1.7 Indicative Swap Pricing Schedule *(01 June 1994)*

now that a firm can issue (sell) fixed–rate five–year debt at 11–5/8 (11.625) percent and can issue floating–rate five–year debt at LIBOR plus 1.50 percent. The firm would like to raise $1 million of five–year fixed–rate money. If the firm borrows in the fixed–rate market, it will pay 11.625 percent. The swap dealer suggests that the firm issue $1 million of floating–rate money at LIBOR plus 1.5 percent and then swap this float-ing–rate debt for fixed–rate debt with the dealer serving as the swap counterparty. In this swap, the dealer will pay the firm LIBOR and the firm will pay the dealer 9.95 percent. There is no need for the firm and the dealer to exchange principals because the principal sums are identical. The cash flows then look as depicted in Figure 1.8.

Observe that the firm is paying its lender LIBOR plus 1.5 percent but the dealer is paying the firm LIBOR flat. At the same time, the firm is paying the dealer 9.95 percent. Thus, the firm's actual cost for its $1 million of five–year money is approximately 11.45 percent (9.95% + LIBOR + 1.5% – LIBOR).[15] Had the firm borrowed fixed–rate five–year money directly, it would have paid 11.625 percent. Thus, the swap strat-egy has saved the firm 17.5 basis points.

By entering into the swap, the swap dealer has assumed the risk that the interest rate it pays the firm will change. This interest rate risk exists because the dealer is paying a floating rate. The ideal solution for the dealer is to enter into another swap with another counterparty who seeks to exchange fixed–rate debt for floating–rate debt. If such a party is found, the dealer can be viewed as standing between its two counterparties in the traditional sense of a **financial intermediary**.

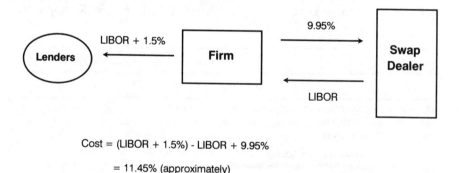

Cost = (LIBOR + 1.5%) - LIBOR + 9.95%

= 11.45% (approximately)

FIGURE 1.8   Interest Flows for a Synthetic Fixed Rate Financing Using an Interest Rate Swap

Suppose that it might take some time for the swap dealer to locate a second counterparty. How can the dealer lay off the risk in the interim? One answer is to short $1 million of five–year T–notes and use the proceeds from this sale to purchase $1 million of 26–week T–bills. If it were necessary to do so, the dealer would roll these bills over every six months for five years. The T–bill rate is viewed as floating in that it will be different with each **rollover**. This is the same sense in which the LIBOR rate is floating. The dealer is then paying a fixed rate (T–note) and receiving a floating rate (T–bill). The dealer's interest rate risk from the swap with its counterparty is thus offset. Importantly, the offset is not perfect because the floating–rate side of the swap is LIBOR based while the Treasury hedge is T–bill based. While these two rates track each other very closely, they are not perfectly correlated and thus there is some residual risk associated with the hedge. This residual risk is called **basis risk**.

It should be noted that cash Treasury hedges for unmatched swaps, once widely used, are no longer the hedge vehicle of choice for most swap dealers. We will consider the dealer's hedging problem more carefully and examine other hedging alternatives in Chapter 8.

There are other risks for banks making markets in swaps. For example, there is credit risk, spread risk, and several forms of mismatch risk. If the floating–rate portions are indexed to different rates, then there is also basis risk. When the swap involves different currencies there will be exchange rate risk and there might also be sovereign risk and delivery risk. We save a detailed discussion of these risks and the management of swap risks for Chapter 8.

1.6 FUTURES

Futures contracts are highly standardized contracts calling for the deferred delivery of some underlying asset or requiring a final cash settlement based on the value of the underlying asset on the contract's final settlement date. Futures contracts trade on futures exchanges. Because they are so highly standardized, futures positions can be easily terminated by making an offsetting transaction. The offset process is facilitated by a clearing association. The clearing association may be viewed as short to all long positions and long to all short positions. This eliminates any concern that futures traders might otherwise have about the financial integrity of the other parties to their trades.

The clearing association, on the other hand, has no net price risk because it is always short and long the same number of contracts. It is protected from default on the part of traders by requiring each trader to secure his or her position by posting margin. Margin serves the function of a performance bond.

Futures have long been used to hedge price risks. For this reason, swaps may be viewed as an over–the–counter substitute for futures. But, futures contracts are single–period instruments. That is, they have a specific termination date. For example, June Eurodollar futures will cash settle on a specific date in June. Once settlement has been reached, the instrument ceases to exist. A swap, on the other hand, can have a long life with a number of settlement dates. For this reason, some persons have described swaps as multiperiod futures. This is a description, however, that is frowned on by both the swaps industry and by futures regulators. Because swaps are tailor–made, like forward contracts, it is more accurate to describe swaps as multiperiod forwards than as multiperiod futures.

Because swaps are multiperiod in nature, they can easily be used to hedge multiperiod price risks. Futures, on the other hand, are best suited to hedging single–period price risks. Of course, a series of futures could be strung together (called a **futures strip**) to replicate the multiperiod nature of a swap. But futures are often not liquid beyond the first few delivery months, called the **front months**. In many cases, they do not even exist with delivery dates beyond one year into the future. Swaps, on the other hand, can be written with any maturity the end user requires. Importantly, the most heavily traded of all futures, namely Eurodollar futures, are liquid out to almost five years. This is largely a consequence of demand for these futures by swap dealers looking to hedge their swap books.

Whether futures or swaps are the best hedging alternative depends on the specifics of the situation and the relative pricing of the different hedge alternatives at the point in time when the hedge is required. As already noted, futures are heavily used by swap dealers to hedge their own price risks when their swap books are not properly balanced. But futures are also used by swap dealers to price their swaps. These are the primary motivations for looking at futures in this book. Interest rate futures are used to hedge and price interest rate swaps, currency futures and interest rate futures are used to hedge and price currency swaps, stock index futures are used to hedge and price equity swaps, and commodity futures are used to hedge and price commodity swaps.

We will concentrate our examples in this book on the use of interest rate futures to price and hedge interest rate and currency swaps. The dealer can use Eurodollar futures, T–bills futures, T–bond and T–note futures, swap futures, and other interest rate futures for these purposes. The prices of these instruments fluctuate inversely with their yields, although the exact relationship between yield and price depends on the pricing convention associated with the specific futures contract. For example, some interest rate futures employ a pricing convention such that the yield is used to discount, via present value arithmetic, the future cash flows on the underlying instrument. The futures price is then quoted as this discounted value. T–bond and T–note futures traded on the Chicago Board of Trade, for example, use this convention. Other futures are priced by simply deducting the yield, in percent form, from 100. Eurodollar futures traded on the International Monetary Market and swap futures traded on the Chicago Board of Trade, for example, use this convention.

1.7   OPTIONS

An **option** is defined, pure and simple, as *a right without an obligation*. More precisely, the holder of an option has a right without an obligation, but the writer (or seller) of the option has an absolute obligation. For the right that the option provides, the option purchaser pays the option writer an up–front onetime fee called the **option premium**.

Most often, options grant the option holder the right to buy or sell some number of units of some underlying asset or to receive a cash payment the size of which is based on what happens to the value of the underlying asset. Because holders of options have no obligations, they are not required to post margin. Option writers, on the other hand, are typically required to post margin.

Options trade both on exchanges (**listed options**) and over–the–counter (**OTC options**). Exchange–traded options have standardized terms while OTC options can be tailored to the specific needs of the end user of the option. Listed options employ a clearinghouse similar to the clearing associations that are used in the futures industry.

There are a great many different types of options. The most commonly discussed are call options and put options. A **call option** grants its holder the right, but not the obligation, to *purchase* the underlying asset from the option writer on or before the option's **expiration date**. If the option holder chooses to exercise the option, he or she must pay the option writer the option's **strike price**.

In recent years, a great many new types of options have been introduced. Some of these are multiperiod in nature. The two most common types of **multiperiod options** are caps and floors. A **cap** may be viewed as a multiperiod call and a **floor** may be viewed as a multiperiod put. This is akin to thinking of swaps as multiperiod forward contracts. These two types of options are particularly important in the swaps trade because swaps are often combined with multiperiod options to engineer special structures.

In addition to caps and floors, a whole array of options with very different characteristics have been introduced in recent years. There are average rate or Asian options, lookback options, bounded options, and dozens of others. These very different new option types are sometimes lumped together and described as **second generation** or **exotic options**. Our only interest in options in this book will be in caps and floors and how caps and floors can be combined with swaps.

1.8 SOME MISCELLANEOUS POINTS ABOUT SWAPS

In this section, we briefly discuss two important considerations involving swaps that don't fit nicely under the other headings. The first is the off-balance sheet nature of swaps and the second is the efforts that have been made to standardize swap documentation.

Swaps are **off–balance sheet** transactions. That is, they do not show up on either the assets side or on the liabilities side of a balance sheet. This accounting treatment of swaps has been an attractive feature of swaps to both corporate users of swaps and to swap dealers. In particular, swap dealers found swap activity to be an easy way to boost bank return on equity—an important measure of profitability—because the off–balance sheet nature of swap activity did not engender a need for additional bank capital. The rapid growth of swap activity eventually led bank regulators to become concerned about bank safety. The regulators then proposed to stiffen capital requirements for such banks.[16] The banks argued that such measures would only increase the cost of swap finance to the end user and drive swap finance overseas.[17] In recent years the Financial Accounting Standards Board (FASB) has developed criteria for reporting many types of off-balance sheet activity.

To address these and related concerns, the Federal Reserve, working with bank regulatory and supervisory bodies from a number of nations, developed a preliminary set of proposals that became known as the **Basle Accord**. The Basle Accord was the culmination of a serious international effort to standardize the measurement of bank capital and to develop capital standards. After a period of public comment and deliberation, the Federal Reserve issued final guidelines for U.S. banks on January 19, 1989. The Federal Reserve's final guidelines provided a risk–based procedure for determining a bank's capital requirements. The guidelines took explicit consideration of swap and related activity. (We address this issue in greater detail in Chapter 8.)

The second major consideration we briefly address is swap documentation. When the swap product was first introduced, each bank that entered the swaps markets as a broker and/or dealer developed its own swap documentation. This documentation included specification of terms, language, pricing conventions, and so on. Different banks used very different terminology and conventions. This lack of standardization limited the ability of banks to assign swaps and slowed the development of a **secondary market** in swap contracts. In June 1985, the New York–based **International Swap Dealers Association** (ISDA) established a code listing standard terms for interest rate swaps. Shortly thereafter, the **British Bankers Association** offered its own set of documentation guidelines (British Bankers Association Interest Rate Swaps or BBAIRS). These codes were later revised and, ultimately, led to the introduction of standard form agreements. The ISDA and BBAIRS alternative codes are referred to, colloquially, by persons in the swap trade as "is da" and "b bears." We address swap documentation and ISDA's efforts toward standardization more fully in Chapter 8. As a side point, in 1993 the ISDA changed its name to the International Swaps and Derivatives Association. It retained the acronym ISDA.

The standardization of documentation has increased the speed of transacting and given an impetus to the development of a secondary market in swaps. The secondary market continues to evolve but is, as yet, not highly developed. For swaps to be easily tradable, they would have to be written with **rights of assignment**. Rights of assignment pose a number of difficulties. In a related effort, some consideration has been given to the creation of a **clearinghouse** for swaps.[18] Such a clearinghouse could, theoretically, function in much the same fashion as the clearing associations used to clear and enforce futures and option contracts. These efforts appear to have been abandoned, and, in any case, the creation of a clearinghouse for swaps would make swaps too much like futures. This could pose serious regulatory problems for the industry. Nevertheless, recent concern about credit risk has once again led to interest in a swaps clearinghouse and other forms of credit enhancements.

The absence of a well–developed secondary market for swaps is not a serious problem for swap counterparties. A counterparty to a swap who finds that the swap no longer serves its purposes can negotiate a cancellation of the agreement directly with the other counterparty. We examine the mechanics for determining cancellation payments later.

This concludes our introduction to the swaps markets. In the next chapter, we will look more carefully at the basic swap structure and we will introduce some additional terminology.

1.9 SUMMARY

Swap finance evolved from parallel and back–to–back loans. These latter financing devices originated as a mechanism to circumvent foreign–exchange controls. The first swaps were currency swaps, but interest rate swaps, first introduced in 1981, account for the bulk of swap activity today. Swaps can be used to reduce financing costs and to manage interest rate and exchange rate risks.

Swap finance is facilitated by the intermediating roles played by swap brokers and dealers. Brokers arrange swaps between parties with matching needs. Dealers become counterparties to swaps and hedge their positions until such time as risk–offsetting swaps can be arranged. Large swap dealers often carry swap portfolios measured in the tens or even hundreds of billions of dollars. A few exceed a trillion dollars.

The off–balance sheet nature of swaps has led to some concern on the part of bank regulators as to the vulnerability of these financial institutions. Traditional bank accounting and regulation did not provide for explicit recognition of off–balance sheet items and the risks associated with them. This deficiency has been addressed by the Federal Reserve's new guidelines for risk–based capital requirements.

In 1985, the first steps were taken by the International Swap Dealers Association (now the International Swaps and Derivatives Association) and the British Bankers Association toward a standardization of swap provisions and language. These efforts have greatly facilitated the writing of swaps and have enhanced the prospects for the emergence of an efficient secondary market in swaps.

REVIEW QUESTIONS

1. Briefly discuss the origins of swaps. What advantages do currency swaps have over back–to–back loans?
2. Discuss the comparative advantage justification for the viability of swaps. How might arbitrage affect this comparative advantage?
3. How might swaps be used to hedge interest rate and exchange rate risk? Discuss. Illustrate by way of cash flow diagrams.
4. Why do swap dealers sometimes use the Treasury market to offset their swaps? How does this relate to the pricing of swaps?
5. Why are the notional principals on interest rate swaps never exchanged while the notional principals on currency swaps are often exchanged?
6. How can swap activity be used to enhance a bank's return on equity? What problems, if any, might this pose for bank safety?
7. What is the rights of set–off problem associated with back–to–back loans and how is this problem solved by swaps?
8. Discuss why caps may be likened to multiperiod options in the same sense that swaps may be likened to multiperiod forwards.
9. Suppose that a corporation wants to borrow fixed–rate money. It can borrow at a fixed rate of 11.75 percent. Suppose now that this same corporation can borrow floating rate at LIBOR plus 1.80 percent and can enter a fixed–for–floating interest rate swap with a swap dealer. The dealer would pay LIBOR flat and the corporation would pay 9.80 percent. Should the corporation borrow fixed–rate money directly or should it borrow floating–rate money and swap into fixed–rate money? Why? Illustrate by way of cash flow diagrams.
10. How might standardization of swap contract documentation facilitate the development of a secondary market in swaps?

NOTES

1. The terms "derivative securities" and "derivative products" are often used as synonyms for the term "derivative instruments." The characterization of swaps as *securities* is technically not correct, but the usage of the term is widely accepted.

2. The term "notionals" is intended to convey the hypothetical nature of the underlying assets. In some swaps, notably currency swaps, the underlying assets can be more than hypothetical. That is, they can be real. In these cases, the term "notional" is not really appropriate. However, not all currency swaps involve real assets. When they do not, the term notionals is appropriate. It is important to be aware of this distinction, and we will note it again in the next chapter. For consistency, however, we will use the term "notionals" for the underlying assets on all swaps, irrespective of whether they are real or hypothetical.

3. For an examination of exchange rate volatility behavior before and after the collapse of the Bretton Woods Agreement, see Wilford (1987).

4. For a discussion of the evolution of swaps from back–to–back and parallel loans, see Powers (1986).

5. For a discussion of the problems which can result from the registration of the rights of set–off, see Price (1986).

6. For an analytical examination of the World Bank's 1981 swap activity, see Park (1984). See also Wallich (1984).

7. See Beckstrom (1986) for details of this swap.

8. Ibid.

9. Exact figures for the volume of swap activity do not exist. The numbers reported here for 1982, 1984, and 1986 are our own composites from estimates by Falloon (1988), Celarier (1987), Baker (1986), Powers (1986), and other sources. The figures for 1987 are more accurate. They represent an aggregation of the values provided by reporting members of the International Swap Dealers Association (ISDA), a trade association founded in 1985. The ISDA now tracks the volume of swap activity worldwide. Nevertheless, the ISDA figures are still estimates, as not all swap dealers report their transactions to the ISDA.

10. The principle of comparative advantage, as the driving force behind international trade, was first formulated by David Ricardo in the early 19th century. For a more detailed discussion of the principle, see Samuelson and Nordhaus (1985, Chapter 38).

11. The term *utility* is used in the economic sense. That is, utility is the benefit or satisfaction that an individual receives or expects to receive from the consumption of some available combination of goods and services.

12. Often, swap dealers do want to bear risk. For example, they may choose to bear exchange rate risk or interest rate risk because they have a "view" on these rates (i.e., a forecast), and they often voluntarily bear credit risk to earn a risk premium.

13. Although there is a near continuum of maturities, the more liquid are the 5-, 7-, 10-, and 30-year instruments, and these are most heavily used by swap dealers.

14. Front–end fees, while once common, are now quite rare and only occur if the swap structure requires special financial engineering, if the swap

involves a buy–up, or if the swap involves an optionlike right. These considerations will be discussed more fully in later chapters.

15. This is an oversimplification. Fixed rates are based on a 365–day year using a yield measure called the bond equivalent yield while floating rates are measured on a 360–day year using a yield measure called the money market equivalent yield. Thus, the premium over LIBOR employed in this example is not directly addable to the fixed rate without first making an adjustment. We consider this adjustment in Chapter 3.

16. See, for example, Celarier (1987), Cooper and Shegog (1987), Whittaker (1987), Riley and Smith (1987), Klein (1986), and Felgran (1987).

17. See, for example, Nelson (1986) and Kennrick (1987).

18. For a more thorough discussion of the standardization of swap documentation, see Stoakes (1985a, 1985b), and Genova and Thompson (1988). For discussion of the role of a swaps clearinghouse, see Crabbe (1986).

REFERENCES AND SUGGESTED READING

Baker, M. "Swaps—Driven Offerings Up." *Pensions & Investment Age* 14, no. 4 (February 1986): 53–4.

Beckstrom, R. "The Development of the Swap Market." In *Swap Finance* 1, Boris Antl, ed., London: Euromoney Publications, 1986.

Celarier, M. "Swaps' Judgement Day." *United States Banker* 98, no. 7 (July 1987): 16–20.

Cooper, R., and A. Shegog. "An Old–Fashioned Tug-of-War." *Euromoney,* Swaps Supplement, July 1987, pp. 22–7.

Crabbe, M. "Clearing House for Swaps." *Euromoney*, September 1986, pp. 345–51.

Falloon, W. "The ABC's of Swaps." *Intermarket Magazine* 5, no. 5 (May 1988): 25–33.

Felgran, S. D. "Interest Rate Swaps: Uses, Risk, and Price." *New England Economic Review* (Federal Reserve Bank of Boston), November/December 1987, pp. 22–32.

Genova, D., and D. Thompson. "A Guide to Standard Swap Documentation." *Commercial Lending Review* 3, no. 2 (Spring 1988): 44–9.

Kennrick, R. "Bank Regulators Suggest Control of Swap Volumes." *Asian Finance* (Hong Kong) 13, no. 9 (September 1987): 16–8.

Klein, L. B. "Interest Rate and Currency Swaps: Are They Securities?" *International Financial Law Review (UK)* 5, no. 10 (October 1986): 35–9.

Nelson, J. F. "Too Good to Last?" *United States Banker* 97, no. 6 (June 1986): 46–50.

Park, Y. S. "Currency Swaps as a Long–Term International Financing Technique." *Journal of International Business Studies* 15, no. 3 (Winter 1984): 47–54.

Powers, J. G. "The Vortex of Finance." *Intermarket Magazine* 3, no. 2 (February 1986): 27–38.

Price, J. A. M. "The Technical Evolution of the Currency Swap Product." In *Swap Finance* 1, Boris Antl, ed., London: Euromoney Publications, 1986.

Riley, W. B., and G. S. Smith. "Interest Rate Swaps: Disclosure and Recognition." *CPA Journal* 57, no. 1 (January 1987): 64–70.

Samuelson, P. A., and W. D. Nordhaus. *Economics.* 12th ed. New York: McGraw–Hill, 1985.

Schwartz, R. J., and C. W. Smith. *The Handbook of Currency and Interest Rate Risk Management.* New York: New York Institute of Insurance, 1990.

Stoakes, C. "The London Inter–Bank Swaps Code." *International Financial Law Review (UK)* 4, no. 10 (October 1985a): 6.

Stoakes, C. "Standards Make Swaps Faster." *Euromoney,* November 1985b, pp. 19–21.

Turnbull, S. M. "Swaps: A Zero–Sum Game." *Financial Management* 16, no. 1 (Spring 1987): 15–21.

Wallich, C. I. "The World Bank's Currency Swaps." *Finance and Development* 7, no. 3 (Fall 1984): 197–207.

Whittaker, J. G. "Interest Rate Swaps: Risk and Regulation." *Economic Review* (Federal Reserve Bank of Kansas City) 72, no. 3 (March 1987): 3–13.

Wilford, D. S. "Strategic Risk Exposure Management." Working paper #3, in *Working Papers in Risk Management,* Chase Manhattan Bank, February 1987.

2

The Generic Swap Structure

2.1 OVERVIEW

The basic structure of a swap is relatively simple and is the same for interest rate swaps, currency swaps, commodity swaps, and equity swaps. The seeming complexity of swaps is more in the extensive documentation needed to fully specify the contract terms and the myriad of specialty provisions that can be included to tailor the swap to some specific need.

In this chapter, we present a simple graphic illustration of the generic or "plain vanilla" swap in the form of cash flow diagrams, and we introduce much of the swaps–specific terminology. By visually depicting the pattern of cash flows associated with swaps and the ways that swaps meld with cash market transactions, one can easily see how a desired end result is achieved. We then apply this basic model in three different settings: 1. an interest rate swap to convert a fixed–rate obligation to a floating–rate obligation; 2. a currency swap to convert an obligation in one currency to an obligation in another currency; and 3. a commodity swap to convert a floating price to a fixed price. While we do not do so in this chapter, the same model is applicable to equity swaps. (A more detailed examination of equity swaps in provided in Chapter 5.)

Also in this chapter, we will take a brief look at how variant forms of the basic swap are created but we will not dwell on variants just yet. Instead, we will examine a number of variants of each of the specific types of swaps in the more narrowly focused chapters that follow. We will end the chapter by introducing some methods of illustrating cash flows that will make it easier to understand the more complex swap structures that we will examine later.

2.2 THE STRUCTURE OF A SWAP

All swaps are built around the same basic structure. Two parties, called counterparties, agree to make payments to one another on the basis of some quantities of underlying assets. For the moment, we will refer to these payments as **service payments**. The underlying assets may or may not be exchanged and are referred to as **notionals**—in order to distinguish them from physical exchanges in the cash markets, which are called **actuals**. Technically, if the notionals are exchanged, then they are not notional because the term "notional" is intended to imply hypothetical. Nevertheless, in order to avoid making frequent distinctions between underlying assets that are *notional* and underlying assets that are *real*, we will simply refer to all underlying assets on swaps as "notionals." The reader should keep in mind that this is an exercise in editorial license on our part. Importantly, this distinction is often not made in practice, just as we will not make it here.

A swap may involve one exchange of notionals, two exchanges of notionals, a series of exchanges of notionals, or no exchanges of notionals. In the **generic swap**, the agreement provides for one real or hypothetical exchange of notionals upon commencement and a reexchange upon termination. The swap commences on its **effective date**, which is also known as the **value date**. It terminates on its **termination date**, which is also known as the **maturity date**. The period of time between these two dates is called the swap's **tenor** or **maturity**. Over its tenor, the service payments will be made at periodic intervals as specified in the swap agreement (documentation) that governs the relationship between the two counterparties. Most typically, these payment intervals are annual, semiannual, quarterly, or monthly. Service payments begin to accrue on the effective date and stop accruing on the termination date.

The notionals exchanged in a swap may be the same or they may be different. Between the exchanges of notionals, the counterparties make the periodic service payments. The service payments of the first counterparty are made at a **fixed price** (or rate) for the use of the second counterparty's notional assets. This fixed price is called the **swap coupon**. The service payments of the second counterparty are made at a floating, or market determined, price (or rate) for the use of the first counterparty's notional assets. This is the basic or plain vanilla structure. By modifying the terms appropriately and/or adding specialty provisions, this simple structure can be converted into hundreds of variants to suit specific end user needs. For purposes of illustration, we shall call the first counterparty "Counterparty A" and the second counterparty "Counterparty B."

The fixed price, as the term implies, does not change over the tenor of the swap. The floating price, on the other hand, is periodically **reset**. That is, it is pegged to some specific spot market price (or rate), called the **reference rate**, which is observed on specific dates, called **reset dates**. Alternatively, the floating price can be set to some average of periodic observations on the reference rate. In the typical case, an observation is made on the reference rate. The floating rate is then set as a function of this observation, and this rate applies to the subsequent payment period for purposes of calculating the floating payment. The actual dates on which the exchanges of payments occur are called the **payment dates**.

It is very difficult to arrange a swap directly between two end users. A much more efficient structure is to involve a financial intermediary that serves as a counterparty to both end users. This counterparty is called a **swap dealer**, a **market maker**, or a **swap bank**. The terms are used interchangeably but the term swap dealer is generally preferred. The swap dealer profits from the **pay–receive spread** it imposes on the swap coupon. The pay–receive spread is also known as a **bid–ask spread**.

The cash flows associated with a typical swap are illustrated in Figures 2.1, 2.2, and 2.3. Figure 2.1 depicts the initial exchange of notionals, which is optional in the sense that it is not required in all swaps; Figure 2.2 depicts the periodic payments between the counterparties; and Figure

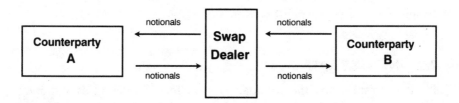

FIGURE 2.1 Swap: Initial Exchange of Notionals (optional)

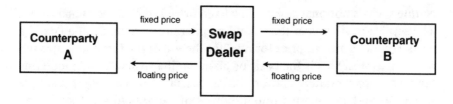

FIGURE 2.2   Periodic Service Payments (required)

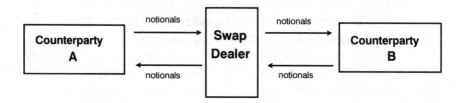

FIGURE 2.3   Swap: Reexchange of Notionals (optional)

2.3 depicts the reexchange of notionals, which, like the initial exchange of notionals, is optional in the sense that it is not required in all swaps.

A swap by itself would generally not make much sense, except as a speculation on the subsequent direction of a price (or rate). But swaps do not exist in isolation. They are used in conjunction with appropriate cash market positions or transactions. There are three such basic transactions: 1. obtain actuals from the cash market; 2. make (receive) payments to (from) the cash market; and 3. supply actuals to the cash market. These possibilities are summarized in Figure 2.4. The cash markets depicted in Figure 2.4 may be the same or different.

By combining the cash market transactions with an appropriately structured swap, we can engineer a great many different outcomes. Here, however, we will only look at the most basic of these. We will examine interest rate swaps first, then currency swaps and, finally, commodity swaps.

2.3   INTEREST RATE SWAPS

In interest rate swaps, the notionals take the form of quantities of money and are consequently called **notional principals**. In such a swap, the notional principals to be exchanged are identical in amount and involve

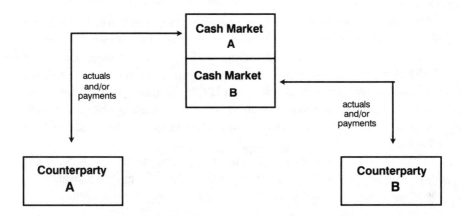

FIGURE 2.4   Cash Market Transactions

the same currency. As such, they can be dispensed with, which explains the origin of the term "notional." Furthermore, since the periodic payments, called interest in this case, are also in the same currency, only the interest differential needs to be exchanged on the periodic payment dates—assuming the payment dates match.

Interest rate swaps have many uses. One that is particularly important, although less so today than in earlier days, is a reduction in financing costs. For an interest rate swap to be viable as a tool for reducing financing costs, one party must have access to comparatively cheap fixed–rate funding but desire floating–rate funding while another party must have access to comparatively cheap floating–rate funding but desire fixed–rate funding.[1] By entering into swaps with a swap dealer, both parties can obtain the form of financing they desire and simultaneously exploit their comparative advantages. (Comparative advantages, which were defined in Chapter 1, are also known in financial circles as **relative advantages**.)

For example, suppose that Party A is in need of ten–year debt financing. Party A has access to comparatively cheap floating–rate financing but desires a fixed–rate obligation. For purposes of illustration, assume that Party A can borrow at a floating rate of six–month LIBOR plus 1/2 percent (50 bps) or at a semiannual fixed rate of 11.50 percent. As it happens, Party B is also in need of ten–year debt financing. Party B has access to comparatively cheap fixed–rate financing but desires a floating–rate obligation. For purposes of illustration, assume that Party B can borrow at a semiannual fixed rate of 10.50 percent and can borrow floating rate as six–month LIBOR flat.

The swap dealer stands ready to enter a swap as either fixed–rate payer (floating–rate receiver) or as floating–rate payer (fixed–rate receiver). In both cases, the dealer's floating rate is LIBOR. In this specific case, if the dealer is fixed–rate payer, it will pay a swap coupon of 10.70 percent semiannual (sa) against six–month LIBOR. If the dealer is fixed–rate receiver, it requires a swap coupon of 10.75 percent sa against six–month LIBOR.[2] (How a swap dealer prices its swaps will be addressed in Chapter 7.)

Party A, now Counterparty A, enters a swap with the swap dealer as fixed–rate payer and Party B, now Counterparty B, enters a swap with the swap dealer as fixed–rate receiver. While there are no exchanges of notional principals in these swaps, there are still three types of exchanges—if we include the borrowings in the cash market. The full set of cash flows are illustrated in Figures 2.5, 2.6, and 2.7. Figure 2.5 depicts the initial borrowings in the cash markets; Figure 2.6 depicts debt service in the cash markets and the cash flows with the swap dealer; and Figure 2.7 depicts the repayment of principals in the cash market.

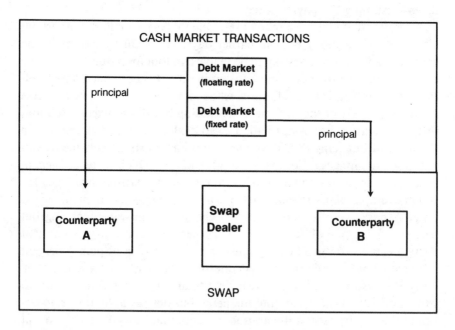

FIGURE 2.5   Interest Rate Swap with Cash Market Transactions (initial borrowing of principals)

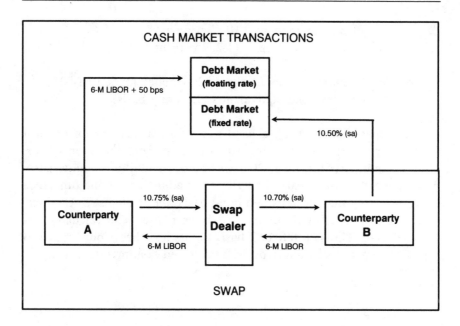

FIGURE 2.6 Interest Rate Swap with Cash Market Transactions (debt service payments with swap service payments)

Examine Figure 2.6. Notice that Counterparty A pays LIBOR + 50 bps on its cash market obligation and receives LIBOR from the swap dealer. The LIBOR components of these payments are, therefore, offsetting. The other obligation of Counterparty A is to pay the swap dealer 10.75 percent. After adjusting for the different **day–count** conventions employed in bond basis and money market basis yields, Counterparty A's final cost is 11.257 percent sa.[3] The calculation is depicted in the following table. Since direct borrowing of fixed rate in the cash market would have cost Counterparty A 11.50 percent, it is clear that Counterparty A has benefited by 24.3 basis points by employing the swap.

Calculation of Counterparty A's Final Cost:

Cost of market obligation:	LIBOR + 50 bps
Less floating rate received:	LIBOR
Net cost differential:	50 bps (money market basis)
MMY to BEY adjustment:	$50 \times \dfrac{365}{360} = 50.7$ bps (bond basis)

Plus swap coupon: 10.75 percent
Final cost of financing: 11.257 percent sa

where: MMY denotes money market yield (money market basis)
        BEY denotes bond equivalent yield (bond basis)

Counterparty B is paying a fixed rate of 10.50 percent on its cash market borrowing and receiving 10.70 percent from the swap dealer. Thus, Counterparty B is up by 20 basis points. In addition, Counterparty B is paying the swap dealer LIBOR. After adjusting for the difference between money market basis and bond basis, the final cost of Counterparty B's debt is LIBOR minus 19.7 basis points. The calculation is depicted here. This is a full 19.7 basis points less than Counterparty B would have paid had Counterparty B borrowed floating rate directly.

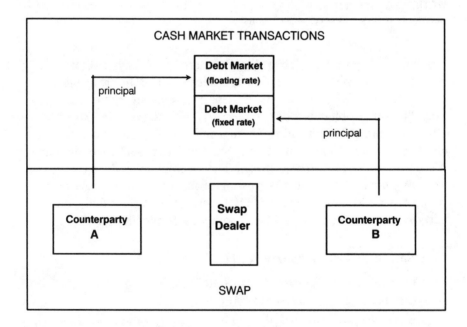

FIGURE 2.7   Interest Rate Swap with Cash Market Transactions (repayment of principals)

Calculation of Counterparty B's Final Cost:

Cost of market obligation:	10.50 percent sa
Less fixed rate received:	10.70 percent sa
Net cost differential:	−20 bps (bond basis)
BEY to MMY adjustment:	$-20 \times \dfrac{360}{365} = -19.7$ bps (MMY)
Plus swap coupon:	LIBOR
Final cost of financing:	6-M LIBOR − 19.7 bps

As a side point, notice that the swap dealer earns 5 basis points for its services in making a liquid swap market. This 5 basis points is the difference between the swap coupon received from Counterparty A and the swap coupon paid to Counterparty B.

2.4 CURRENCY SWAPS

We should preface this section by noting that the floating rate on currency swaps is most often LIBOR. LIBOR is the rate of interest quoted for interbank lendings of Eurocurrency deposits and is an acronym derived from London Interbank Offered Rate. For example, there is a LIBOR quoted for interbank lendings of dollar deposits (USD LIBOR), deutsche-mark deposits (DEM LIBOR), yen deposits (JPY LIBOR), and so on. Unless specifically indicated otherwise, LIBOR is assumed to be USD LIBOR in all cases used in this book.

In a currency swap, the currencies in which the principals are denom-inated are different and, for this reason, usually (but not always) need to be exchanged. A currency swap is viable whenever one counterparty has comparatively cheaper access to one currency than it does to another.[4] To illustrate, suppose that Counterparty A can borrow deutschemarks for seven years at a fixed rate of 9 percent and can borrow seven–year dollars at a floating rate of one–year LIBOR.[5] Counterparty B, on the other hand, can borrow seven–year deutschemarks at a rate of 10.1 percent and can borrow seven–year floating–rate dollars at a rate of one–year LIBOR. As it happens, Counterparty A needs floating–rate dollar financing and Coun-terparty B needs fixed–rate deutschemark financing.

Now suppose we have a swap dealer that makes deutschemark–for–dollar currency swaps. It is currently prepared to pay a fixed rate of 9.45 percent on deutschemarks against one–year LIBOR, and it is prepared to pay one–year LIBOR against a fixed–rate of 9.55 percent on deutsche-marks. The counterparties borrow in their respective cash markets—Counterparty A borrows fixed–rate deutschemarks and Counterparty B borrows floating–rate dollars—and then both enter into swaps with a swap dealer. Figure 2.8 depicts the initial borrowings in the cash markets and the initial exchange of notional principals at the commencement of the swap. Figure 2.9 depicts the ongoing debt service in the cash markets and the exchanges of interest payments on the swap. Figure 2.10 depicts the reexchange of notional principals on the termination of the swap and the repayment of borrowings.

Notice that while Counterparty A borrows deutschemarks, the swap converts the deutschemarks to dollars. Notice also that these dollars have a floating–rate character with a net cost of LIBOR minus 45 basis points.[6] This represents a 45 basis point savings compared to a direct borrowing in the floating–rate dollar market. Similarly, Counterparty B borrows dollars but uses the swap to convert the dollars to deutschemarks. These deutschemarks have a net cost of 9.55 percent. This represents a 55 basis

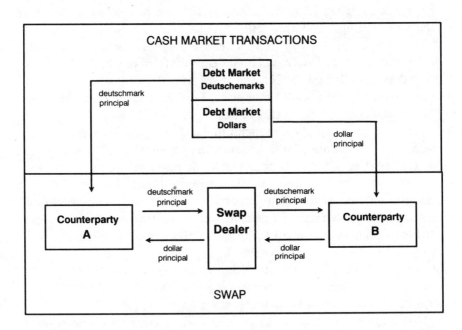

FIGURE 2.8 Currency Swap with Cash Market Transactions (initial borrowings and exchanges of notional principal)

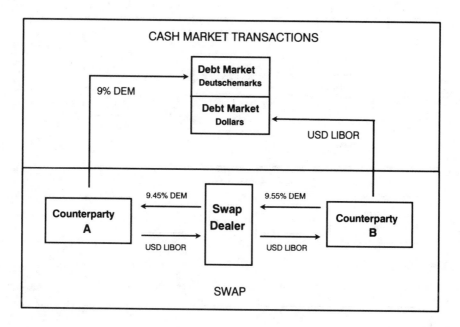

FIGURE 2.9 Currency Swap with Cash Market Transactions (debt service with swap payments)

point savings compared to a direct borrowing in the fixed–rate deutsche-mark market. (See the following calculations.) Thus, we see that a swap can be used with the appropriate cash market transactions to convert both the currency denomination of a financing and the character of the interest cost.

Counterparty A's objective:	Seven-year floating-rate dollars
Cost of borrowing directly:	One-year LIBOR, resets annually
Strategy:	
Borrow fixed-rate deutschemarks:	9.00% DEM
Pay floating rate on swap:	LIBOR
Receive fixed rate on swap:	−9.45% DEM
Final cost =	9.00% DEM + LIBOR − 9.45% DEM
=	LIBOR − 45 bps
	(USD) (DEM)

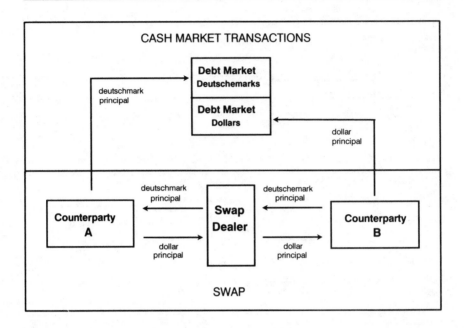

FIGURE 2.10 Currency Swap with Cash Market Transactions (repayment of actuals and reexchanges of notional principal)

Counterparty B's objective:	Seven-year fixed-rate deutschemarks
Cost of borrowing directly:	10.1% DEM
Strategy:	
Borrow floating-rate dollars:	LIBOR
Pay fixed rate on swap:	9.55% DEM
Receive floating rate on swap:	−LIBOR
Final cost =	LIBOR + 9.55% DEM − LIBOR
=	9.55% DEM

2.5 COMMODITY SWAPS

The final type of swap we will consider in this chapter is the commodity swap. In a commodity swap, the first counterparty makes periodic payments to the second counterparty at a per–unit fixed price for a given notional quantity of some commodity. The second counterparty pays the first a per–unit floating price (usually an average price based on periodic observations on a spot price) for a given notional quantity of some commodity. The commodities may be the same (the usual case) or different. No exchanges of notional commodities take place between the counterparties to the swap. All exchanges of commodity, if any, take place in the cash markets.

Consider a simple case. A crude oil producer (Counterparty A) wants to fix the price it *receives* for its oil for five years, and its monthly production averages 8,000 barrels. At the same time, an oil refiner and chemicals manufacturer (Counterparty B) wants to fix the price it *pays* for oil for five years, and its monthly need is 12,000 barrels. To obtain the desired outcomes, they enter into swaps with a swap dealer but continue their transactions in actuals in the cash markets.

At the time these end users enter into their swaps, the commodity swap dealer's mid–price for the appropriate grade of crude oil is $15.25 a barrel. Counterparty B agrees to make monthly payments to the dealer at a rate of $15.30 a barrel and the swap dealer agrees to pay Counterparty B the average daily price for oil during the preceding month. At the same time, Counterparty A agrees to pay the swap dealer the average daily spot price for oil during the preceding month in exchange for payments from

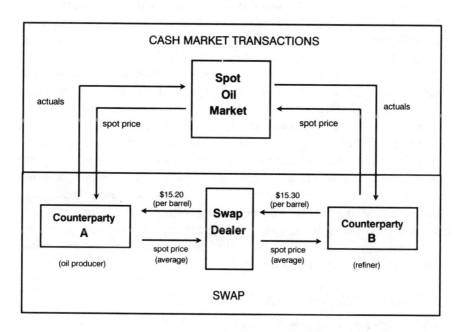

FIGURE 2.11 Commodity Swap with Cash Market Transactions

the dealer at the rate of $15.20 a barrel. As can be seen in Figure 2.11, these payments have the effect of fixing the price of crude oil for both the oil producer and the oil refiner.

The difference in the notional quantities in these two swaps raises an interesting point. If Counterparty A and Counterparty B had attempted a swap with each other directly, it would have failed because the parties have different notional requirements. But, by using a swap dealer, both swaps are viable. The swap dealer can offset the risk from the mismatched notionals by entering a third swap as fixed–price payer on 4,000 barrels. And, until an appropriate counterparty can be found, the swap dealer can hedge in oil futures.

2.6 VARIANTS

There are two basic ways to create a swap variant. The first is to enter into two separate commitments. Both might be swaps or only one might be a swap. For example, by entering a fixed–for–floating dollar–based interest rate swap as floating–rate receiver and simultaneously entering a fixed–for–floating dollar–for–deutschemark currency swap as floating–rate payer, a counterparty can convert a fixed–rate dollar obligation to a fixed–rate deutschemark obligation. If both floating legs are tied to LIBOR, the usual case, then this particular combination is called a **circus swap**. The circus swap is depicted in Figure 2.12.

As a second example, a floating–rate paying counterparty to an interest rate swap might also enter a multiperiod interest rate option, such as an interest rate cap. The cap has the effect of placing a ceiling on the floating rate that might, at any given time, have to be paid.

The second way to create a swap variant is to alter the terms of the swap itself. There are a great many ways by which a swap can be tailored to suit some specific end user need. For example, while the notionals are normally nonamortizing over the life of a swap, they can be made amortizing; swap agreements can be entered with options to extend or to shorten their stated lives; swaps can be entered with delayed setting of the swap coupon; and so on. We will illustrate these variants, and many others, in the chapters that follow.

2.7 ILLUSTRATING CASH FLOWS

Boxed cash flow diagrams like the ones we have been using to illustrate the cash flows between swap counterparties are very useful for under-

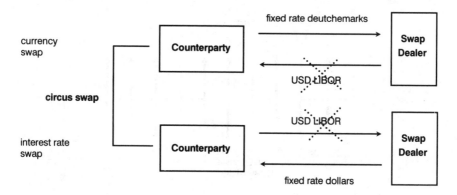

Definition: A synthetic structure is a combination of instruments that replicates the cash flows associated with a real instrument.

FIGURE 2.12   The Circus Swap (synthetic fixed–for–fixed currency swap)

standing the relationship between the counterparties. Another useful way to depict the cash flows associated with a swap is by way of a cash flow line. In this form of representation, a horizontal line is drawn to reflect the passage of time. Then, arrows pointing up are drawn to indicate cash inflows (payments received) and arrows are drawn pointed down to indicate cash outflows. If all the arrows are the same size, the cash flows represent a fixed rate. (Alternatively, fixed rates are often denoted $\bar{R}$.) If the size of the cash flows vary, the cash flows represent a floating rate. (Alternatively, floating rates are often denoted by $\tilde{R}$.) A typical scenario is depicted in Figure 2.13. Importantly, these diagrams only illustrate the cash flows for one of the two counterparties. But, of course, the other counterparty's cash flows from the swap are the mirror image of these cash flows.

When the cash flows are in different currencies, we often represent the different currencies by giving the arrows different colors or different patterns. For example, we might have a swap with the fixed–rate deutsche-marks (hatched arrows) and floating-rate dollars (solid arrows) that is depicted in Figure 2.14.

The locations of the up and down arrows on the time line indicate the points in time when the cash flows occur. This is very useful, particularly if the timings of the two sets of cash flows are different. An example of this is depicted in Figure 2.15.

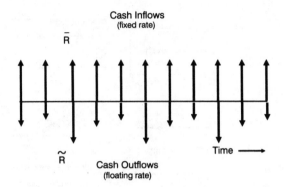

FIGURE 2.13   Arrow Cash Flow Diagram (fixed versus floating-rate payments)

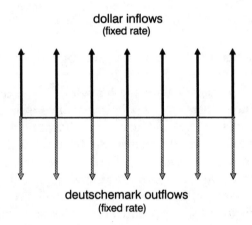

FIGURE 2.14   Arrow Cash Flow Diagram (multiple currency representation)

Finally, it may be that some of the cash flows are uncertain for one reason or another. For example, some swaps allow one party to elect to terminate the swap on or after a specific date but prior to the swap's scheduled maturity. Other swaps allow one party to extend the swap for an additional period of time, that is, to extend the swap beyond the scheduled termination date. In either case, some of the cash flows are uncertain until the party with the right to terminate or extend the swap,

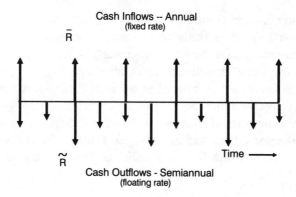

FIGURE 2.15 Arrow Cash Flow Diagram (different payment dates and/or frequencies)

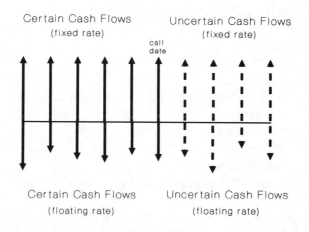

FIGURE 2.16 Arrow Cash Flow Diagram (certain versus uncertain cash flows)

as the case may be, makes an election to do so or not to do so. In order to indicate that some of the cash flows are uncertain, we often represent the uncertain ones with broken lines. This is illustrated in Figure 2.16.

2.8 SUMMARY

All swaps are predicated on the same basic model. This is true of interest rate swaps, currency swaps, commodity swaps, and equity swaps. In the basic, or generic, forms, one counterparty pays the other counterparty a fixed price on a given quantity of notional underlying assets while the second counterparty pays the first counterparty a floating price on a given quantity of the same or different notional assets. This simple structure has many uses and can be altered in an incredible number of ways to achieve very specific outcomes.

There are a number of different ways to represent the cash flows associated with swaps. Each has its own special uses. The two most widely used are the "boxed cash flow approach" and the "arrow cash flow approach."

REVIEW QUESTIONS

1. Define the following terms as they pertain to swaps:
   (a) floating price (or rate)
   (b) fixed price (or rate)
   (c) LIBOR
   (d) swap coupon
2. Define the following terms as they pertain to swaps:
   (a) reset dates
   (b) effective date
   (c) termination date
   (d) payment dates
3. Define the following terms as they pertain to swaps:
   (a) tenor
   (b) notionals
   (c) actuals
   (d) reference rate
4. Define the concept of a "quality spread differential" and explain why early swap literature defined this differential as the potential gains from a swap (see Note 1).
5. Why might one firm in one country have a comparative borrowing advantage in its domestic capital markets relative to a foreign firm of equivalent credit quality? Discuss.
6. In brief, why should we not add money market yield differentials to bond basis yield differentials without first making an adjustment? Can a failure to make such an adjustment cause errors in judgment with respect to the benefits from swap finance? Why?

7. Fixed–rate financings created by floating–rate borrowings coupled with a fixed–for–floating interest rate swap are often referred to as "synthetic fixed–rate financings." What is the word "synthetic" in this term meant to imply?

8. Why might a counterparty to a swap prefer some variant of the plain vanilla structure to the plain vanilla structure itself? Can you think of a few examples?

9. What benefits might there be to using the "boxed cash flow" approach (as in Figures 2.1, 2.2, and 2.3) relative to the "arrow cash flow approach" (as depicted in Figures 2.14, 2.15, and 2.16) and vice versa?

10. Why is it important to state an interest rate on an annual basis but to also make it very clear that the rate applies to a borrowing of a specific term, such as specifying six–month LIBOR or three–month LIBOR?

NOTES

1. The comparative advantage is explained by **quality spread differentials** among borrowers in the cash markets. In brief, the poorer a credit, the greater the premium it must pay for a long–term fixed rate over a floating rate if that floating rate is established by short–term borrowings with roll-overs. The difference between the long–term fixed rate of the poorer credit and the long–term fixed rate of the better credit represents a quality spread. Similarly, the difference between the short–term floating rate for the poorer credit and the short–term floating rate for the better credit is a quality spread. Since the long–term quality spread is greater than the short–term quality spread, there is a quality spread differential. On the surface, it would seem that this quality spread differential is a direct measure of the gains to be achieved with an interest rate swap. Some, including the authors, have argued that quality spread differentials can seriously overstate the gains to be achieved from the use of swaps. The overstatement of gains is a consequence of a number of quantitative and qualitative factors that are often overlooked. This issue is addressed in Chapter 7. For further discussion, see Bansal, Bicksler, Chen, and Marshall (1993).

2. If required, the swap dealer can write the swap with other payment frequencies: fixed–rate annual against one–year LIBOR or fixed–rate quarterly against three–month LIBOR, etc.

3. Bond basis assumes that a year has 365 days and pays interest on each and every one of those days. (Alternatively, bond basis can assume that interest is paid on a 360-day basis and each month has exactly 30 days.)

Money market basis, on the other hand, assumes that a year has 360 days but pays interest on all 365 days. Because the two measures employ different day-count conventions, an adjustment is needed to equalize bond basis and money market basis differentials. Assuming that the payment frequencies on the bond basis and money market basis yields are the same, the adjustment is straightforward. Bond basis is converted to money market basis by multiplying bond basis by 360/365 and money market basis is converted to bond basis by multiplying money market basis by 365/360. (This adjustment is more fully described in Chapter 3.)

4. As with interest rate swaps, there are other motivations for currency swaps besides comparative advantage. For example, the end user might have an existing obligation that it wishes to offset, or the swap might be just one component in a complex structure, or the end user might lack direct access to debt markets in the desired currency.

5. LIBOR, like all interest rates, is quoted for different borrowing terms but is always stated on an annual basis. For example, one-year LIBOR (1-Y LIBOR) denotes the annual rate of interest on a one-year Eurodollar deposit. Similarly, six-month LIBOR (6-M LIBOR) denotes the annual rate of interest on a six-month Eurodollar deposit, and so on.

6. For purposes of this example, we are assuming that deutschemark interest differentials and dollar interest differentials are directly comparable. We are also assuming that fixed-rate differentials and floating-rate differentials in the same currency are directly comparable. Neither of these treatments is technically correct but insufficient information has been provided to make the necessary adjustments. Little is lost in employing these treatments for purposes of illustrating the concepts involved. The necessary adjustments are fully described in later chapters.

REFERENCES AND SUGGESTED READING

Bansal, V. K., J. L. Bicksler, A. H. Chen, and J. F. Marshall. "The Gains from Interest Rate Swaps: Fact or Fancy." *Journal of Applied Corporate Finance*, forthcoming, 1993.

Liaw, T. "Interest Rate Swaps and Interest Rate Savings." In *The Swaps Handbook: 1991-92 Supplement*, K. R. Kapner and J. F. Marshall, eds., New York: New York Institute of Finance, 1991.

3
Interest Rate Swaps

3.1 OVERVIEW

In this chapter we will discuss interest rate swaps in more detail. We will examine how swap dealers quote interest rate swap coupons on generic interest rate swaps. Next, we will consider how swap quotations are adjusted when the required terms differ from those of the generic swap. Specifically, we will consider how dealers adjust their swap coupons for payment frequencies that are different from those of the generic swap, how dealers adjust their pricing to account for amortization of notional principal, and how dealers adjust their pricing when the client requires off–market pricing. Swap pricing and adjustments to swap pricing are of interest to both those who work on swap desks and those who use swap products. End users, for example, might want to compare the pricing of swaps offered by several swap dealers and compare the all–in cost of these swap alternatives to the all–in cost of other financing and/or other risk-management opportunities available to them.

Next, we will consider a few of the uses for interest rate swaps other than reducing financing costs. Specifically, we will consider how interest rate swaps are used to hedge interest rate exposures and how interest rate swaps can be used to manage seasonal cash flows. (In a later chapter we will consider some of the other uses for interest rate swaps, including the creation of synthetic securities.) Finally, we will look at some of the many variants of interest rate swaps and touch on a few of their uses.

We will not delve into the methodology used by swap dealers to arrive at their swap pricing for their generic at-market swaps in this chapter. For now, we will take this as given. Later, in Chapter 7, we will look more closely at the pricing issue. We do not mean to imply, by postponing a discussion of swap pricing, that the pricing of swaps is unimportant. On the contrary, it is extremely important. But, it is also technically difficult. For this reason, it is better postponed until we have a better grasp of the basic concepts and terminology. For now, suffice to say that the pricing of swaps will hinge on a number of factors. These include: 1. the maturity of the swap; 2. the structure of the swap; 3. the availability of other counterparties with whom the dealer can offset the swap; 4. the existence and the pricing of other instruments in which a swap dealer can synthesize a swap; 5. the creditworthiness of the counterparty; 6. the demand and supply conditions for credit generally and for swaps in particular in all countries whose currencies are involved in the swap; and 7. any regulatory constraints on the flow of capital that influence the efficiency of the markets.

3.2 INDICATIVE PRICING SCHEDULES: THE INTEREST RATE SWAP

Swap dealers regularly prepare **indicative pricing schedules** for use by their capital market personnel. These schedules provide the dealers' traders with guidelines for pricing swaps, and they are updated frequently to take account of changing market conditions. Prices take the form of interest rates, called swap coupons, and are stated in terms of basis points (bps). Each basis point is $1/100$ of one percent. In the case of dollar-based interest rates, the fixed-rate side of the swap is usually stated as a spread over prevailing yields on **on the run** U.S. Treasury securities. On the runs are the securities of a given maturity that were most recently auctioned. For example, five years ago the Treasury auctioned ten-year notes. With the passage of time, these ten-year notes have become five-year notes. If the Treasury were now to auction a new issue of five-year notes, then there would be at least 2 five-year T-note issues simultaneously trading. The most recent issues (the on the run) have the more current coupon and tend to be more liquid than the older issues. The floating-rate side of an interest rate swap is most often taken to be LIBOR flat. The pricing structure assumes **bullet transactions**. That is, the notional principal is assumed to be **nonamortizing**.

A minor complication introduced by this pricing scheme is that the interest rate on the fixed–rate side of a swap is quoted as a semiannual **bond equivalent yield**, that is, semiannual bond basis. Bond equivalent yields employ either an "actual over 365" day-count convention or a "30 over 360" day-count convention.[1] (The "30 over 360" day-count convention means that every month is assumed to have 30 days and a year is assumed to have 360 days.) We will employ the "actual over 365" version in all of our references to "bond basis." The floating–rate side is usually tied to LIBOR. LIBOR is quoted as a **money market yield**, that is, money market basis. Money market yields employ an "actual over 360" day-count convention. This difference in day-count conventions often necessitates some conversions to make the rates more directly comparable. This issue, which was touched on in both Chapters 1 and 2, will be addressed in more detail in this chapter.

In the early days of swaps, it was quite common for a swap dealer to require a front–end fee for arranging a swap. The front–end fee was negotiable and could run as much as one–half of a percentage point. The justification for the front–end fee was the time it took to write the swap documentation and the time it took to work with the client to design a swap that would accomplish the client's objectives. With the increasing standardization of swaps, front–end fees have all but disappeared. Today, a front–end fee will only be imposed when some fancy financial engineering is required or when the client is purchasing a special optionlike feature. In the latter case, the front–end fee is best viewed as an option premium. Front–end fees have never been common on interbank swaps.[2]

Consider a typical indicative pricing schedule for swaps with various maturities as depicted in Table 3.1. The prices indicated are for fixed–for–floating interest rate swaps and assume semiannual compounding (sa). Although we always state interest rates on an annual basis, it is customary to call an annual rate of interest compounded semiannually a "**semiannual rate**." For example, the phrase "a semiannual rate of 8 percent" means an annual interest rate of 8 percent that is compounded semiannually. The phrase "an annual rate of 8 percent" means an annual interest rate of 8 percent that is compounded annually.

Let us consider a simple example: A corporation has determined that it can sell $25 million of five–year nonamortizing debt at par by offering a semiannual coupon of 9.675 percent.[3] It prefers floating–rate liabilities to fixed–rate liabilities and approaches the capital markets group of our

Table 3.1   Indicative Pricing for Interest Rate Swaps

Maturity	Dealer Pays Fixed Rate	Dealer Receives Fixed Rate	Current TN Rate
2 years	2-yr TN sa + 38 bps	2-yr TN sa + 44 bps	8.55%
3 years	3-yr TN sa + 46 bps	3-yr TN sa + 52 bps	8.72%
4 years	4-yr TN sa + 50 bps	4-yr TN sa + 58 bps	8.85%
5 years	5-yr TN sa + 52 bps	5-yr TN sa + 60 bps	8.92%
6 years	6-yr TN sa + 58 bps	6-yr TN sa + 66 bps	8.96%
7 years	7-yr TN sa + 62 bps	7-yr TN sa + 70 bps	9.00%
10 years	10-yr TN sa + 74 bps	10-yr TN sa + 84 bps	9.08%

The schedule assumes semiannual rates and bullet transactions and it assumes that the counterparty is a triple-A credit. TN denotes the Treasury note rate. All rates are quoted against six-month LIBOR flat.

swap dealer to arrange an interest rate swap. Call this firm Counterparty 1.

The swap dealer has been asked to pay fixed rate and receive floating rate. Since the dealer has been asked to pay fixed rate, the dealer offers to pay 9.44 percent (5-year TN rate + 52 bps) in exchange for six-month LIBOR. The firm's net cost of funds, after the interest rate swap, *appears* to be LIBOR plus 0.235 percent (9.675% + LIBOR – 9.440%). This is not, however, quite correct. Because the fixed-rate sides are bond equivalent yields, the difference between them, 0.235 percent, is also a bond equivalent. This difference cannot be added directly to LIBOR without first converting it to a money market yield equivalent. Remember, six-month LIBOR is quoted as a money market yield (MMY) and based on the assumption of a 360-day year, while the fixed-rate side of a fixed-for-floating rate swap is quoted as a semiannual bond equivalent yield (BEY) and based on the assumption of a 365-day year. The importance of the difference in yield conventions when pricing swaps now becomes apparent. For this reason, we will reiterate some of what has already been said on this subject.

To combine these values correctly, we must transform the fixed-rate differential, 0.235 percent, to its money market yield equivalent. The conversion formula appears as Equation 3.1.[4] This conversion is simple because both six-month LIBOR and the swap coupon are semiannual rates. When the payment frequencies are mismatched (annual vs. semiannual, for example) the conversions are somewhat more complex.

$$\text{MMY differential} = \text{BEY differential} \times \frac{360}{365}$$

$$= 0.235\% \times \frac{360}{365} \qquad (3.1)$$

$$= 0.232\%$$

The final floating–rate cost of funding for the firm is then LIBOR plus 0.232 percent. The cash flows associated with this swap are depicted in Figure 3.1. As it happens, had this firm borrowed directly in the floating–rate market, it would have been required to pay LIBOR plus 0.75 percent. The firm thus enjoyed a cost savings by engaging in the swap.

The swap dealer in Figure 3.1 would look for an opportunity to offset this swap with another swap. Until it can do so, however, the dealer will hedge in T–notes and Eurodollars (or T–bills). For example, since the swap dealer has agreed to pay fixed rate and receive floating rate on the swap, it might borrow $25 million in the six–month Eurodollar market (or sell $25 million of T–bills short) and use the proceeds from this borrowing (or short sale) to purchase $25 million of five–year Treasury notes.[5]

If a short sale of securities is involved, the dealer can obtain the securities for the short sale by a **reverse repurchase** agreement (a reverse) with another institution. In a reverse, the dealer "purchases" a security from another party and agrees to "sell" the security back to this same party at a specific later date for a specific price. An alternative way to obtain securities for a short sale exists when the swap dealer holds a portfolio of Treasuries separate and distinct from its swap operations. This is not unusual, because most swap dealers are major commercial or investment banks. For example, the portfolio might represent an

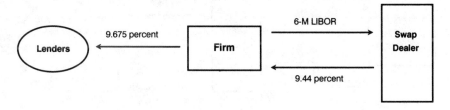

Net cost = LIBOR + 23.2 bps (MMY)

FIGURE 3.1 Synthetic Floating–Rate Financing

investment portfolio that the dealer bank manages either for itself or for its clients, or the swap dealer bank might be a market maker in Treasuries (known as a government securities dealer). These portfolios can serve as the source of the securities that the swap dealer sells short. The swap desk will pay other departments of the bank for these securities. The cost of these intrabank borrowings is called the **transfer pricing rate (TPR)**. The transaction may be viewed as equivalent to a reverse repurchase agreement between departments within the bank. For purposes of this text, we assume that the TPR is the prevailing rate on Treasuries of the maturity borrowed. In practice, the TPR will often be at a premium to Treasuries. The cash flows for the swap dealer are depicted in Figure 3.2.

The swap dealer prefers to offset the swaps to which it is a counterparty with matching swaps with other counterparties. The Treasury/Eurodollar positions represent hedges placed only until such time as a matched swap can be arranged. It is important to note that if the swap dealer hedges in T–bills, as opposed to Eurodollars, it will have a residual basis risk because LIBOR and the T–bill rate are not perfectly correlated.

Suppose now that another firm approaches the swap dealer in need of $30 million of fixed–rate dollar financing. This firm has a comparative advantage in the floating–rate (LIBOR) market. It can sell five–year nonamortizing floating rate notes at par by paying six–month LIBOR plus 150 basis points. (**Floating rate notes**, also known as **FRNs** or **floaters**, are debt securities in which the coupon is periodically reset to some prevailing reference rate of interest.) Through the vehicle of the swap, the firm would like to convert this floating–rate liability into a

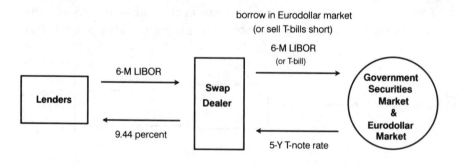

FIGURE 3.2   Dealer's Position with Hedge in Cash Markets

fixed–rate liability. The swap dealer is asked to receive fixed rate and pay floating rate. Call this firm Counterparty 2.

Assume that the indication pricing schedule depicted in Table 3.1 is still in effect. Since the dealer has been asked to receive fixed rate, it would require that Counterparty 2 pay 9.52 percent (5–year TN rate + 60 bps) in exchange for the dealer paying six–month LIBOR flat. To calculate Counterparty 2's net cost of funds, we must first convert the floating–rate spread over LIBOR (i.e., 1.5%), which is stated on a money market basis, to a bond basis. Equation 3.1 allowed us to move from a bond equivalent yield to a money market yield; in this case, however, we need to move in the opposite direction. Equation 3.2 allows us to move from a money market yield to a bond equivalent yield. Again, this conversion is simple because both rates are already stated on a semiannual basis. If the payment frequencies were mismatched, the conversions would be more complex.

$$
\begin{aligned}
\text{BEY differential} &= \text{MMY differential} \times \frac{365}{360} \\
&= 1.5\% \times \frac{365}{360} \\
&= 1.521\%
\end{aligned}
\tag{3.2}
$$

The conversion renders the value 1.521 percent. Counterparty 2's net cost of funds, after the interest rate swap, is then 11.041 percent (LIBOR + 1.521% – LIBOR + 9.52%). As it happens, this firm could have borrowed fixed–rate funds directly at a cost of 11.375 percent. Thus, this firm has also enjoyed a benefit from its swap.

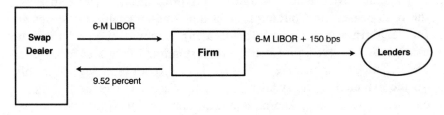

Net cost = 11.041 percent sa

FIGURE 3.3 Synthetic Fixed–Rate Financing

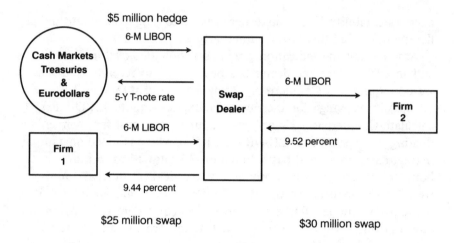

FIGURE 3.4 Partially Matched Swaps with Remaining Hedge

The cash flows between the dealer and Counterparty 2 are depicted in Figure 3.3. The swap dealer could offset its position with Counterparty 2 by selling $30 million of five–year Treasury notes short and by using the proceeds from this short sale to lend $30 million in the Eurodollar market (or to purchase T–bills).

Notice that the dealer's cash flows with Counterparty 2 are very nearly the mirror image of its cash flows with Counterparty 1. In fact, if the swap dealer lifts its Treasury market positions that it is using to hedge its swap with Counterparty 1, it will only require a $5 million position in Treasuries/Eurodollars to hedge the interest rate exposure that stems from its swap with Counterparty 2. The flows, from the swap dealer's perspective, are depicted in Figure 3.4.

The indicative pricing schedule used to price the swaps made between the swap dealer and Counterparties 1 and 2 assumes that the swaps are of the plain vanilla fixed–for–floating rate variety and that the counterparties have a satisfactory credit standing in the eyes of the swap dealer. Thus, the indicative pricing schedule provides starting prices only. To the extent that the swap will require a special structure, or that a counterparty's credit standing is not first rate, or that the swap exposes the dealer to special risks, the swap pricing will have to be adjusted to reflect these factors. Price adjustments can take the forms of a wider swap pay–receive spread or a front–end fee or both.

3.3 ADJUSTMENTS TO INDICATIVE PRICING

The indicative pricing schedule assumes that 1. the swap's notional principal is nonamortizing (i.e., bullet transactions); 2. payments are to be made semiannually; 3. the swap is at–market; and 4. the floating rate is six–month LIBOR. An **at–market swap**, also known as a **par swap**, is a swap on which the present values of the payments on the floating and fixed legs are equal and, therefore, does not require any front-end fee to compensate one side or the other.

It is not unusual for an end user to require amortizing notionals or to require a payment frequency other than semiannual. Occasionally, a swap end user has reason to want a swap that is written off–market. In the several subsections that follow, we will examine how swap prices are adjusted to accommodate these requirements.

3.3.1 Amortizing Swaps: A Role for Average Life

The indicative pricing schedule assumes that the swap is nonamortizing so that the interest payments are calculated on the same notional principal throughout the term of the swap. Suppose instead that the swap dealer's client requires a swap that is based upon amortizing principal. Any number of amortization schedules are possible. For example, the client might require that: 1. the notional principal underlying the swap be reduced by a fixed dollar amount each year (often called a **sinking fund** schedule); 2. the notional principal be reduced by a fixed dollar amount each year beginning *after* some defined **grace period**, during which no amortization of notional principal occurs; or, 3. the principal amortizes at an increasing rate, as is customary with mortgage–type amortization schedules.

As already described, most swap dealers quote the fixed–rate side of an interest rate swap as a spread over Treasury securities. Treasury debt is always nonamortizing. That is, the Treasury pays periodic (semiannual) interest but does not repay any principal on a Treasury note or bond until such time as the note or bond matures. At maturity, the Treasury repays all principal in a single transaction. Given the nonamortizing nature of Treasury securities, it is not appropriate to base the price of an *N*–year *amortizing* swap on the prevailing yield of an *N*–year *nonamortizing* Treasury security.

Operatives in the debt markets, including commercial banks, investment banks, and government securities dealers, know that, all other things being equal, the longer the maturity associated with a given debt instrument, the more price sensitive the debt instrument will be to fluctuations in yield levels. It is partly for this reason that long–term debt instruments are regarded as more risky than short–term debt instruments. This fact forms the foundation for one well–known, though not universally accepted, explanation for the shape of the Treasury **yield curve**—the liquidity preference theory—which holds that the yield on a debt instrument is directly related to its price sensitivity to interest rate fluctuations.[6] It has also long been known that maturity alone is not the sole determinant of a debt instrument's price sensitivity to changes in interest rates. Two other important factors are the speed with which the debt principal amortizes and the size of the coupons. Other less important factors include the frequency of the coupon payments and the yield presently afforded by the instrument. In 1938, Frederick Macaulay developed a measure of price sensitivity to yield changes that incorporated all five of the factors that influence price sensitivity. This measure is known as **duration**.

Assuming equal basis point changes in yield, two debt instruments with identical durations will have identical interest rate sensitivities. In addition, the ratio of two debt instruments' durations is an accurate measure of their relative price sensitivities to equivalent yield changes when such price sensitivity is stated on a percentage basis. Duration, which is measured in years and denoted here by D, is a weighted–average time to the maturity of the instrument. The weights are the ratios of the present values of the future cash flows (including both interest and principal) to the current market price of the instrument. The current price of the instrument is, of course, the sum of the present value of all future cash flows associated with the instrument. The duration formula appears below as Equation 3.3.

$$D = \sum_{t}^{mT} w_t \times (t/m) \qquad (3.3)$$

$$\text{where} \quad w_t = \frac{CF_t(1 + y/m)^{-t}}{\sum_{t} CF_t(1 + y/m)^{-t}} \qquad t = 1,2,3,...mT$$

CF_t = cash flow for period t
   y = present yield on instrument
  m = number of periods per year
   T = number of years

Because of its long–standing role as a measure of a debt instrument's price sensitivity to fluctuations in yield, it seems logical to use duration in the pricing of the fixed–rate side of swaps. Unfortunately, duration has proven unsatisfactory for this purpose. The duration equation allows one to determine an instrument's duration *if* one knows its yield. A problem occurs when the instrument's duration *and* the appropriate yield—which is the fixed rate of interest used for the swap coupon for an at–market swap—are both unknown.

One widely used solution to pricing the fixed–rate side of a swap is to use a weighted–average measure of the times at which notional principal is amortized where the weights are formed without reference to yield. **Average life** is such a measure.[7]

The average life of an instrument is found by forming the products of the principal repayments and the times at which those principal repayments will be made. These products are then added and the sum is divided by the notional principal at the start of the swap. The average life formula appears as Equation 3.4.

$$AL = \frac{\sum P_t \times (t/m)}{IP} \qquad (3.4)$$

AL = average life
P_t = principal repaid (or canceled) at time t
IP = initial principal (principal at start of swap)
m = number of payments per year

It is important to remember that in interest rate swaps the principal repayments are only notional. The notional nature of the principal, however, does not affect the calculation of the average life.

Let's consider a simple example: Suppose a firm requires an amortizing swap with an initial notional principal of $9.5 million and a tenor of nine and one–half years with semiannual payments. The principal will amortize under a semiannual sinking–fund type schedule with notional principal payments of $0.5 million each. Thus, the first payment is due at the end of period 1 (i.e., $t = 1$ so $t/m = 0.5$ years), the second is due at the end of period 2, and so on until the last, which is due at the end of period 19 (i.e., $t = 19$ so $t/m = 9.5$ years). The first product is formed by multiplying \$0.5 million by 0.5, the second is formed by multiplying \$0.5 million by 1, and so on.

These products are then added to get 47.5 million. Finally, this sum is divided by the initial notional principal of 9.5 million to get an average life of five years. Thus, the swap has an average life of five years. The calculation of this average life follows.

Time	Principal Repaid	Product
0.5	$\times$ \$0.5 M =	\$0.25 M
1.0	$\times$ \$0.5 M =	\$0.50 M
.	.	
.	.	
.	.	
9.5	$\times$ \$0.5 M =	\$4.75 M
	Sum	47.50 M

$$AL = \frac{47.5}{9.5} = 5 \text{ years}$$

Once the average life has been determined, the swap's average life is used in lieu of its maturity for purposes of pricing the swap as a spread over Treasuries. Thus, this particular swap would be priced from the five-year T-note. While the average life of an amortizing instrument is not the same as its term to maturity, the average life of a nonamortizing instrument, such as a T-note, is identical to its term to maturity.

When pricing swaps, an important argument in favor of the use of average life, as opposed to duration, lies in the treatment of interest. With a typical debt instrument, interest payments flow only one way. With a swap, interest payments flow two ways and are therefore largely offsetting. The offsetting nature of the interest payments suggests a strong argument for focusing on the principal alone—which is precisely what average life does. Additionally, zero coupon instruments have a duration that is identical to their average life and also identical to their maturity. As we will demonstrate in Chapter 8, zero coupon yield curves play an important role in pricing and hedging swaps.

3.3.2 Payment Frequencies

Interest rate swaps priced as a spread over Treasuries assume semiannual interest payments. When the dealer's client requires annual payments, as opposed to semiannual payments, the dealer must adjust the fixed rate of interest to reflect this difference.

Consider again the case of Counterparty 2, which had approached the swap dealer for a five-year fixed–for–floating interest rate swap. This party would pay fixed rate and receive floating rate. The dealer quotes a semiannual fixed rate of 9.52 percent (5-year TN + 60 bps). Counterparty 2 now indicates that it prefers *annual* fixed–rate payments, although it still wishes to receive semiannual floating–rate payments based on six-month LIBOR.

The swap dealer is agreeable but must now determine the annual rate that is *equivalent* to a semiannual rate of 9.52 percent. The procedure for determining the equivalent annual rate is founded on basic time value arithmetic. That is, we calculate the annual interest rate that would provide the same future value, for a given starting sum, as would the semiannual rate. This calculation appears as Equation 3.5.

$$r_{an} = \left(1 + \frac{r_{sa}}{2}\right)^2 - 1 \qquad (3.5)$$

In Equation 3.5, r_{an} denotes the annual interest rate and r_{sa} denotes the semiannual interest rate. More generally, an interest rate stated on one payment frequency can be converted to an interest rate stated on another payment frequency by using the relationship given in Equation 3.6.

$$r_m = m \times \left[\left(1 + \frac{r_z}{z}\right)^{z/m} - 1\right] \qquad (3.6)$$

r_m = rate of interest assuming m compoundings per year.
r_z = rate of interest assuming z compoundings per year.

In this more general formulation, m would be 1 if the rate r_m were annual; z would be 2 if the rate r_z were semiannual; and so on. These conversions ignore the issue of reinvestment risk. **Reinvestment risk** is the risk that income received from an investment will be reinvested at a rate that differs from the rate that prevailed at the time the investment was acquired. The swap dealer might be expected to attach a small premium to its swap pricing when the swap structure gives rise to reinvestment risk. In a large swap portfolio, reinvestment risk is largely diversified away, so we will ignore it.

Now let's return to Counterparty 2. Counterparty 2 requires a payment schedule that provides for annual, rather than semiannual, payments of fixed–rate interest. The dealer calculates the annual fixed rate using Equation 3.6.

$$r_1 = 1 \times [(1 + .0952/2)^{2/1} - 1] = 9.747\%$$

The swap dealer now offers counterparty 2 a fixed–for–floating rate swap in which the dealer would pay semiannual interest to Counterparty 2, at the rate of six–month LIBOR, in exchange for counterparty 2's annual payments to the dealer, at the rate of 9.747 percent.

There is one additional problem with this swap from the swap dealer's perspective. Since the dealer pays the client semiannually but the client only pays the dealer annually, there is a payment mismatch that exposes the dealer to additional credit risk. For example, suppose that the floating–rate side is initially set at 8.5 percent and that six months after the swap documents are executed, the dealer pays its counterparty client $1.275 million—calculated as one–half of 8.5 percent on $30 million. Next, suppose that, six months later, the client defaults at the time that it is due to make its first payment to the dealer. While the client's default frees the dealer from its obligation to make the current and future interest payments, as per the rights of set–off contained in the terms and conditions of the swap agreement, the dealer has already made its first payment to the client. It must now utilize the swap's default provisions to try to recover its losses.

This example illustrates the extra level of risk associated with entering into swaps that have payment timing mismatches. This is one special form of risk that is associated with a swap book. We will consider this problem, and the steps the swap dealer might take to alleviate it, again in Chapter 8. One final point is, however, in order. Because payment timing mismatches increase the risk exposure of the swap dealer, we might expect that the swap dealer will insist on additional compensation from its client. For example, the dealer might add a few basis points to the fixed rate its client is required to pay.

3.3.3 Off–Market Pricing

The off–market pricing problem arises when, for one reason or another, a client of the swap dealer requires a swap coupon that is different from that quoted for par swaps. Most often, a need for off–market pricing arises when the client has an existing commitment that it cannot perfectly offset at the par coupon.

Adjustments to swap pricing to reflect the off–market requirements of a counterparty can be handled in three ways. These are all based on equating present values and they are equivalent in a present value sense. The first method is to determine the present value differential between the at–market swap and the required off–market swap. The counterparty receiving the greater present value would then pay that identical sum to the other counterparty. If the off–market swap has a swap coupon below that for at–market swaps, the payment is called a **buy down**. If the off–market swap has a swap coupon above that for at–market swaps, the payment is called a **buy up**. Let's consider a complete example.

Suppose that a counterparty wants to be the fixed–rate payer on a five-year swap. At–market pricing requires a swap coupon of 9.52 percent sa. The client, however, would like a swap with a coupon of only 9.30 percent. The notional principal is $20 million. We need to determine the present value of the required differential. The differential is 0.22 percent (22 bps) per year or 11 basis points per six–month period. Since this same differential will be exchanged each period, we can view it as an annuity. The problem is then to determine the present value of 11 basis points on $20 million (.0011 × $20 million = $22,000) for ten periods (5 years × 2 periods per year) using a semiannual discount rate of 9.52 percent. The present value annuity formula, given by Equation 3.7, is used for this purpose. The calculation follows immediately.

$$PVA = PMT \times \left[\frac{1 - (1 + y/m)^{-nm}}{(y/m)} \right] \tag{3.7}$$

PVA = present value of the annuity
PMT = annuity payment (per period)
y = yield or discount rate (annual)
m = periods per year
n = number of years (tenor)

$$PVA = \$22,000 \times \left[\frac{1 - (1 + .0952/2)^{-10}}{.0952/2} \right]$$
$$= \$171,875.65$$

We conclude that the off–market swap required by the client has a present value of $171,875.65 in favor of the client. Thus, to obtain a lower rate than the current swap coupon for at–market swaps, the client will have to pay the dealer an up–front fee of $171,875.65. Because the client is looking for a coupon below the current market rate, this constitutes a **buy down**.

The second method for adjusting the present values is to require a payment upon the termination of the swap. Since we know the present value from our previous calculation, we can easily project the terminal value (TV) using the same rate. This calculation appears below:

$$TV = PVA \times (1 + 0.0952/2)^{10}$$
$$= \$171,875.65 \times 1.59204$$
$$= \$273,633.49$$

Terminal value adjustments are rarely, if ever, used to adjust the pricing on off–market swaps and we will not consider them further.

The final method, and one that is often used, is to adjust the floating–rate side of the swap to maintain the present value equality of the two legs of the swap. In this particular case, we know that the client wants a swap coupon that is 22 basis points less than the at–market swap coupon. This 22 basis point differential is, of course, quoted bond basis. Before adjusting the floating–rate side of the swap, we will need to determine the money market basis equivalent. This adjustment has been illustrated several times before. It appears below:

$$\text{Floating leg adjustment} = -22 \text{ bps} \times \frac{360}{365}$$
$$= -21.7 \text{ bps}$$

The swap would then have a swap coupon of 9.30 percent sa and a floating rate of 6-M LIBOR minus 21.7 bps. The buy down and floating leg off–market adjustments are contrasted in Figure 3.5.

3.4 MARKET IMBALANCES AND PAY/RECEIVE RATE ADJUSTMENTS

The difference between the fixed rate a swap dealer must receive and the fixed rate it is willing to pay at any given average life is its pay–receive spread for swaps with that average life. In preparing its indicative pricing schedules and implied spreads, the swap dealer must take several things into consideration. Of major importance, of course, are the competitive

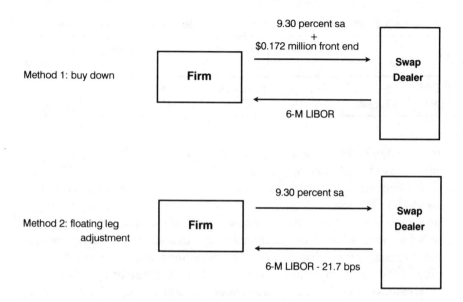

FIGURE 3.5 Off–Market Pricing

pressures of the market. The swap dealer must offer competitive swap pricing if it is to attract rate–conscious corporate clients.

Suppose that the swap dealer using the indicative pricing schedule appearing in Table 3.1 finds that it is attracting considerable five–year average life fixed–for–floating swap activity on the dealer–pays–fixed–rate side but very little swap activity on the other side. The swap dealer prefers to offset its swaps with other swaps rather than resorting to hedging in the cash market for Treasury securities. Look again at the dealer's current pricing for five–year average life swaps and assume that the dealer needs to attract additional swap activity on the dealer–receives–fixed–rate side. At present, the dealer's base pricing requires the Treasury note rate plus 60 basis points (TN + 60 bps) from fixed–rate payers. The dealer can attract additional activity on the dealer–receives–fixed–rate side by lowering the fixed rate it requires of fixed–rate paying counter-parties. For example, it could lower its price on five–year average life swaps to the Treasury note rate plus 58 basis points. At the same time, it might lower the rate that it will pay so as to discourage new swaps on the dealer–pays–fixed–rate side until such time as it can fully offset its existing portfolio of swaps. For example, it might lower its dealer–pays

Table 3.2   Pay-Receive Pricing Adjustment to Correct Market Imbalance

	Maturity	Dealer Pays Fixed Rate	Dealer Receives Fixed Rate	Current TN Rate
Old	5 years	5-yr TN sa + 52 bps	5-yr TN sa + 60 bps	8.92%
New	5 years	5-yr TN sa + 49 bps	5-yr TN sa + 58 bps	8.92%

rate to the Treasury note rate plus 49 basis points. These pricing adjustments are summarized in Table 3.2.

By frequently adjusting its pay-receive rates, the swap dealer is able to attract additional counterparties on the side of the market it prefers and to thereby correct market imbalances. In some cases, the swap dealer will find that some of the counterparties attracted to its prevailing rate are themselves swap dealers who have developed imbalances on the other side of the fixed–for–floating rate market. This is one of the reasons for **interbank swaps**—defined as swaps between banks. Recall that most swap dealers are banks.

3.5   VARIANT FORMS OF THE INTEREST RATE SWAP

The original swap structure, now known as the plain vanilla or generic swap structure, has given rise to literally hundreds of different variants. Some of these are considerably different from the plain vanilla structure while others are only minor variations. Often, the variant structures can be created by combining two or more swaps with the generic structure. We cannot possibly review all interest rate swap variants in this book. What follows is, therefore, limited to those variants that are widely used or that we feel will become widely used.

Amortizing and accreting swaps.   Amortizing swaps are swaps on which the notional principal is *reduced* at one or more points in time *prior* to the termination of the swap. Accreting swaps are swaps on which the notional principal is *increased* at one or more points in time prior to the termination of the swap. Both types of swaps require a separate schedule providing for the amortization or accretion of the notionals.

Roller coaster swaps.   These swaps provide for a period of accretion followed by a period of amortization of the notionals.

Mortgage-indexed and Collateralized Mortgage Obligation (CMO) swaps. Special classes of swaps that provide for the amortization of the notionals in a fashion consistent with the amortization of a mortgage or CMO pool.

Basis swaps. Also called floating-for-floating swaps, these are swaps on which both legs are floating but tied to two different indices. For example, one leg might be tied to LIBOR while the other is tied to the T-bill rate. Or, one leg might be tied to 6-M LIBOR while the other is tied to 3-M LIBOR.

Yield curve swaps. These are swaps on which both legs are floating but, unlike basis swaps, the floating legs may be tied to long-term rates. For example, one leg might be pegged to the auction rate on the 30-year Treasury bond and the other leg might be pegged to the auction rate on the 10-year Treasury note.

Zero coupon swaps. These are fixed-for-floating swaps on which the fixed rate is a zero coupon. That is, no payments are made on the fixed-rate leg of the swap until maturity. At maturity, the fixed rate settles for a single large payment.

Forward swaps. Also called deferred swaps, these are swaps in which the swap coupon is set on the transaction date but the swap does not commence (i.e., start to accrue interest) until a later date. This might be 30 days forward, 60 days forward, a year forward, and so on.

Delayed-rate setting swaps. Also called deferred-rate setting swaps. These swaps are swaps that commence immediately but on which the swap coupon is not set until a later date. The time of the rate setting is left, within contractual bounds, to the discretion of the end user. When it is set, it is set according to a previously agreed upon formula.

Callable swaps, putable swaps, and extendable swaps. These are swaps on which one party has the right, but not the obligation, to either extend or shorten the tenor of the swap. On a callable swap, the fixed-rate payer has the right to terminate the swap early. In a putable swap, the floating-rate payer has the right to terminate the swap early. In an extendable swap, one party has the right to extend the tenor of the swap beyond its scheduled termination date.

Rate–capped swaps.   These are swaps on which the floating rate is capped. This cap can be obtained by incorporating the cap directly into the terms of the swap or it can be purchased separately from an interest rate cap dealer. These types of swaps are discussed more fully in Chapter 6.

Reversible swaps.   These are swaps on which the fixed–rate payer and the floating–rate payer reverse roles one or more times during the life of the swap. That is, the floating–rate payer becomes the fixed–rate payer and the fixed–rate payer becomes the floating–rate payer.

Seasonal swaps.   These are broadly defined as any swap that is designed to deseason a firm's cash flows. There are a number of structures that can do this. One is for the swap to be fixed–for–fixed with mismatched payment dates. This type of swap is described more fully later in this chapter.

Swaptions.   Swaptions are options on swaps. That is, a firm expects to be in need of a swap at a later date but it is not sure the swap will be needed. At the same time, it finds the current swap pricing attractive and would like to lock–in that pricing. It then purchases a swaption on a par swap, which gives it the right but not the obligation to enter into that swap for some period of time.

Asset–based swaps.   This is a misnomer, in our opinion. Most swaps are undertaken to transform the character of the end user's liabilities. In recent years, many swaps have been undertaken to transform the character of the end user's assets. Such swaps are called asset–based swaps but, in reality, there is usually no structural difference between an asset–based swap and any other swap. The issue is really one of motivation and not structure.

3.6   OTHER USES FOR INTEREST RATE SWAPS

In this section, we will consider two specific and important uses for interest rate swaps that have nothing to do with reducing the cost of financing for the end user—at least not directly. Specifically, we will consider interest rate swaps as tools for hedging interest rate risk and tools for managing a firm's seasonal cash flows.

3.6.1 Hedging Interest Rate Risk

Many firms are exposed to interest rate risk. Sometimes this interest rate risk is single-period in nature. When an interest rate risk is single-period in nature, it can easily be hedged with interest rate futures contracts or with a forward rate agreement (FRA). At other times, the interest rate risk is multiperiod in nature. In these cases, the risk can be hedged with a strip of futures, a strip of FRAs, or a swap. If the exposure extends far into the future, then the futures strip alternative is usually not workable because futures are rarely liquid beyond a year forward. (As noted in an earlier chapter, Eurodollar futures are an exception. They are liquid out to almost five years.) Forwards may also be illiquid or they may simply not be cost effective. In any event, the swap alternative is often preferred.

Consider a specific case. Imagine a finance company that finances automobile purchases. It funds its operations in the commercial paper market. Suppose that it sells commercial paper with a six-month maturity and rolls this paper over every six months. Suppose further that the firm is a top credit and its commercial paper rate averages 6–M LIBOR plus 25 bps. The auto loans the firm funds carry a fixed rate of 14.50 percent and have a term of four years. The principal on the auto loans is amortizing.

At present, 6–M LIBOR stands at 8 percent. At this rate, the firm's interest margin is 6.25 percent [14.50% – (8.00% + 0.25%)]. (We will ignore the difference between yield conventions in this example.) As it happens, the firm's other operating costs amount to the equivalent of 4.00 percent on its loan portfolio. Thus, the firm's profit margin is 2.25 percent.

If the firm's commercial paper rate does not change, implying that 6–M LIBOR does not change, the firm could sit back and enjoy a 2.25 percent profit margin for four years. But, commercial paper rates and LIBOR change every day. Indeed, these rates can change quite dramatically in a very short period of time. The volatility of these rates exposes the finance company to considerable interest rate risk. For example, if LIBOR rises to 10.00 percent, then the firm's profit margin declines to 0.25 percent. If LIBOR rises to 12.00 percent, then the firm's profit margin becomes negative. This sort of interest rate volatility explains a large part of the losses that were experienced by the savings and loan industry over the last decade.

If the finance company ignores its interest rate risk, it exposes itself to the possibility that a significant rise in the rate of interest it pays could put it out of business. The firm would like to hedge this risk but continue to fund its operations in the commercial paper market. A swap is ready-made for this finance company. The firm enters into a four–year fixed–for–floating swap with a swap dealer with itself as fixed–rate payer (float-ing–rate receiver). The swap requires the firm to pay 8.20 percent in exchange for 6–M LIBOR. The notionals on the swap are scheduled to amortize at the same rate as the finance company's loan portfolio. The swap and the associated cash market transactions are depicted in Figure 3.6.

It is clear that the swap has eliminated the finance company's interest rate risk. Its interest margin is now fixed at 6.05 percent [14.50 – 8.20 – (LIBOR + 0.25) + LIBOR] for the next four years and its profit margin is fixed at 2.05 percent. (The reduction in expected profit of 0.20 percent, relative to no hedge, may be viewed as a cost of hedging.)

While the new structure renders a bit less profit for the firm, the re-duction in risk has several significant ancillary benefits. First, the firm's

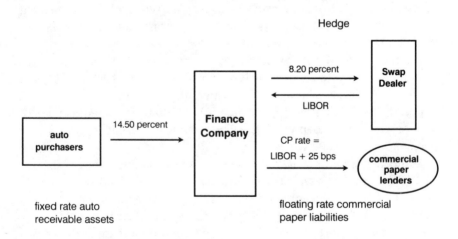

rate mismatch exposes finance company to interest rate risk

FIGURE 3.6 Using Swaps to Hedge Interest Rate Risk

profits are less volatile and it is less risky. Suppliers of long–term debt capital, and even purchasers of the firm's commercial paper, are certain to consider the diminished risk in their lending decisions. This is likely to result in lower borrowing costs for the firm, which was not reflected in Figure 3.6. Second, the firm's shareholders are, presumably, risk averse and the reduction in risk is likely to lead to a higher price for the firm's stock. Third, given the risk reduction, the firm is able to operate on a larger scale with the same capital base. The firm's capital base serves as a cushion against losses. With a reduction in risk, the same capital base can support a greater volume of lending. With larger scale operations, the firm can enjoy the economies of scale that accompany larger scale operations. Finally, by reducing the volatility of the firm's profits, the firm stands to benefit from a lower rate of taxation. That is, all other things being equal, two firms with the same average income will not pay the same average tax in an economy with a progressive tax structure. Firms with more volatile profits tend to pay a higher average tax rate.

Once all of the ancillary benefits of hedging are considered, the cost of hedging can be, and often is, negative. For example, our initial calculation indicated that the cost of hedging was 0.20 percent. But, suppose that lenders will reduce the required rate on the firm's debt by 10 basis points as a consequence of its hedging; and suppose that the economies of scale the firm enjoys have a value of another 10 basis points; and suppose that the tax consequences are worth 3 basis points and that the shareholders attach a value of 7 basis points to the risk reduction. Then, the ancillary benefits have a value of 30 basis points *which is more than the firm's explicit cost of hedging.* The true cost of hedging is thus negative for this firm.

3.6.2 Deseasoning a Firm's Cash Flows

Swaps can be defined as contracts that entail the transfer of cash flows at recurrent intervals. Because swaps entail the periodic transfer of cash flows, they should be useful as a cash flow management tool. In this section, we provide a simple framework for using swaps to deseason an end user's cash flows.

Define CF_p as a periodic cash flow. For instance, CF_p may represent a corporation's annual profit. Also, define CF_i, $i = 1, 2, 3, \ldots, n$ as intraperiod cash flows. For instance, CF_i may represent quarterly profits ($n = 4$) or monthly profits ($n = 12$). Thus, $CF_1 + CF_2 + CF_3 + \ldots +$

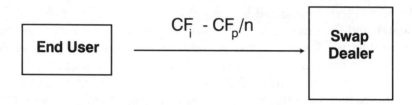

FIGURE 3.7 Fixed-for-Fixed Interest Rate Swap with Mismatched Payment Dates

$CF_n = CF_p$. Finally, let $CF_i \neq CF_j$, $i \neq j$, $j = 1, 2, 3, \ldots, n$. In other words, intraperiod cash flows are uneven or seasonal. The end user's goal is to deseason these intraperiod cash flows. That is, the end user desires that $CF_i = CF_j = CF_p/n$.

To achieve equivalent intraperiod cash flows, the end user can engage in a swap in which it pays the swap dealer the amount $CF_i - CF_p/n$ each intraperiod i. Figure 3.7 illustrates this swap. Recognize that for any intraperiod i in which $CF_i < CF_p/n$, the end user would "pay" the swap dealer a negative amount; that is, the end user would receive net cash flow.

As a simple example, suppose that a firm experiences annual profit of $CF_p = \$1,200,000$ with seasonal quarterly profits of $CF_1 = \$400,000$, $CF_2 = \$100,000$, $CF_3 = \$600,000$, and $CF_4 = \$100,000$. By engaging in a swap in which the firm pays $CF_i - \$300,000$ for each quarter i, it achieves a constant quarterly profit of \$300,000.

It is important to recognize that the swap arrangement described above and illustrated in Figure 3.7 is equivalent to a fixed–for–fixed interest rate swap with mismatched payment dates. For example, the firm might pay the swap dealer fixed sums during the first and third quarters of the year, while the swap dealer pays the firm fixed sums during the second and fourth quarters of the year. Let's consider a more detailed and less abstract example.

A Case Study

Consider the following situation.[8] World Tours, Incorporated (WTI), a travel agent that books overseas, primarily European, tours, aggressively markets its product. Company policy requires that tours be booked and paid for at least 90 days prior to departure. Tour payments are nonrefundable after the payment due date unless a cancellation is dictated by a demonstrable medical condition. Revenue is recorded, for reporting purposes, on the tour departure date. The firm receives 15 percent of tour revenue for its booking services. The remainder is paid to the tour organizers. The firm has a fixed overhead of $160,000 per quarter. Its variable costs amount to 7 percent of tour revenue. Of this, 4 percent represents commissions to its salespeople and 2 percent represents advertising expenditures. The remaining 1 percent covers miscellaneous variable costs. The firm's quarterly revenue can be converted to before-tax profit as follows:

$$\text{Before Tax Profit} = [(15\% - 7\%) \times \text{Revenue}] - \$160,000$$

WTI's bookings and profits have been growing over time. However, profit is highly variable from quarter to quarter. The historic quarterly profit for the 24 calendar quarters from the first quarter of 1985 to the last quarter of 1990 are depicted graphically in Figure 3.8.

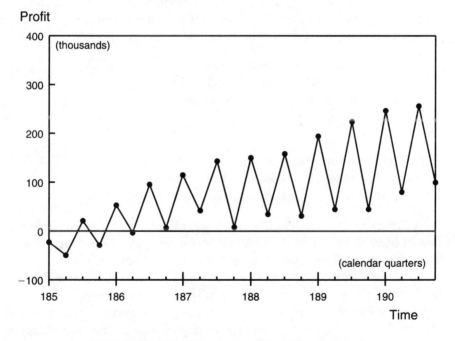

FIGURE 3.8 World Tours, Inc.—Raw Historical Profit

Until early 1991, WTI was entirely equity financed and had no out-standing debt. In late 1990, the firm's management began to consider issuing debt in an effort to increase leverage. Its underwriters suggested that WTI could sell its debt at a lower coupon if it reduced its quarterly profit volatility. Management believed that shareholders would also pre-fer greater profit stability. In order to remove some of the volatility from profit, management sought to identify the sources of the firm's profit volatility and then to reduce the volatility by properly structured swaps.

Since sales had been growing over the years, management believed that there was a secular trend to sales which was explained by its in-creasing expenditures on advertising and customers' word–of–mouth en-dorsements. Management also noted that recorded revenues tended to rise in the first quarter (explained by the popularity of its winter ski tours) and in the third quarter (explained by the popularity of its summer tours). Management also believed that sales revenue exhibits a significant ran-dom component.

A statistical decomposition of the revenue history confirmed the trend and seasonal components of WTI's business. There was also a random component to revenue but this proved considerably less important than originally believed. Specifically, the decomposition revealed the following relation between revenue and the various revenue components:

$$\text{Revenue} = \text{Trend} + \text{Seasonal} + \text{Random}$$
$$\text{Trend} = 1200 + (200 \times \text{Period})$$
$$\text{Seasonal} = .2 \times D \times \text{Trend}$$

where

Period: quarter number (1 through 24)
D: seasonal dummy $= +1$ for quarters 1 and 3
$\qquad\qquad\qquad = -1$ for quarters 2 and 4

In an effort to reduce volatility, WTI considered how its profit history would have differed had it employed an interest rate swap designed to offset the seasonal component of its profit. The notional principal on the swap was structured to increase quarter by quarter with the revenue base dictated by the secular trend. That is, it is an accreting swap. The swap requires WTI to pay the swap dealer an intertemporally increasing sum during the first and third quarters of each year and for the swap dealer to pay WTI an intertemporally increasing sum during the second and fourth quarters of each year. That is, the fixed rates stay the same but the notional principal increases over time to reflect the secular trend.

This swap can be described as a fixed–for–fixed accreting interest rate swap with mismatched payment dates. The payments are based on the profit pattern *implied* by the relation between revenue and profit.[9] The payment requirements are summarized in Table 3.3, which also depicts the combined profits from operations and the interest rate swap. The combined profits are also portrayed graphically in Figure 3.9. As the table and figure clearly demonstrate, had the swap been in place over the 1985 through 1990 period, it would have reduced quarterly profit volatility considerably.

Table 3.3   Quarterly Profit after Seasonal Offset with Swap
(*all values in thousands*)

Calendar Quarter	Operating Profits Before Swap		Interest Rate Swap Payments to WTI		Operating Profit + Swap Payment
185	−23.93	+	−22.40	=	−46.33
285	−51.62	+	25.60	=	−26.02
385	20.01	+	−28.80	=	−8.79
485	−30.18	+	32.00	=	1.82
186	50.38	+	−35.20	=	15.18
286	−4.67	+	38.40	=	33.73
386	91.44	+	−41.60	=	49.84
486	6.22	+	44.80	=	51.02
187	111.81	+	−48.00	=	63.81
287	37.16	+	51.20	=	88.36
387	138.86	+	−54.40	=	84.46
487	4.84	+	57.60	=	62.44
188	145.38	+	−60.80	=	84.58
288	30.38	+	64.00	=	94.38
388	151.61	+	−67.20	=	84.41
488	26.88	+	70.40	=	97.28
189	188.86	+	−73.60	=	115.26
289	40.52	+	76.80	=	117.32
389	218.12	+	−80.00	=	138.12
489	40.62	+	83.20	=	123.82
190	240.23	+	−86.40	=	153.83
290	76.07	+	89.60	=	165.67
390	250.34	+	−92.80	=	157.54
490	94.09	+	96.00	=	190.09

Profit

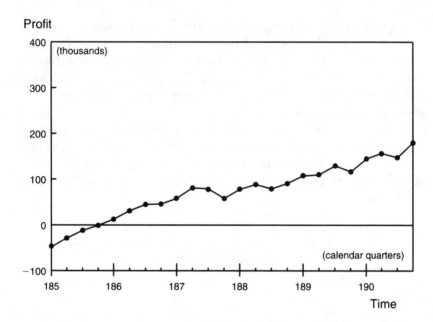

FIGURE 3.9   Quarterly Profit with Seasonal Swap Hedge

It is important to appreciate that the specially engineered swap described here does not increase or decrease the firm's profits. Its function is to smooth out the firm's cash flows from quarter to quarter. Thus, it represents a "swap alternative" to the traditional borrow/lend strategy that most firms use to achieve the same result. Importantly, however, it might be cheaper than a borrow/lend strategy.

3.7   SUMMARY

In this chapter we have considered the structure of an interest rate swap in more detail and we have considered how the indicative swap coupon for a generic swap is adjusted to accommodate an end user when the end user requires terms that differ from those of the generic swap. We have seen how we can adjust pricing when the payment frequencies differ, when the swap is amortizing, and when the swap is off–market. We also briefly considered some of the many variants of the basic interest rate swap and we considered two important additional uses for swaps in greater detail. These uses include the use of interest rate swaps to hedge interest rate risk and the use of swaps to deseason a firm's cash flows.

REVIEW QUESTIONS

1. Using cash flow diagrams, show how a savings and loan association might use interest rate swaps to hedge its fixed–rate mortgage portfolio. What special problems are involved in hedging a mortgage portfolio and what provisions might be required in a swap to solve these problems?

2. Distinguish between a "callable swap" and a "putable swap."

3. What is a "rate–capped swap" and how might one be created?

4. What is a "swaption" and what might it be used for?

5. Suppose that a swap dealer enters into two different interest rate swaps with end users. One requires the dealer to pay fixed rate against floating LIBOR and the other requires the dealer to receive fixed rate against floating T–bill. What residual risk is the swap dealer exposed to and how might the swap dealer use an interbank swap to hedge this residual risk?

6. What is meant by the "cost of a hedge"? Why might the cost of hedging be exaggerated? Give some specific examples.

7. If you were told that a rate is quoted 9.50 percent *money market basis*, what is the equivalent rate stated on a *bond basis*? Assume the same payment frequencies.

8. Suppose that a $5 million loan will repay $1 million in principal each year beginning *after* a two–year grace period. What is the *average life* of this seven–year loan?

9. What special property do zero coupon instruments have with respect to the relationship between their duration, their maturity, and their average life?

10. Suppose that a dealer is quoting dealer–pays–fixed–rate swaps at 10.32 percent sa against 6-M LIBOR. Now suppose that a client would like to receive fixed rate from the dealer but requires *quarterly* payments rather than *semiannual* payments. What quarterly fixed rate is equivalent to the dealer's current semiannual rate?

11. Suppose that a dealer is quoting dealer–pays–fixed–rate swaps at 10.32 percent sa against 6-M LIBOR. Now suppose that a client would like the dealer to pay 11.48 percent sa rather than 10.32

percent. The dealer is willing to accommodate the client and offers the client two choices: a buy up or an adjustment to the floating rate. Calculate each off–market solution for the client.

NOTES

1. Treasury notes and bonds employ the "actual over 365" day version of bond basis while U.S. corporate bonds employ a "30 over 360" day version of bond basis. The version used with Treasuries, which pay a semiannual coupon, begins by dividing the annual coupon rate by 2 to get the half–year coupon. This half–year coupon is then divided by the actual number of days in the half–year period. This provides a daily interest accrual rate for that coupon period. The accrued interest is then the number of days that have elapsed since the last coupon payment times the daily rate. In the corporate method, the annual coupon rate is divided by 360 to get a daily rate. The interest accrual days are determined by treating each month as having 30 days. If a month has 31 days, then the extra day does not pay interest. If the month has 28 days, then the bond pays two extra days' interest on the 28th. The two alternative forms for bond basis are equivalent over full coupon payment periods but can differ modestly over shorter intervals. But, both are different from "actual over 360" day counts over any period.

2. **Interbank swaps** are swaps made between banks. Banks enter into interbank swaps for a variety of purposes including: 1. to hedge other bank positions, 2. to close an interest rate gap, 3. to speculate on the direction of interest rates and exchange rates, and 4. to better manage their own swap portfolios.

3. The corporation will, of course, also encounter some flotation costs in the form of underwriting fees. While these flotation costs must be factored in to obtain the firm's all–in cost in any actual financing, we ignore them here in order to concentrate on the pricing of swaps.

4. For a fuller discussion of yield conversions and yield conventions, see Fage (1986).

5. When the swap dealer's objective is simply to hedge a swap until a matched swap can be booked or until the swap can be assigned to another party, the dealer will often hedge the swap in T–note and Eurodollar (or T–bill) futures. This is important as futures hedges, like swaps themselves, are off–balance sheet positions while cash market positions are on–balance sheet positions. This use of futures to hedge unmatched swaps is discussed more fully in Chapter 8.

6. The liquidity premium theory explains the shape of the yield curve in terms of ever greater interest rate risk associated with ever longer maturities. Greater risk requires higher levels of interest as compensation.

7. For an examination of the relationship between duration and average life, see Leibowitz (1986).
8. This particular example is based on an actual case described by Marshall, Bansal, and Tucker (1991).
9. In this specific case, the swap coupon on both sides of the swap was assumed to be fixed at 10 percent. (In any practical application, of course, the dealer's receive rate will be higher than its pay rate.) The notional principal on the swap (*NP*) was set to increase quarter by quarter according to the following rule (all values in thousands):

$$NP = (64 \times Q) + 384$$

where *Q* denotes calendar quarter.

REFERENCES AND SUGGESTED READINGS

Abken, P. A. "Beyond Plain Vanilla: A Taxonomy of Swaps." *Economic Review*, March/April 1991.

Arak, M., L. S. Goodman, and J. Snailer. "Duration Equivalent Bond Swaps: A New Tool." *Journal of Portfolio Management*, Summer 1986, pp. 26–32.

Fage, P. *Yield Calculations*. London: Credit Swiss First Boston, October 1986.

Gay, G. D., and R. W. Kolb. "Removing Bias in Duration Based Hedging Models: A Note." *Journal of Futures Markets* 4, no. 2 (Summer 1984): 225–28.

Kopprasch, R., J. MacFarlane, D. R. Ross, and J. Showers. "The Interest Rate Swap Market: Yield Mathematics, Terminology and Conventions." In *The Handbook of Fixed Income Securities*, 2d ed., edited by F. Fabozzi and I. Pollock. Homewood, IL: Dow Jones Books, 1987.

Leibowitz, M. L. "The Dedicated Bond Portfolio in Pension Funds—Part II: Immunization, Horizon Matching and Contingent Procedures." *Financial Analysts Journal*, March/April 1986, pp. 47–57.

Litzenberger, R. H. "Swaps: Plain and Fanciful." *Journal of Finance* 47, no. 3 (July 1992): 831–50.

Macaulay, F. R. *Some Theoretical Problems Suggested by the Movement of Interest Rates, Bond Yields, and Stock Prices in the United States Since 1856*. New York: Columbia University Press for the National Bureau of Economic Research, 1938.

Marshall, J. F., V. K. Bansal, and A. L. Tucker. "Fixed–for–Fixed Interest Rates Swaps." *Corporate Risk Management*, April 1991.

Marshall, J. F., V. K. Bansal, and A. L. Tucker. "Using Swaps as a Cash Management Tool." *Advances in Working Capital Management*, forthcoming, 1993.

Nadler, D. "Eurodollar Futures/Interest Rate Swap Arbitrage." Quantitative Strategies Group, Shearson Lehman Hutton, April 1989.

Weston, J. F., and T. E. Copeland. *Managerial Finance*. 8th ed. New York: Dryden Press, 1986.

4

Currency Swaps

4.1 OVERVIEW

As with interest rate swaps, the notionals on currency swaps take the form of notional principals. However, as noted twice in earlier chapters, it is not really correct to call the principals on a currency swap "notional principals" in those cases in which the principals are actually exchanged. This would not be consistent with the accepted meaning of the term notionals to imply "hypothetical." Nevertheless, the term notionals is often used with reference to currency swaps even when the principals are exchanged. In this chapter, we try to avoid the use of the term notionals when it is not appropriate.

We begin this chapter with a review of the plain vanilla currency swap and its use as a tool for reducing financing costs. We then examine some of the other uses for currency swaps. Specifically, we consider how a currency swap can be used to hedge exchange rate risk and how a currency swap can enable a firm to operate in foreign markets that it might not otherwise be easily able to enter. We will also consider how currency swap prices are quoted and some of the adjustments in pricing that are necessary when the end user has requirements that are at odds with the indicative pricing assumptions. Finally, we will briefly examine some of the more common variants of the basic structure.

In order to better understand the currency swap discussion that follows, a few introductory definitions are in order. Since, by design, currency swaps involve two or more currencies, currency swaps will require a specification of exchange rates. An exchange rate is simply the price of one currency stated in terms of another currency. For example, a deutschemark–for–dollar (DEM/USD) exchange rate of 1.5 means that one dollar will purchase 1.50 deutschemarks. Exchange rates are quoted for both exchange transactions that are to be effected immediately (defined by convention as two days from the current date) and for transactions that are to be effected at some point in the future. The former are called **spot exchange rates** and the latter are called **forward exchange rates**.

There is an important foundation relationship between exchange rates and interest rates called the **interest rate parity theorem**. This theorem states that spot and forward exchange rates will be related to one another in such a fashion as to equate the rate of interest in each country. Thus, exchange rates embody interest rate information and interest rates imply exchange rates.

4.2   THE BASIC STRUCTURE OF A CURRENCY SWAP

The basic currency swap involves three distinct sets of cash flows: 1. the initial exchange of principals; 2. the interest payments made by each counterparty to the other; and 3. the final exchange, or reexchange, of principals. These cash flows are depicted in Figures 4.1, 4.2, and 4.3 for a swap between an end user and a swap dealer. Both the initial exchange of principals and any reexchanges of principals are made at the spot exchange rate prevailing at the time of contracting. While this may initially seem strange, it is logical once one realizes that the difference between the forward and spot exchange rates has already been accounted for in the interest rates on the swap.

The early currency swaps, like the early interest rate swaps, were made directly between two end users. A swap broker served to identify and to match the two end users and collected commission for its trouble. In these early currency swaps, each end user would typically borrow funds in its domestic market and then turn these borrowed funds over to its swap counterparty. A typical currency swap between two end users, together with the accompanying cash market transactions, is depicted in Figures 4.4, 4.5, and 4.6. These early currency swaps were called, and sometimes still are called, **exchanges of borrowings**. The origin of the term is readily apparent from the structure.

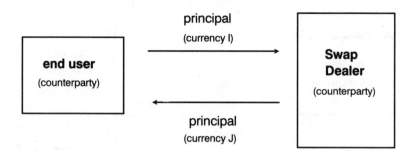

FIGURE 4.1   The Initial Exchange of Principals

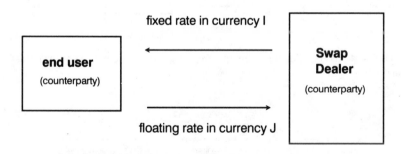

FIGURE 4.2   The Service Payments on the Swap

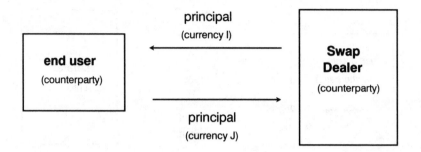

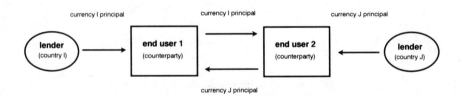

FIGURE 4.3   The Reexchange of Principals

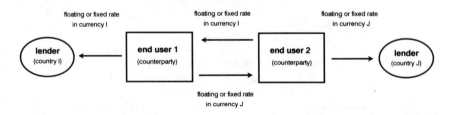

FIGURE 4.4   Basic Currency Swap: Exchange of Principals (*an exchange of borrowings*)

FIGURE 4.5   Basic Currency Swap: Service Payments (*an exchange of borrowings*)

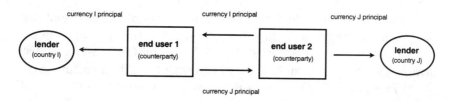

FIGURE 4.6 Basic Currency Swap: Reexchange of Principals (*an exchange of borrowings*)

The earliest currency swaps, like the back–to–back and parallel loans that preceded them, were created as a vehicle to circumvent controls on capital flows. It was not long, however, before the real value of these instruments as a vehicle to reduce finance costs was discovered. Let's consider a complete example of how currency swaps can be used to reduce costs. The specific swap we will look at is a variant of the plain vanilla fixed–for–floating currency swap. In this particular swap both counter-parties are paying a fixed rate of interest. Such swaps are called **fixed–for–fixed currency swaps**.

Suppose that a British firm needs fixed–rate U.S. dollars funding (USD) for a period of five years. At the same time, an American firm needs fixed–rate pound sterling funding (GBP) for a period of five years. Now assume that the British firm can borrow fixed–rate pounds in its domestic capital markets at a rate of 9.50 percent and it can borrow dollars in the Eurobond market at a fixed rate of 11.50 percent. The American firm, on the other hand, can borrow fixed–rate dollars in its domestic capital markets at a rate of 11.75 percent and it can borrow pounds in the Eurobond market at a rate of 10.25 percent. It is clear that the British firm has an absolute borrowing advantage in both pounds and dollars. Nevertheless, as we will see, the American firm has a comparative advantage in the dollar market. The proof of this is simple. If there is any set of interest rates for this swap that is cost reducing for both firms, then each firm had to have had a comparative advantage in one of the markets.

	Cash Market Borrowing Costs	
	GBP Market	USD Market
American Firm	10.25% GBP	11.75% USD
British Firm	9.50% GPB	11.50% USD

Suppose now that each firm borrows in its domestic market and that the two firms then enter into a fixed–for–fixed currency swap with the American firm paying the British firm 9.75 percent GBP and the British firm paying the American firm 11.50 percent USD. The structure is depicted in Figure 4.7. (Only the interest payments are shown.)

Ignoring the fact that USD interest rate differentials and GBP interest rate differentials are not directly comparable, except as first approximations, we can see that both firms have obtained the form of financing that they required and, at the same time, have reduced their financing costs. The British firm, for example, has obtained five–year fixed–rate dollars at a cost of approximately 11.25 percent. The cost calculation is provided below.

$$\text{British firm's cost} = 11.50\% \text{ USD} + 9.50\% \text{ GBP} - 9.75\% \text{ GBP}$$
$$= 11.50\% \text{ USD} - 0.25\% \text{ GBP}$$
$$\approx 11.25\% \text{ USD}$$

Had the British firm borrowed dollars directly, its cost would have been 11.50 percent. Thus, the British firm has saved approximately 25 basis points each year for five years. With the average swap transaction having notionals of $25 million, a 25 basis point savings for five years can be quite considerable. (The correct adjustment to make interest rate differentials in different currencies directly comparable is discussed later in this chapter.)

It is easily seen that the American firm also saved 25 basis points compared to a direct borrowing of pounds. We leave it to the reader to do the calculation. The fact that the two firms both saved 25 basis points in this example was purely coincidental. There is nothing about a swap that requires the benefits to be divided evenly between the two counterparties. (Importantly, for reasons that will be discussed in Chapter 7, the gains from the synthetic structures described here may be

FIGURE 4.7 A Fixed–for–Fixed Currency Swap

exaggerated because certain factors that contribute to the cost of a financing have been ignored.)

4.3 INDICATIVE PRICING SCHEDULES: CURRENCY SWAPS

This section concentrates on the pricing of fixed–for–floating currency swaps. The swap dealer's international capital markets team will estimate appropriate pay and receive fixed rates for all of the currencies in which the dealer makes a market. We will suppose that all fixed rates are quoted against LIBOR flat. The fixed rates may be stated on an annual or a semiannual basis and the adjustment from annual to semiannual or vice versa is exactly the same as that described in our discussion of rate adjustments for interest rate swaps. Whether indicative pricing is provided using annual rates or semiannual rates depends on the accepted convention in the country whose currency is involved. For example, in the United States, the convention is to quote semiannual rates while the convention in most European countries is to quote annual rates. To keep things simple, we will assume that the rates in the following examples are all stated on a semiannual basis.

In the case of currency swaps, indicative pricings are often stated as a midrate to which some number of basis points are added or subtracted depending on whether the swap dealer is receiver or payer of the fixed rate. Such a schedule is depicted for deutschemark–to–dollar rates in Table 4.1.

Table 4.1 Indicative Pricing for Deutschemark–to–Dollar Swaps

Maturity	Midrate DEM
2 years	6.25% sa
3 years	6.48% sa
4 years	6.65% sa
5 years	6.78% sa
6 years	6.88% sa
7 years	6.96% sa
10 years	7.10% sa

The rates above are midrates. To these rates, deduct 5 basis points if the dealer is paying fixed rate and add 5 basis points if the dealer is receiving fixed rate. All principal transactions are assumed to be bullet transactions. Quotes are against 6-M LIBOR flat.

The structure of the DEM–to–USD indicative pricing schedule in Table 4.1 is typical of currency swaps, although the size of the pay–receive spread varies by currency. The swap dealer would likely offer similar schedules for the other major hard currencies including the Swiss franc, French franc, British pound, Canadian dollar, and Japanese yen. A spread of 4 to 12 basis points is a rough approximation of the range of the pay–receive spreads. The 10 basis points used in this example is actually a bit high, by current standards, for DEM–to–USD swaps.

As already mentioned, the rates in Table 4.1 are midrates. The actual pay-receive rates are found by deducting/adding the appropriate premium to the midrate. For straight U.S. dollar interest rate swaps, the indicative pricing schedule depicted in Table 3.1 lists both the dealer's pay and receive rates. Table 3.1 is repeated below as Table 4.2.

We can obtain a midrate for interest rate swaps by simply taking the average of the pay and receive rates. For example, for the five–year interest rate swap the midrate is 9.48 percent, which is calculated as (9.44 + 9.52)/2.

Consider now a simple example: A German firm approaches our swap dealer looking to convert a DEM 35 million five–year semiannual fixed–rate liability into a floating–rate dollar liability. The swap dealer offers a fixed–for–floating currency swap at the current spot exchange rate of 1.75 DEM/USD. At the current exchange rate, the principal is $20 million. Since the dealer will be paying fixed rate, the rate is found by taking the

Table 4.2   Indicative Pricing for Interest Rate Swaps

Maturity	Dealer Pays Fixed Rate	Dealer Receives Fixed Rate	Current TN Rate
2 years	2-yr TN sa + 38 bps	2-yr TN sa + 44 bps	8.55%
3 years	3-yr TN sa + 46 bps	3-yr TN sa + 52 bps	8.72%
4 years	4-yr TN sa + 50 bps	4-yr TN sa + 58 bps	8.85%
5 years	5-yr TN sa + 52 bps	5-yr TN sa + 60 bps	8.92%
6 years	6-yr TN sa + 58 bps	6-yr TN sa + 66 bps	8.96%
7 years	7-yr TN sa + 62 bps	7-yr TN sa + 70 bps	9.00%
10 years	10-yr TN sa + 74 bps	10-yr TN sa + 84 bps	9.08%

The schedule assumes semiannual rates and bullet transactions and it assumes that the counterparty is a top credit. TN denotes the Treasury note rate. All rates are quoted against six-month LIBOR flat.

five-year midrate and deducting 5 basis points. This calculation produces a rate of 6.73 percent (6.78 − 0.05). Thus, the German firm would pay the swap dealer six-month LIBOR on principal of $20 million and the swap dealer would pay the German firm 6.73 percent sa on DEM 35 million.

Unlike an interest rate swap, in which there is no exchange of principals, there is often an exchange of principals in the straight currency swap. That is, at the commencement of the swap, the German firm would exchange its DEM 35 million for the dealer's $20 million. For the next five years, the two parties would pay each other interest at the rates indicated. After five years, the two parties would reexchange principals at the same exchange rate used for the initial exchange of principals, that is, 1.75 DEM/USD. The straight currency swap clearly involves three separate cash flows: 1. the initial exchange of principals; 2. the interest payments; and 3. the reexchange of principals.

In the event that the dealer experiences a demand imbalance on one side of the currency swap market, the dealer will have to raise or lower its midrate. For example, suppose that the dealer experiences a surge in demand for currency swaps by clients who want to pay five-year fixed-rate deutschemarks and receive floating-rate dollars. To discourage this side of the market and encourage the other, the dealer might raise its five-year midrate from 6.78 percent to, say, 6.85 percent.

Determining the correct midrates to serve as the basis of swap pricing is typically a function of the bank's international capital markets group (of which the swap dealer is a part). **Capital markets groups** operate with an international perspective and continuously monitor the capital markets worldwide. They watch their own banks' swap portfolios closely and adjust rates quickly when they suspect that an imbalance is developing. A capital markets group may find, for instance, that they must lower the dealer's four-year midrate while simultaneously raising the dealer's five-year midrate.

4.4 CURRENCY SWAPS WITH NO INITIAL EXCHANGE OF BORROWINGS

The straight currency swap involves an initial exchange of principals and an eventual reexchange of principals. Not all currency swaps involve two exchanges of principals. Let us consider such a case.

Suppose it is now 1 February 1993. As a consequence of an earlier financing, a firm is committed to making semiannual floating-rate (six-month LIBOR) dollar payments on an amortizing loan for four more years. The payment dates are 1 August and 1 February. By the nature of the firm's business, the firm receives revenue in deutschemarks. The firm's current payment schedule is depicted in Table 4.3.

Recent fluctuations in the DEM/USD exchange rate and U.S. interest rates have caused the firm's management to become increasingly concerned about its dollar liabilities and have led the firm to look for a way to convert its floating-rate dollar liabilities to fixed-rate deutschemark liabilities. At the same time, it would like to lock in the current DEM/USD exchange rate (1.75 DEM/USD) for all future exchanges. The swap dealer offers a currency swap with no initial exchange of principals. The dealer offers to pay LIBOR on the amortizing balance *and* to pay $0.5 million every six months. The swap has an average life of two and one-half years, and the dealer's current midrate for two and one-half year deutschemark-to-dollar swaps is 6.36 percent. In exchange for the dealer's paying LIBOR, the dealer requires the firm to pay 6.41 percent (midrate plus 5 basis points). In addition, the dealer will pay the firm $0.5 million of principal every six months in exchange for the firm's principal payments to the bank of 0.875 million deutschemarks every six months. This latter sum reflects principal translations at a DEM/USD exchange rate of 1.75. These payments are depicted in Table 4.4.

The firm's dollar commitments to its earlier financing source are now assured. The dealer will pay the firm $0.5 million plus LIBOR flat every six months and the firm will then pay this identical sum to its creditor. The firm's net liability is now to pay DEM 0.875 million plus 6.41 percent

Table 4.3 Amortization Schedule on Floating-Rate Loan

Date	Loan Balance Before Payment	Loan Balance After Payment	Payment Amount
1 Feb 1993		$4.0 million	—
1 Aug 1993	$4.0 million	$3.5 million	$0.5 million + LIBOR
1 Feb 1994	$3.5 million	$3.0 million	$0.5 million + LIBOR
1 Aug 1994	$3.0 million	$2.5 million	$0.5 million + LIBOR
1 Feb 1995	$2.5 million	$2.0 million	$0.5 million + LIBOR
1 Aug 1995	$2.0 million	$1.5 million	$0.5 million + LIBOR
1 Feb 1996	$1.5 million	$1.0 million	$0.5 million + LIBOR
1 Aug 1996	$1.0 million	$0.5 million	$0.5 million + LIBOR
1 Feb 1997	$0.5 million	$0.0	$0.5 million + LIBOR

Table 4.4 Currency Swap Payment Schedule

Date	Dealer Pays Firm	Firm Pays Dealer
1 Feb 1993	—	—
1 Aug 1993	$0.5 million + LIBOR	DEM 0.875 million + 6.41%
1 Feb 1994	$0.5 million + LIBOR	DEM 0.875 million + 6.41%
1 Aug 1994	$0.5 million + LIBOR	DEM 0.875 million + 6.41%
1 Feb 1995	$0.5 million + LIBOR	DEM 0.875 million + 6.41%
1 Aug 1995	$0.5 million + LIBOR	DEM 0.875 million + 6.41%
1 Feb 1996	$0.5 million + LIBOR	DEM 0.875 million + 6.41%
1 Aug 1996	$0.5 million + LIBOR	DEM 0.875 million + 6.41%
1 Feb 1997	$0.5 million + LIBOR	DEM 0.875 million + 6.41%

sa. That is, it has a fixed–rate deutschemark commitment—exactly what it was looking for. It is now fully hedged with respect to exchange rates and interest rates.

Unlike the straight currency swap, which is best understood as an exchange of borrowings, this currency swap is best viewed as a series of forward contracts all made at the current spot rate of 1.75 DEM/USD with the normal forward–spot exchange rate differential reflected in the interest payments made by the two counterparties.

4.5 OFF–MARKET PRICING

Just as it is necessary to make pricing adjustments to interest rate swaps when payment frequencies differ from those assumed in the indicative pricing schedules and when amortization schedules differ from those assumed in the indicative pricing schedules, it is also frequently necessary to make pricing adjustments for variations in currency swap requirements. For example, the straight currency swap assumes semiannual payments and bullet transactions. If the currency swap requires annual fixed–rate payments instead of semiannual payments, an adjustment is required. If the swap is amortizing, then average life must replace maturity. These currency swap pricing adjustments are identical to those for interest rate swaps, and we will not address them again. But when the swap is off–market, the pricing adjustment is more complex than it is for an interest rate swap, and this adjustment is, therefore, worth some additional consideration. (As a side note, certain of the conversions required in pricing off–market currency swaps are the same conversions that would be used to make interest rate differentials in one currency equivalent to interest rate differentials in another currency. These conversions, for example, would be employed to determine the precise interest rate savings to the American firm and the British firm that were only approximated in Section 4.2. We leave it to the reader to make the connection.)

The need for an off–market swap arises when a firm has an existing liability at a rate that differs from that which is currently prevailing in the market. Consider the following case: A U.S. firm is committed to making semiannual interest payments to holders of its deutschemark bonds that were issued five years ago. The bond principal covers DEM 18 million, all of which will be repaid at maturity in ten more years. The bond carries a fixed coupon of 9.50 percent. The U.S. firm wants to swap this liability for a floating–rate dollar liability. Its purpose is to eliminate exchange rate risk. Note that this swap requires no initial exchange of principals and is similar in this regard to the case discussed in the preceding section.

The dealer's current indicative pricing schedule (Table 4.1) calls for the dealer to pay a fixed rate of DEM 7.05 percent sa (midrate less 5 basis points) against six–month USD LIBOR flat. However, the client requires the dealer to pay DEM 9.50 percent. Any rate other than DEM 9.50 percent will leave the firm with a residual exchange rate risk. This swap calls for off–market pricing.

The trick to pricing off–market swaps is to create cash flow streams with equivalent present values. This requires that we exploit our knowledge of the ten–year USD fixed rate and the ten–year DEM fixed rate. We use midrates for this purpose. The latter is 7.10 percent (Table 4.1) and the former is 9.87 percent (Table 4.2).

The first step is to determine the rate differential between that which the client firm requires, 9.50 percent, and that which the dealer would ordinarily pay, 7.05 percent. The differential, in this case, is 2.45 percent. That is, the client firm requires that the dealer pay a premium of 2.45 percent on the DEM fixed–rate side.

The next step is to determine the dollar–rate premium that has the *same* present value as this 2.45 percent DEM premium. Since this DEM premium payment takes the form of an annuity, we can compute the present value of the payment using present value annuity arithmetic. Importantly, because the rates involved are semiannual rates, the annuity payment is 1.225 every six months rather than 2.45 each year. The necessary relationship is given by Equation 4.1.[1]

$$PVA = PMT \times \left[\frac{1 - (1 + R/m)^{-mn}}{R/m} \right] \qquad (4.1)$$

PVA = present value of the annuity
PMT = annuity payment
   R = midrate (for deutschemarks)
   n = tenor of swap
   m = frequency of interest payments

The values of PMT, R, m, and n are, in this case, 1.225, 7.10 percent, 2, and 10, respectively. Plugging these values into Equation 4.1 provides a present value of 17.332.

Now, we use the 17.332 present value to determine the dollar–interest premium. To obtain the dollar–interest premium Equation 4.1 is again employed, but this time the current midrate for dollars is used for R (9.87%). Substitute the value 17.332 for PVA and solve for PMT. The value of PMT that solves this particular case is 1.3831, which we must double in order to annualize. The annual rate differential is then 2.766%. This value is interpreted as the dollar–rate premium on this off–market transaction. However, this rate premium was derived from fixed–rate bond basis yields and, consequently, cannot be added directly to LIBOR, which is stated on a money market basis. The necessary adjustment was demonstrated in Chapter 3. That is, the bond basis rate differential is multiplied by 360/365. The adjustment provides a yield premium of 2.728 percent, which can be added directly to LIBOR.

The final result is a swap that calls for the dealer to pay its client deutschemarks at the semiannual fixed rate of 9.50 percent in exchange for the client paying the dealer dollars at the rate of six–month LIBOR plus 2.728 percent. At maturity, the parties will exchange principals at the rate of 1.75 DEM/USD, which is the spot rate that prevailed at the time the swap was negotiated. The cash flows associated with this swap are depicted in Figures 4.8 and 4.9 and the calculations are summarized as follows:

Summary calculation of off-market pricing adjustment

Step 1: Determine the *DEM* rate differential required:

> Differential = required off-market coupon – at-market coupon
> = 9.50% *DEM* sa – 7.05% *DEM* sa
> = 2.45% *DEM* sa
> = 1.225 *DEM* per period

Step 2: Determine the present value of the *DEM* rate differential:

$$PVA = DEM\ PMT \times PVAF$$
$$= 1.225 \times 14.1486$$
$$= 17.332$$

where *PVAF* is the present value annuity factor embedded in Equation 4.1.

Step 3: From the present value, determine the *USD* fixed-rate differential:

$$PVA = USD\ PMT \times PVAF$$
$$17.332 = USD\ PMT \times 12.5533$$

implying that:
$$USD\ PMT = 17.332/12.531$$
$$= 1.3831$$

Since the 1.3831 *USD* rate differential is for a six-month period, the annual rate differential is 2.766% sa.

Step 4: Convert the *USD* fixed-rate differential to its money market yield equivalent and add to six-month LIBOR.

$$MMY\ differential = BEY\ differential \times \frac{360}{365}$$
$$= 2.766\% \times \frac{360}{365}$$
$$= 2.728\%\ MMY$$

Floating leg = six-month LIBOR + 2.728%

The firm is now fully hedged against exchange rate fluctuations. The deutschemark payments, including both interest and principal, that the firm must make to its creditors are perfectly matched by the dealer's

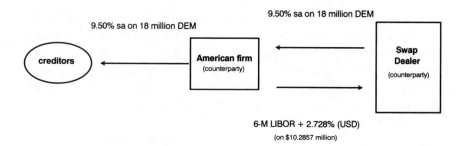

FIGURE 4.8 Service Payments on Off–Market Swap

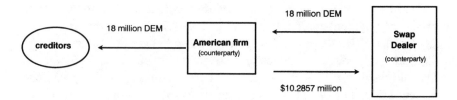

FIGURE 4.9 Principal Exchanges at Maturity

payments to the firm. The firm's net position consists of its LIBOR plus 2.728 percent payments to the dealer.

As with interest rate swaps, it is not necessary to build the fixed–rate coupon premium for an off–market swap into the floating leg in order to equate the present values of the two legs. An alternative is for the firm to engage in a buy–up of the swap coupon at the outset of the swap. That is, the firm could have made a onetime up–front payment, equal to the present value of the off–market rate differential, to the swap dealer for a swap having a coupon of DEM 9.50 percent sa against six–month LIBOR flat.

4.6 CIRCUS SWAPS

Earlier, in Section 4.2, we employed a currency swap in which *both* interest rates were fixed. We described this swap as a fixed–for–fixed currency swap. In our example, one leg was a fixed dollar rate and the other leg was a fixed pound rate. We had noted in the last chapter that a floating–for–floating interest rate swap, also known as a basis swap, can be created by combining two fixed–for–floating interest rate swaps. In the same fashion, a fixed–for–fixed currency swap can be created by combining a fixed–for–floating currency swap with a fixed–for–floating interest rate swap. When the two fixed–for–floating swaps each have LIBOR as the floating leg, then the combination is often referred to as a **circus swap**. The creation of a fixed–for–fixed currency swap by way of the circus swap structure is depicted in Figure 4.10.

The pricing of circus swaps follows directly from the mechanics of the two swap components. Consider one last time the off–market swap discussed in the preceding section. The U.S. firm has swapped a 9.50 percent fixed–rate deutschemark commitment for LIBOR plus 2.728 percent. This same client can now convert its dollar floating–rate payments to fixed–rate payments using the rates in Table 4.2. That is, the dealer will pay the firm LIBOR plus 2.728 percent in exchange for the firm paying the dealer the "dealer–receives" rate of 9.92 percent plus 2.766 percent. The end result for the firm is a fixed–rate semiannual payment of 12.686 percent USD. The net cash flows from the combined components of the circus swap are depicted in Figure 4.11.

4.7   OTHER USES FOR CURRENCY SWAPS

We have argued that currency swaps can be used to reduce an end user's financing costs and we have provided examples of how this works. But

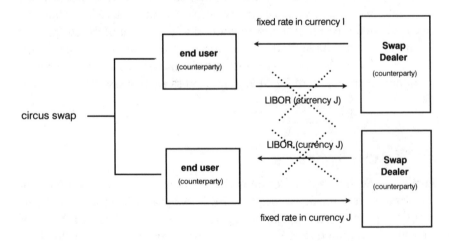

FIGURE 4.10   The Circus Swap Structure

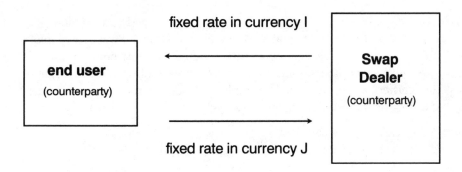

FIGURE 4.11 Net Flows on the Circus Swap

one cannot help but ask why exploitable comparative advantages might exist in the first place. If markets are efficient, after all, then comparative advantages *should not* exist. Indeed, the existence of comparative advantages implies market imperfections.

Imperfections in the world's capital markets include controls on the movement of capital across national borders, unequal access to the world's capital markets due to differences in borrower size and market acceptance, government–granted loan guarantees, differing tax treatments of interest paid and/or received (both internationally and intranationally), and, finally, different yield curve behaviors in different countries for both fixed–rate and floating–rate borrowings. In addition to these obvious imperfections, there are less obvious ones as well. For example, a potential lender may have unequal access to, or knowledge of, legal protections afforded to lenders in the world's capital markets. Concern over the validity and enforceability of protective covenants can diminish a potential lender's willingness to lend to a nondomestic borrower. The end result is a higher cost of funds for the nondomestic borrower. Thus, domestic borrowers often enjoy a comparative borrowing advantage over nondomestic borrowers.

Swap finance can lower borrowing costs for both counterparties to a swap by exploiting these comparative advantages. But with the rapid growth in swap finance and increasing competition among the banks that act as swap brokers and dealers, much of the potential cost–reducing benefits of swap finance have been arbitraged away and market efficiency has increased. It is for this reason that swap finance has served to integrate the world's capital markets.

Even if the world's financial markets become perfectly efficient, the swap product will still be viable. The reason is simple. Swaps have many uses besides lowering financing costs. One of the most common uses is as a multiperiod hedging instrument. While we looked at an example of this earlier, a more detailed example will help to reinforce our understanding of this use for currency swaps.

4.7.1   Hedging Price Risks: A Case Analysis

Suppose a Swiss provider of retirement annuity contracts sells its policies worldwide. With its most popular policy, the Swiss firm provides fixed quarterly payments to its policyholder (payable at the end of each calendar quarter) for a period of 15 years in exchange for a single up–front payment by the policyholder to the Swiss firm. The Swiss firm does not necessarily invest the funds it receives from its policyholders in the policyholders' country. Rather, the firm looks worldwide for the most attractive investment opportunities it can find.

The Swiss firm is planning a policy offering in the United States. It determines that it can convert any dollars it receives to deutschemarks at the current spot exchange rate of 2.000 DEM/USD and lend these deutschemarks to a German firm for a return of 10 percent quarterly (qr). The loan would be a 15–year amortizing loan providing quarterly payments. On the strength of its knowledge of this investment opportunity, the Swiss firm offers its prospective U.S. policyholders a fixed rate of 9 percent qr. From the 1 percent receive/pay rate differential, the Swiss firm must cover its administrative costs and try to earn a reasonable profit for its shareholders. Suppose that the policy offering brings the Swiss firm a total of $50 million from 1,000 new policyholders.

The Swiss firm will receive quarterly revenues from its German investment in the amount of DEM 3,235,340.[2] At an exchange rate of 2.000 DEM/USD, this is equivalent to $1,617,670 for each of the next 60 quarters. At the same time, the Swiss firm must make aggregate quarterly payments to its U.S. policyholders in the amount of $1,526,767. The rate differential then translates, at the current spot exchange rate, to a net quarterly revenue of $90,903 or an annual net revenue of $363,612. The Swiss firm estimates the annual administrative costs associated with providing these policies at $135,000. Thus, if all of its expectations are realized, the new policy offering should contribute $228,612 to the firm's annual profit.

Suppose, for the moment, that the Swiss firm does not hedge its currency commitments. If the deutschemark strengthens against the dollar, the Swiss firm will profit in excess of its expectations. On the other hand, it will suffer unexpected losses if the deutschemark weakens against the dollar. A small adverse change in the value of the deutschemark could easily wipe out all profit from this offering. For example, if the exchange rate were to rise to just 2.073 DEM/USD, representing a weakened deutschemark, the annual profit contribution from the policy offering would be reduced to near zero. A more substantial weakening of the deutschemark could irreparably impair the financial integrity of the Swiss firm. The effects of an increase in the exchange rate are illustrated in Table 4.5.

The Swiss firm is in the business of providing annuity contracts and not in the business of currency speculation and, so, it seeks to hedge its foreign–exchange exposure. The firm often hedges its short–term currency exposures in foreign–exchange forward and futures contracts. But these hedging instruments are not adequate to hedge this multiyear commitment.

The Swiss firm approaches a U.K.–based swap dealer for a solution. The dealer, which makes a market in both currency and interest rate swaps, offers to pay the Swiss firm dollars at 9.85 percent qr in exchange

Table 4.5 Illustration of Foreign–Exchange Exposure

		Exchange Rate (DEM/USD)		
		2.000	2.073	2.146
Firm receives DEM quarterly	DEM	3,235,340	3,235,340	3,235,340
Converted to dollars	USD	1,617,670	1,560,704	1,507,614
Less USD payments to policyholders	USD	1,526,767	1,526,767	1,526,767
Gross quarterly profit (USD)	USD	90,903	33,937	(19,153)
Less quarterly administrative costs	USD	33,750	33,750	33,750
Net quarterly profit	USD	57,153	187	(52,903)
Net annual profit	USD	228,612	748	(211,612)

The actual zero profit exchange rate occurs at 2.0732. For purposes of this example, we treat the second column net quarterly and net annual profits as approximately zero.

for the Swiss firm paying the dealer deutschemarks at 10 percent qr, that is, a fixed–for–fixed currency swap. For both payment streams, we will assume quarterly compounding and a 15–year amortization schedule. The principal on the dollar side of the swap is $50 million, and the principal on the deutschemark side is DEM 100 million. The latter is obtained by converting the dollar side to deutschemarks at the current spot exchange rate.

The Swiss firm now has two separate sets of cash flows. Figure 4.12 depicts the cash flows between the German firm, the Swiss firm, and the Swiss firm's U.S. policyholders. Figure 4.13 depicts the cash flows associated with the swap between the Swiss firm and the swap dealer. We can now combine the cash flows depicted in Figures 4.12 and 4.13. The *net* cash flows are depicted in Figure 4.14.

The Swiss firm is now fully hedged against fluctuations in the DEM/USD exchange rate. Assuming that the Swiss firm's management has no

FIGURE 4.12   Quarterly Cash Flows from Commercial Transaction

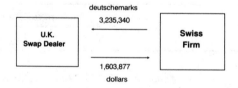

FIGURE 4.13   Service Payments on the Swap

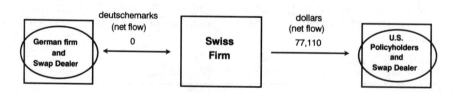

FIGURE 4.14   Net Cash Flows

reason to believe the DEM/USD exchange rate is more likely to rise than fall in the coming years (that is, the current 2.000 spot DEM/USD exchange rate is an unbiased estimate of future spot DEM/ USD exchange rates), the firm's expected annual profit from the policy offering is reduced by the swap hedge to \$173,440 [(4 × \$77,110) − \$135,000]. The **cost of the hedge** to the Swiss firm is the amount by which the expected annual profit from the policy offering is reduced as a consequence of hedging. In this case, the annual cost of hedging is \$55,172, that is, \$228,612 minus \$173,440.

It is premature to conclude that the positive hedging costs incurred when hedging with swaps would prevent the Swiss firm from hedging in this instrument. The **risk averse** shareholders of this firm enjoy a utility gain from the risk reduction that accompanies hedging. For this risk reduction, the swap hedger would likely be willing to pay a price—just as futures hedgers are willing to pay a price for the risk reduction made possible by hedging in futures.[3]

There are two ancillary benefits from hedging that are easily overlooked but that should be of considerable importance to the hedger when considering the cost of hedging. The first involves reduced financing costs and the second involves economies of scale.

By hedging, the Swiss firm has reduced the uncertainty of its cash flows. This has implications for the firm's cost of funds completely separate from the reduced financing costs associated with swap finance itself. By reducing the uncertainty of its cash flows, the firm is viewed as more **creditworthy**. To the extent that the markets recognize this reduction in uncertainty, the firm's cost of debt and equity capital should decline. This, in turn, implies higher prices for the firm's stock.

The second ancillary benefit of hedging cash flows with swaps is associated with the scale on which the firm can operate. This benefit is addressed in the next section.

4.7.2   Exploiting Economies of Scale

Hedging its risks makes it possible for a firm to operate on a larger scale. Consider again the case of the Swiss provider of annuity contracts. The annuity provider that does not hedge cannot operate on the same scale, for a given capital base, as the annuity provider that does hedge. Suppose that the prudent annuity provider holds \$1 of equity capital for each \$0.40 of annual profit volatility. Next, suppose that, in the absence of hedging, each $1 of annuity policies gives rise to $0.05 of profit volatility. The unhedged annuity provider can then carry, at most, $8 of annuity policies for each $1 of equity capital it holds.

Now suppose that a complete swap hedge, like the one described for the Swiss firm above, reduces profit volatility by 90 percent. The residual risk, called **basis risk**, that remains is then 10 percent of the risk that existed in the absence of hedging. The same annuity provider can then carry $80 of annuity policies for each $1 of its equity capital. Thus, in this example, the hedged annuity provider can operate on a scale ten times that of the unhedged annuity provider without bearing any greater risk.

Even when hedging is costly, as it is in the example of the Swiss firm above, the cost incurred from hedging may be a small price to pay for the increased scale at which the hedged firm can operate. The annuity provider is capable of operating on a larger scale by hedging benefits from the greater profits associated with a larger policy base, but it may also benefit from **economies of scale**. That is, to the extent that the provision of annuity policies involves a high fixed cost and relatively little variable cost per policy, there may be significant cost savings to be enjoyed by annuity providers that can operate on a large scale. These savings alone may be sufficient in some cases to completely offset the costs of hedging.

4.7.3 Gaining Access to New Markets

There are many ways that swaps allow firms to access markets that they might otherwise be unable to profitably enter. Consider just one such possibility. Suppose the Swiss annuity provider would like to offer its annuity contracts to Italian citizens who require annuity payments in lira. In the absence of swap opportunities, the Swiss firm, which cannot afford to take foreign-exchange risk, is limited to finding investment opportunities in Italy. These opportunities might be inferior to opportunities in other nations. In fact, given the investment opportunities in Italy, the Swiss firm might decide that it cannot currently invest in Italy at a return sufficient to offer Italians an attractive annuity rate and still earn a reasonable profit. Given this situation, the Swiss firm judges the Italian market to be closed to it at the present time.

By engaging a swap dealer that makes a market in lira-for-dollar swaps, lira-for-deutschemark swaps, and so on, the annuity provider can seize an investment opportunity outside Italy and then transform this non–lira asset into a lira–denominated asset. With lira assured, the annuity provider can obtain lira financing by offering its policies to Italian citizens in the same way that it offered its policies to U.S. citizens.

There are many other ways in which a firm can use swaps to access markets that would otherwise be closed to it or for which the cost of entering the market is judged to be prohibitive. We will examine some of these opportunities, in the context of equity swaps, in Chapter 5.

4.8 VARIANTS

Just as the plain vanilla interest rate swap is not always adequate to meet the needs of an interest rate swap end user, the plain vanilla currency swap can fail to meet the needs of a currency swap end user. To meet end users' needs, swap dealers have created a number of currency swap variants. These variants can be used individually or can be combined with other variants to produce very effective solutions to financing and foreign–exchange risk management problems. We will now briefly examine fixed–for–fixed currency swaps, floating–for–floating currency swaps, and amortizing swaps. Unlike interest rate swaps, which do not require an exchange of principals, currency swaps generally do require such an exchange. This is not an absolute, however, and many currency swaps are structured in such a way that no principal exchanges are required.

Fixed–for–fixed rate nonamortizing currency swaps. The fixed–for–fixed rate nonamortizing currency swap is identical to the fixed–for–floating rate currency swap except that both counterparties pay a fixed rate of interest. This type of swap can be created via a single swap agreement or via two separate swap agreements. In the latter case, a fixed–for–floating rate currency swap can be used for the initial exchange of currencies with the corporate user paying the floating rate. A fixed–for–floating rate interest rate swap can then be used to convert the floating-rate side to a fixed rate. The end result is a cash flow pattern identical to a fixed–for–fixed rate currency swap. As already noted, when the floating leg of both swaps is LIBOR, this combination is called a circus swap.

Floating–for–floating rate nonamortizing currency swaps. The floating–for–floating rate nonamortizing currency swap is identical to the fixed–for–floating rate currency swap except that both counterparties pay a floating rate of interest. This type of swap can be created via a single swap agreement or via two separate swap agreements. In the latter case, a fixed–for–floating rate currency swap can be used for the initial transaction with the corporate user paying the fixed rate. A fixed–for–floating rate interest rate swap can then be used to convert the fixed–rate side to a floating rate. The end result is a cash flow pattern identical to a floating–for–floating rate currency swap.

Amortizing currency swaps.   Unlike the single reexchange of principals associated with nonamortizing swaps, amortizing currency swaps are reexchanged in stages. That is, the principals amortize over the life of the swap. These currency swaps can be fixed–for–floating, fixed–for–fixed, or floating–for–floating.

Accreting currency swaps.   Like accreting interest rate swaps, accreting currency swaps are swaps on which the notional principal is scheduled to increase over the life of the swap. These swap structures are very useful for hedging exchange rate risk when the size of the cash position giving rise to the exchange rate risk is expected to increase over time.

This look at swap variants is not meant to be exhaustive or detailed. Other types of interest rate and currency swaps exist, and new ones are evolving all the time. Our cursory examination of these products is sufficient, however, to provide an appreciation of the versatility associated with these instruments. It is also sufficient to appreciate the complexities associated with pricing these products and the difficulties encountered by swap dealers in managing their swap portfolios.

4.9 SUMMARY

Currency swaps have made it possible to raise funds in any currency and use those funds to invest in an asset denominated in any other currency. This ability of currency swaps to transform the currency of a liability or an asset makes it possible to exploit comparative advantages that different firms hold in different currencies for the purpose of reducing financing costs. Currency swaps have also made it possible to hedge multiperiod foreign exchange exposures, to enter new markets, and to exploit economies of scale.

The pricing of currency swaps is a complex undertaking. Typically, the bank, of which the swap dealer is a part, has a capital markets group that is charged with developing and periodically revising indicative swap pricing schedules. These schedules provide base rates. The base rates are adjusted to reflect any special features the client requires, the creditworthiness of the client, the frequency of interest payments, and whether the swap will be at–market or off–market. The arithmetic of swap pricing depends heavily on the mathematics of the time value of money.

A need for off–market pricing arises whenever a client of the dealer requires a swap to be written at a rate that differs from the prevailing swap rates. This situation is most likely to arise when a firm seeks to transform the type of interest rate or the currency associated with an existing obligation.

Circus swaps, by combining interest rate and currency swaps, allow the end user to convert fixed–rate debt in one currency to fixed–rate debt in a different currency, or to convert floating–rate debt in one currency to floating–rate debt in another currency. These swaps are priced in exactly the same fashion as other swaps but the pricing is a two–stage process.

REVIEW QUESTIONS

1. Why are the notional principals on a currency swap sometimes exchanged while the notional principals on an interest rate swap are never exchanged?

2. Why are some currency swaps often described as "exchanges of borrowings"? Draw a typical cash flow scenario, including the cash market transactions, that would illustrate your arguments.

3. The swap described in Section 4.2 allows the British firm and the American firm to each reduce their borrowing costs by 25 basis points. If the GBP swap coupon was 9.80 percent and the USD swap coupon was 10.45 percent, what would the gains of the two parties have been? Show your calculations.

4. What is meant by the term "midrate" and how can it be obtained for an interest rate swap from an indicative pricing schedule that depicts dealer–receive and dealer–pay rates?

5. In the example of off–market pricing given in Section 4.5, it was noted that the firm could have employed a buy–up rather than adjusting the rate on the floating leg of the swap, in order to obtain the off–market swap coupon that it required. How much

would this buy–up have cost the firm in the form of a front–end fee? Show your calculations.

6. Describe a situation in which a firm might desire a swap with no initial exchange of notional principals.

7. Describe and illustrate how a fixed–for–fixed currency swap can be created from a fixed–for–floating interest rate swap and a fixed–for–floating currency swap. What is a circus swap?

8. What do swap dealers mean when they say that the secret to swap pricing is to equate present values?

9. Why do measures of hedging costs that focus only on the difference between expected profit without a hedge and expected profit with a hedge often overstate the true costs of hedging when all factors are considered? Discuss.

10. How might swaps be used to achieve greater economies of scale? How might swaps be used to enter new markets?

NOTES

1. For a discussion of the arithmetic of annuities, see Chapter 2. For a more detailed discussion, see any good text on corporate finance.
2. This sum is found using standard annuity arithmetic, which is applicable when the amortization schedule is of the mortgage–type. The annuity formula is given by Equation 4.1.
3. There is an extensive literature on whether or not there is a cost associated with hedging in futures. The focus of this debate is whether or not futures prices embody a risk premium. That is, since speculators bear the risk that hedgers are trying to shed and since speculators are, presumably, rational and risk averse, it follows that speculators demand a reward for bearing the hedgers' risk. Early empirical evidence generally fails to find risk premiums in futures prices but more recent literature, using more sophisticated techniques, has reported finding risk premiums in futures prices.

REFERENCES AND SUGGESTED READING

Park, Y. "Currency Swaps as a Long–Term International Financing Technique." *Journal of International Business Studies*, Winter 1984, pp. 47–54.

Schwartz, R. J., and C. W. Smith. *Handbook of Currency and Interest Rate Risk Management*. New York: New York Institute of Finance, 1990.

Schwartz, R. J., and C. W. Smith. *Advanced Strategies in Financial Risk Management*. New York: New York Institute of Finance, 1993.

5
Commodity Swaps
and Equity Swaps

5.1 OVERVIEW

Commodity swaps were introduced by The Chase Manhattan Bank in 1986. There was immediate interest in these instruments as vehicles to hedge commodity price risks. Both commodity producers and commodity users, many of whom were already familiar with basic hedging theory and the use of futures contracts to hedge price risks, were drawn to the new commodity swap products to hedge their longer–term multiperiod price risks. As the market for commodity swaps began to grow, the Commodity Futures Trading Commission (CFTC) questioned the legality of the contracts. Most activity in them in the United States immediately ceased. In 1989, the CFTC reversed itself and granted the contracts safe harbor provided that certain requirements were met. Most of these requirements were already established practice in the swaps industry. The only important requirement that was not an established practice was a ban on the use of a margining system to guarantee contract performance. Those dealers that wished to continue with swaps were forced to accept this condition, and many chose to limit their dealings to counterparties that were best credits. Some continued to deal with counterparties more generally but factored the greater credit risk into their pricing.

Also in 1989, financial engineers at Bankers Trust introduced the basic equity swap and a number of novel variants. In the short time since their introduction, this new line of over–the–counter equity derivatives has attracted many major players.

As with many financial engineering innovations, commodity and equity swaps began as low–volume, high–margin custom designs. But, as with interest rate swaps and currency swaps before them, these swaps were quickly transformed into high–volume, low–margin products. This "productizing" of financial innovations, as it is called by financial engineers, occurs whenever a structured solution to one client's problem has a significant market potential beyond the client for whom it was first designed.

In this chapter we provide a general overview of commodity and equity swaps. We demonstrate the use of commodity swaps to hedge price risks and we explore some of the specific uses for equity swaps. We begin with commodity swaps.

5.2 COMMODITY SWAPS

The basic structure of a commodity swap was explained in Chapter 2. For this reason, we will only briefly review the basic structure here. The remainder of our focus will be on the use of commodity swaps as a hedging tool.

In a commodity swap, the first counterparty makes periodic payments to the second at a per unit fixed price for a given quantity of some commodity. The second counterparty pays the first a per unit floating price (usually an average price based on periodic observations of the spot price) for a given quantity of some commodity. The commodities may be the same (the usual case) or different. As a general rule, no exchanges of notionals take place—all transactions in actuals take place in the cash markets.

Consider a simple case. A copper producer wants to fix the price it *receives* for its copper output for six years. Suppose that its monthly production averages 3 million pounds. To obtain the desired outcome, the copper producer enters into a swap with a commodity swap dealer but continues its transactions in actuals in the cash markets.

At the time this firm enters the swap, the commodity swap dealer's mid–price for copper is $0.620 per pound. To this, the dealer adds $0.0025

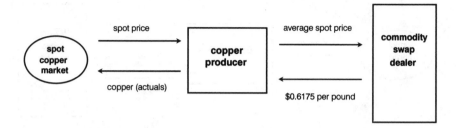

FIGURE 5.1 The Basic Copper (Commodity) Swap

per pound if it is fixed–price receiver and deducts $0.0025 if it is fixed–price payer. In either case, the floating–price side is determined by an average of weekly observations on the spot price of copper.

Given the dealer's pricing, the copper producer can expect to receive $0.6175 per pound of copper and to pay the average spot price for the month. As can be seen in Figure 5.1, these payments have the effect of fixing the price of copper for the copper producer. To the extent that the dealer has an imbalance in the copper portion of its commodity swap book, the dealer will hedge in copper futures.

5.3 THE PLAIN VANILLA EQUITY SWAP

Like any other basic swap, the basic equity swap involves a notional principal, a specified tenor, prespecified payment intervals, a fixed rate (swap coupon), and a floating rate pegged to some well–defined index. The novel twist in these swaps is that the floating rate is pegged to the total return on some stock index. Total return includes both dividend and capital appreciation.[1] This can be a broadly based stock index such as the S&P 500, the London Financial Times Index, or the Nikkei Index. Alternatively, the swap can be pegged to a narrower index such as that for a specific industry group (an oil industry index, a gold mining index, an electric utility index, and so on).

To provide an example of a basic equity swap, suppose that an end user, who holds a diversified stock portfolio highly correlated with the S&P return, wants to pay the S&P return and to receive a fixed rate, thereby hedging the preexisting equity position against downside market risk over the tenor of the swap. The payments are to be made quarterly on a notional principal of $100 million. The tenor is three years. The

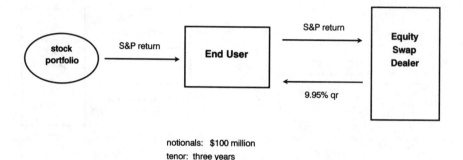

notionals: $100 million
tenor: three years

FIGURE 5.2   An Equity Swap at Work

dealer prices the swap at 9.95 percent qr (a periodic rate of 2.4875%). The swap is written so that the notional principal is fixed over the life of the swap. The cash flows of the swap together with the cash flows of the cash position are depicted in Figure 5.2.

The swap depicted in Figure 5.2 demonstrates that a properly structured equity swap can be used to convert a volatile equity return into a stable fixed income return. Thus, the equity swap bridges the debt and equity markets. It is important to observe that, because an equity return can be positive or negative, the cash flow on the equity–pegged leg of the swap can go in either direction. In the swap depicted in Figure 5.2, if the equity return is negative for the quarter, then the dealer pays the end user the negative sum as well as the swap coupon on the fixed leg.

The basic equity swap just described was structured to have a floating leg tied to an equity index and a fixed leg that pays a fixed rate of interest. Call this an equity–for–fixed equity swap. An alternative, but equivalent, structure for an equity swap is to have one leg tied to a floating equity index and to have the other leg tied to a floating rate of interest, most often LIBOR. Call this an equity–for–floating–equity swap. These two alternative structures are, in fact, equivalent because either can be converted to the other by employing a fixed–for–floating interest rate swap. The conversion of an equity–for–fixed rate equity swap to an equity–for–floating rate equity swap is depicted in Figure 5.3.

5.4   EQUITY SWAP DEALERS

Like other swap dealers, equity swap dealers look to offset their risk through effective hedging. Ideally, the dealer seeks a direct hedge involving a perfectly matched swap counterparty. For instance, from Figure 5.2, the dealer would seek a counterparty that wants to pay fixed and receive the S&P return on a quarterly basis for a tenor of three years on a notional principal of $100 million. Perfect matching of every swap is impractical, however, and so the dealer will focus on hedging any residual risks associated with a mismatched swap book. In many cases, the equity swap dealer will trade stock index futures to accomplish the task.

Consider Figure 5.4 in which the equity swap dealer from Figure 5.2 has offset a portion of its exposure with Counterparty D and the re-

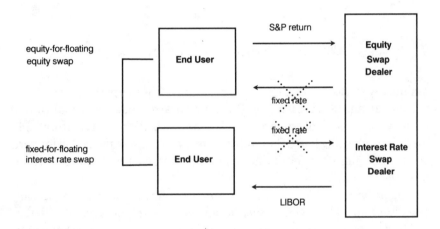

FIGURE 5.3   Creating an Equity–for–Floating Rate Equity Swap

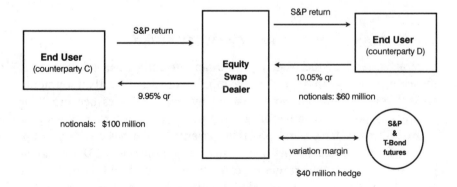

FIGURE 5.4   Hedging an Equity Swap Dealers Book

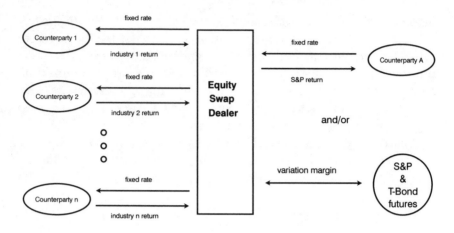

FIGURE 5.5   Hedging Industry–Index Specific Swaps

mainder with stock index futures. Specifically, Counterparty D pays 10.05 percent qr and receives the S&P return on a notional principal of $60 million for a tenor of three years. The dealer hedges the remaining $40 million by shorting listed S&P futures contracts, rolling the hedge forward as required until the $40 million can also be offset with another counterparty.

The hedging problem is more complex for dealers who write industry specific swaps. However, if such swaps are written on several different industry groups, they may collectively mimic a broader market index. Thus, they can be effectively hedged with, say, S&P swaps or S&P futures. This concept is illustrated in Figure 5.5.

5.5   VARIANTS OF THE BASIC EQUITY SWAP

Several variants of the basic equity swap currently exist. Moreover, as the use of equity swaps increases, the number of variants will undoubtedly grow. Some variants are accompanied by front–end fees because their complexity poses problems for keeping the swap book properly hedged.

We will consider several possible variants of the basic equity swap. The first variant is a simple one. Instead of employing a fixed notional principal, the notional principal can fluctuate on the basis of the net amount of the cash flow received each period. For example, suppose that the initial notional principal is $100 million, the floating rate is the S&P

return, and the swap coupon is 10.00 percent qr (i.e., a periodic rate of 2.5%). The end user is the fixed rate payer/S&P receiver. Suppose now that for the first payment period, the *periodic* S&P return is 6 percent and the fixed rate is 2.5 percent. Thus, the dealer must pay the end user 3.5 percent (i.e., 6% − 2.5%) on $100 million or $3.5 million. For the next payment period, the notional principal is then $103.5 million. Now suppose that during the next period the S&P return is −3.25 percent. The fixed rate is, of course, still 2.5 percent, so the end user must pay the dealer 5.75 percent on $103.5 million for a total of about $5.95 million. The notional principal for the next period then declines to about $97.55 million. This structure would be useful for a portfolio manager who is trying to obtain a portfolio IRR that precisely matches the S&P IRR.

The second variant we will briefly consider involves a cap on the equity (S&P) side of the equity swap. A cap is a multiperiod cash–settled option. Such options are usually tied to LIBOR or some other interest rate index, but there is absolutely no reason why a cap cannot be tied to an equity return. A capped–equity swap, for lack of a better name, can be created in either of two ways. One way is to enter a capped equity swap directly with an equity swap dealer. The alternative is to purchase the cap separately from the swap. Since these two alternatives would generate identical cash flows, we will not distinguish between them. Now consider an example of a capped equity swap. Suppose that an end user, who is the S&P payer/fixed rate receiver on a four-year equity swap with annual payments, purchases an S&P cap with a cap rate of 16 percent. In any year in which the S&P return is above 16 percent, the cap dealer pays the firm the excess. This imposes an upper limit on the end user's potential payout.

The third variant, sometimes called an **asset allocation swap,** is an even more novel twist wherein the equity return is pegged to the *greater* of two stock indexes. Consider, for example, an equity swap in which the equity return side pays the greater of the S&P return or the Nikkei return. Since such a swap is more attractive to the equity receiver than is a swap pegged to a single index, we can expect that the former will command a higher swap coupon. Alternatively, in lieu of a higher swap coupon, a front–end fee may be imposed.

Another variant, similar in concept to a basis swap, has two equity legs rather than one. That is, a counterparty *pays* the total return on one index, say the S&P 500, and *receives* the total return on another stock index, say the Nikkei 225. This type of swap, sometimes called a quantro swap, can be used by asset allocators who hold an equity portfolio of one country and who wish to convert it, or a portion of it, to an equity portfolio of another country.

The final variant we note uses a blended index on the equity–pay side. A **blended index** is a weighted average of other indexes—usually two. For example, the equity leg of the swap can be 40 percent S&P and 60 percent Nikkei. A blended index consisting of many indexes from different countries is sometimes called a **rainbow**.

Note that both of the last two variants can be created by combining individual equity swaps. The logic of combining swaps is discussed in more detail in the next chapter.

5.6 INSTITUTIONAL CONSIDERATIONS

At the time of this writing, it is not possible to offer a definitive assessment of the size of the equity swap market. In its 1991 survey of swap dealers, the International Swap Dealers Association (ISDA) included questions, for the first time, on equity swap activity. Members were not obligated to respond to these questions, and most chose not to do so. ISDA officials characterized the survey response rate to the equity swap questions as "poor."

While not authoritative, *Risk* magazine reported that the market doubled in size during the first half of 1991, albeit from a still small base.[2] Most of the swaps written during this period were indexed to the S&P 500 and the Nikkei 225, but activity was also considerable in Germany's DAX, France's CAC–40, and the UK's FT–SE 100. The average size of the transactions was in the $50 million to $100 million range, but transactions of $500 million and more were reported.

There are natural players on the equity–receive side of equity swaps with index–funds being the most obvious. There are fewer natural players on the equity–pay side. (The equity paying player can be viewed as having taken a long–term short position on the index.) Consequently, most of the earlier equity swaps involved dealers themselves (on the equity–pay side) whose motivation was to hedge other aspects of their portfolios— most notably their options books.

Index–fund managers are drawn to index swaps on the equity–receive side partly because the swap structure guarantees 100 percent correlation with the index—a strong argument for fund managers whose performance is judged by how closely their fund tracks the targeted index. In addition, equity swap dealers claim that end users of equity swaps can outperform a straight equity position by from 5 to 125 basis points (depending on the index and the investor's country).[3] If true, this would be a compelling motivation for fund managers to engage in equity swaps. These arguments are most often made on the assumption that the nonequity leg of the swap is LIBOR–based. There is some question, however, as to whether these excess returns are "clean." Some have argued that they represent credit arbitrage and are, in fact, a reward for bearing additional risk.[4]

Nevertheless, there are reasons to expect that a synthetic equity portfolio can outperform a real equity portfolio. In general, these benefits accrue from circumventing market imperfections. Probably the dominant source of savings is the elimination of transaction costs associated with acquiring the cash portfolio. The transaction costs associated with acquiring the portfolio are significantly greater than the transaction costs associated with entering a swap. But there are numerous potential savings beyond initial transaction costs. For example, many countries attach a withholding tax to dividends paid to foreign investors (e.g., United States, Germany, and the Netherlands). A U.K. investor holding a U.S. stock portfolio has to pay a 15 percent withholding tax on the dividends. If the dividend rate is, say, 3 percent, then the swap alternative translates to an immediate pickup of 45 basis points. Thus, we see that equity swaps can be used to engage in regulatory and tax arbitrage. In other countries the underlying securities included in an index are often illiquid or, through monopoly control, bid–ask spreads are kept large (e.g., Japan). In some countries, there is a "turnover" tax on transactions in securities (e.g., United Kingdom). In most countries, foreign securities are held through custodial banks, as is the case with ADR's in the United States. This results in the payment of custodial fees. There is also a transactions cost to rebalancing a cash equity portfolio when there is a change in the composition of an index. Collectively, the initial transactions costs, the withholding taxes, the monopoly control in some markets, turnover taxes, custodial fees, and rebalancing costs can be substantial. To the extent that an equity swap can reduce or eliminate these costs, the benefits accrue directly to the fund's shareholders.

We should note some incidental considerations that have a monetary value. For example, for the international investor, the swaps alternative eliminates the problems associated with different settlement, accounting, and reporting procedures among countries. We would suggest that measuring the gains from engaging in equity swaps is fertile ground for empirical study.

An equity swap can be viewed, as demonstrated earlier, as a series of in-arrears forward contracts. Alternatively, and almost equivalently, an equity swap can be viewed as a long-dated futures contract. Little, if anything, is required in the way of margin. This affords considerable leverage to those who might seek to use equity swaps as speculative instruments. There is, however, considerable credit risk since swaps are not marked-to-market daily as are futures contracts. Dealers cite this risk as the reason why most equity swaps employ a quarterly payment frequency, rather than a semiannual payment frequency, and why many have been written with a monthly payment frequency. (Each payment may be regarded as a mark-to-market.)

In closing this section, we would point out that the equity swap provides a new vehicle to engage in that dynamic hedging strategy commonly called portfolio insurance. A pension fund manager, for example, can hold a stock portfolio and achieve a conversion to fixed income by overlaying his or her equity portfolio with an equity swap in which the fund is the equity-paying counterparty. This, in essence, removes any uncertainty from the fund's overall return. The swap can be written with a tenor to precisely match the horizon necessary to achieve the fund's minimum target return.

5.7 SUMMARY

In this chapter, we demonstrated the basic commodity swap and the basic equity swap. We demonstrated how commodity swaps can be used to hedge commodity price risk for both industrial producers and industrial consumers of commodities. We also introduced the basic equity swap in two forms, and we introduced some variants of the basic equity swap. Finally, we considered the equity swap dealer's hedging problem and some important institutional details.

REVIEW QUESTIONS

1. Suppose that a large grain company enters into a long-term contract to buy wheat for a fixed price. It sells the wheat, however, at market-determined spot prices. How might the grain company

use a commodity swap to convert its fixed-price grain purchases to a floating price? Illustrate the cash flows with a boxed cash flow diagram.

2. Suppose that an oil producing country that also consumes a great deal of rice would like to use swaps to structure a solution such that it pays for rice purchases with oil production. Show how such a solution could be effected using a combination of commodity swaps.

3. Explain how commodity swap dealers, with no facilities to handle, process, or transport commodities, can nevertheless be significant players in the commodity markets.

4. Show how an equity swap can be used to convert the income from a fixed–income bond portfolio into a variable equity return.

5. Equity–for–equity swaps, often called quantro swaps, have two equity legs. How might such swaps be used?

6. Show how an equity–for–equity swap can be created from two plain vanilla equity swaps (i.e., from two equity–for–LIBOR swaps or from two equity–for–fixed swaps).

7. What role would a cap on an equity swap play? Discuss.

8. How might an equity swap having a "rainbow" on the equity leg be hedged by an equity swap dealer?

9. What arguments have been made in the text as to why synthetic equity, created with an equity swap, might return more than real equity? Discuss. Are there any counterarguments?

10. What is "portfolio insurance" and how can an equity swap be used to effect a portfolio insurance strategy?

NOTES

1. The equity return leg of an equity swap is sometimes written with respect to the value changes in the index only, as opposed to the more common total return.
2. See Chew (1991).
3. Ibid.
4. Ibid.

REFERENCES AND SUGGESTED READING

Apsel, D., J. Cogen, and M. Rabin "Hedging Long Term Commodity Swaps with Futures." *Global Finance Journal*, Fall 1989, pp. 77–93.

Chew, L. "Sex, Swaps, and Arbitrage." *Risk* 4, no. 6 (June 1991).

Hansell, S. "Is the World Ready for Synthetic Equity?" *Institutional Investor*, August 1990, pp. 54–62.

Krzyzak, K. "Copper–Bottomed Hedge." *Risk* 2 (September 1989) 35–39.

Lewis, J. "Oil Price Jitters? Try Energy Swaps." *Institutional Investor*, December 1990, pp. 206–8.

Marshall, J. F., and V. K. Bansal. *Financial Engineering: A Complete Guide to Financial Innovation.* New York: New York Institute of Finance, 1992.

Marshall, J. F., E. H. Sorensen, and A. L. Tucker. "Equity Derivatives: The Plain Vanilla Equity Swap and Its Variants." *Journal of Financial Engineering* 10, no. 2 (September 1992).

Salomon Brothers, Inc. "Equity–Linked Index Swaps." Sales brochure, 1990.

Spraos, P. B. "The Anatomy of a Copper Swap." *Corporate Risk Management,* 2, January/February, 1990.

6

Swaps, Structured Solutions, and Financial Engineering

6.1 OVERVIEW

One of the most fascinating developments in finance in recent years has been the birth of the financial engineering profession. Financial engineering involves the development and the application of financial technology to solve problems in finance and to exploit financial opportunities. Financial engineering takes a very proactive, as opposed to reactive, approach to financial problems. That is, the financial engineer determines the form of the outcomes he or she desires and then structures a solution to achieve those outcomes.

Swaps, and other derivative instruments, have played a major role in the development of financial engineering. Indeed, many in the profession regard swaps, and related derivatives, as the key building blocks for structuring such solutions. In this chapter, we are going to examine some of the many ways that swaps can be used to structure solutions to complex problems. Specifically, we will demonstrate how swaps can be combined with other swaps to produce seemingly impossible outcomes. We will also examine how swaps can be combined with other instruments and how swaps can be used to create synthetic instruments. Finally, we will illustrate a few of the ways that swaps can be used to arbitrage markets. We begin, however, with a few observations about financial engineering as a profession.

6.2   FINANCIAL ENGINEERING AS A PROFESSION

Financial engineering is a profession that focuses on the use of financial technology to solve problems. Financial technology includes the current body of financial theory and the collection of available financial instruments and processes. It is important to appreciate that financial engineering is not limited to activity in derivatives markets and need not involve activity in the derivatives markets at all. In any case, after your reading of this chapter, you might be seriously interested in a career as a financial engineer. It is challenging and rewarding, but it is also hard work. You must be prepared to be a "lifetime student" and innovator, willing to challenge conventional wisdom, and refusing to accept the excuse that "it can't be done."

Financial engineering emerged as a formal discipline during the 1980s. The consensus in the profession is that the term itself first appeared in a Chase Manhattan Bank advertisement around 1986 that used the term to describe the activities of the bank's risk management team. It wasn't long, however, before those involved in financial engineering activities more generally began to claim the title of financial engineer for their own. In 1988, financial engineering was formally defined by John Finnerty in a *Financial Management* article.[1] In 1990 and 1992, the first full texts focusing exclusively on financial engineering and describing the profession in all of its dimensions appeared.[2] In 1992, a professional association of financial engineers[3] emerged with the stated goals of defining the profession, networking the practitioner and academic communities that are mutually responsible for the rapid development of financial engineering, fostering education and research into financial engineering, and studying public policy issues affecting or affected by financial engineering.

6.3   COMBINING SWAPS TO BUILD COMPLEX STRUCTURES

We have repeatedly stressed that the basic structure of a swap is relatively simple. Yet, these simple structures can be used to solve complex problems. The secret is to use a number of individual swaps as building blocks in formulating the solutions. We will demonstrate this using two specific examples. The first one will be thoroughly described with all of its steps. It involves the use of a commodity swap, an interest rate swap, and a currency swap to achieve a desired outcome. The second case will only be outlined and the cash flows illustrated. The mathematical detail is basically the same as that employed in the first case and need not be described again. The second case involves an equity swap, an interest rate swap, and a currency swap to achieve a specific outcome.

6.3.1 Structured Solutions Using Commodity Swaps: A Case

Suppose a German chemicals manufacturer uses 250,000 barrels of oil every three months. The firm has contracted to sell its output at a fixed price for seven years and would like to fix its input costs for the same period. Its largest expenditure is for oil.

Oil is priced in the world's markets in dollars, and this exposes the German firm to two forms of price risk. The first is the price of oil in dollars and the second is the price of dollars (USD) in deutschemarks (DEM). The German firm would like to engineer a structure that would allow it to fix the price of oil in deutschemarks. The current spot DEM/ USD exchange rate is 1.5000.

As it happens, a commodity swap dealer's current mid–price for seven–year oil swaps is $15.25 a barrel and the swap dealer will enter a seven–year oil swap with itself as fixed–price receiver at $15.30 a barrel. (The dealer adds $0.05 to its mid–price when it is fixed–price receiver.) Seven–year USD interest rate swaps are currently available at a rate of 10 percent (quarterly bond basis, denoted here by qr) against three–month LIBOR. Seven–year DEM–for–USD currency swaps are currently available at a rate of 8 percent qr against three–month LIBOR.

The solution for this chemicals manufacturer is to simultaneously enter three carefully constructed swaps. One is a USD interest rate swap, one is a DEM–for–USD currency swap, and the last is a commodity swap involving oil. Both the interest rate swap and the currency swap will be nonamortizing and neither will require any exchanges of notional principal.

Structuring the swaps is a six-step process, illustrated in the following.

Step 1: *Determine the number of dollars the German firm will need every three months to pay the fixed-price leg of its commodity swap.*

This is 250,000 barrels times $15.30 a barrel for a total of $3,825,000.

Step 2: *Determine the notional principal required on a USD interest rate swap for the fixed–rate side to generate $3,825,000 every three months using the current 10 percent qr for USD interest rate swaps.*

This is found by simply dividing the quarterly cash flow requirement by the periodic rate of 2.5 percent (10% qr). The notional principal on the interest rate swap is found to be $153 million (i.e., $3,825,000/0.025).

Step 3: *Calculate the present value of the cash flows on the fixed–rate side of the interest rate swap using the current 10 percent rate.*

This is found using the present value annuity formula. The periodic payments are $3,825,000, there are 28 periods (four per year times seven years), and the periodic discount rate is 2.5 percent (10% divided by 4). The present value is found to be about $76,365,699.

Step 4: *Translate the present value of the dollar annuity to its equivalent in deutschemarks using the current spot rate.*

Since the current spot rate is 1.5000 DEM/USD, the present value in deutschemarks is DEM 114,548,550.

Step 5: *Determine the DEM cash flow on the fixed–rate side of the DEM–for–USD currency swap having a present value of DEM 114,548,550 at the current 8 percent deutschemark rate.*

We use the same present value annuity approach used in Step 3. This time, however, we know the present value and we need to find the quarterly payments. There are again 28 periods, but the periodic discount rate is 2 percent (8% divided by 4). The quarterly deutschemark cash flows are found to be DEM 5,382,599.

Step 6: *Last, we need to determine the DEM notional principal that would generate the quarterly payments of DEM 5,382,599 at the 8 percent qr.*

This is done using the same procedure as in Step 2. That is, we divide the required periodic cash flow in deutschemarks by the periodic deutschemark rate of 2 percent. The required notional principal is found to be DEM 269,129,950 (i.e., 5,382,599/0.02).

We can now combine the three swaps that form the structured solution. This is depicted in Figure 6.1. Notice that the structure has fixed the price of oil for the German firm at DEM 21.53 per barrel for the next seven years.

As a side point, in this structured deal we assumed that we would build the structure using nonamortizing swaps and that there would be no exchanges of notionals on the currency swap. We could have, alternatively, used amortizing swaps with ongoing exchanges of notionals. If properly structured, this alternative would have produced exactly the same end result for the German firm but it would have allowed us to employ a currency swap with much smaller notional principals. To the extent that the swap dealer's capital requirements might have been adversely affected by the size of the swap, the swap with the smaller notionals might be preferred.

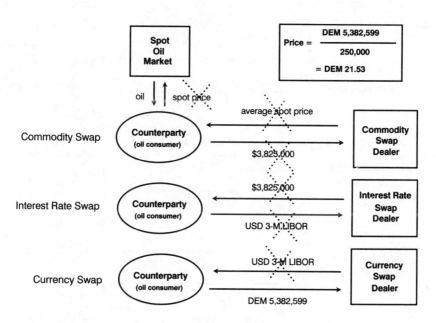

FIGURE 6.1 Structured Solution Using Commodity Swaps

6.3.2   Structured Solutions Using Equity Swaps: A Case

Suppose that a Japanese pension fund holds a U.S. stock portfolio on which it earns a volatile equity return that is highly correlated with the S&P 500 index. This volatile return is in dollars. The firm would prefer to have its income in the form of fixed–rate yen. We can engineer the desired result with the proper combination of a dollar–based interest rate swap, a USD–to–JPY currency swap and a dollar–based equity swap. This is illustrated in Figure 6.2.

Notice that the S&P dollar–based return from the stock portfolio is canceled by the equity leg of the equity swap. The dollar coupon of the equity swap is canceled by the dollar coupon of the interest rate swap. Finally, the floating–rate leg of the interest rate swap is canceled by the floating–rate leg of the currency swap. The net result is a fixed cash flow in yen from holding a U.S. stock portfolio.

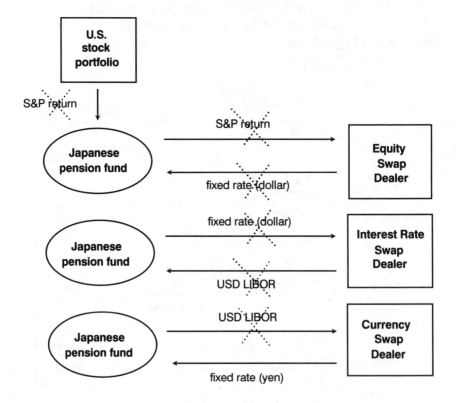

FIGURE 6.2   Structured Solutions Using Equity Swaps

6.4   STRUCTURING SOLUTIONS WITH SWAPS AND OTHER DERIVATIVES

Just as some solutions require swaps to be combined to achieve the desired outcome, other solutions require that swaps be combined with other derivative instruments to achieve the desired outcome. For example, swaps are often combined with interest rate caps to place a cap on a floating rate payout, or combined with interest rate floors to place a floor on a floating rate return. Let's consider one example of each.

Suppose that a firm wants rate–capped floating–rate debt but the firm has a comparative advantage in the fixed–rate market. It can thus reduce its borrowing cost if it borrows at a fixed rate, swaps its fixed–rate payments for floating–rate payments with a swap dealer, and then caps its floating–rate payments to the swap dealer with an interest rate cap. The interest payment flows associated with these transactions are depicted in Figure 6.3. For obvious reasons, there are economies of scale for swap dealers to also make markets in rate caps. The swap/cap dealer depicted in Figure 6.3 happens to be a commercial bank.

Now, let's consider the usage of an interest rate floor to place a lower limit on the return from some floating rate asset. We will follow this with an extension involving a combination of a floor and a swap. Suppose that an insurance company has obtained funds by selling 7.00 percent ten–year fixed–rate annuities. These annuities constitute fixed–rate liabilities. Because the insurance company's managers believe that interest

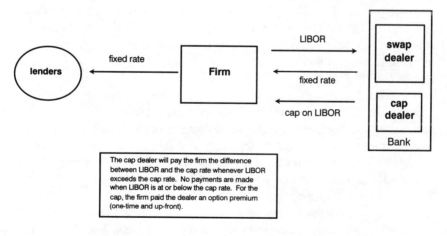

FIGURE 6.3 A Synthetic Capped Floating Rate

rates are going to rise, they decide to invest the proceeds from the sale of the annuities in floating–rate assets (six–month T–bills) that are currently yielding 7.25 percent. Management's plan is to sell the floating–rate assets after rates rise and then invest the funds in fixed–rate assets.

While management's plan seems quite rational—*fix interest costs now by the sale of the annuities while interest rates are low, invest in floating–rate assets until rates rise, and then move to fixed–rate assets*—management still runs the risk that its interest rate projections might prove wrong. To deal with this risk, the firm's financial engineer suggests the purchase of an interest rate floor. The firm buys a ten–year floor with a floor rate of 7.00 percent and the six–month T–bill rate as the reference rate. Suppose for this floor the firm pays an up–front premium of 2.24 percent of the notional principal, which is equivalent to an annual percentage cost of 0.34 percent at a discount rate of 7 percent (compounded semiannually). The firm is now protected from declines in rates.

As it happened, management's interest rate projections proved wrong—at least for a time. Rates declined and stayed below the floor rate for four years. During this time, the insurance company received payments from the floor dealer. These payments made it possible for the insurance company to meet its obligations to the holders of its annuity policies. About four and a half years after the commencement of the floor, interest rates began to rise, and about five years after the commencement of the floor, the insurance company converted its floating–rate assets into five–year fixed–rate assets yielding 8.375 percent. At the same time, the insurer sold what remained of the floor back to the dealer for 0.82 percent of the notional principal. While the firm held it, the floor performed exactly as required. It spared the insurance company serious financial damage by guaranteeing a minimum return on its floating–rate assets. The cash flow diagram corresponding to the structure we have described is depicted in Figure 6.4.

The preceding example illustrated the use of an interest rate floor. Now consider the case of a firm that holds fixed–rate assets funded by floating–rate liabilities. The firm would like to transform its assets to floating–rate in order to get a better match with its liabilities. However, the firm expects that interest rates are far more likely to fall than to rise, and it would like to place a floor on the floating–rate return from its assets. What steps are appropriate?

First, we would use a fixed–for–floating interest rate swap to convert the nature of the fixed–rate assets to floating-rate assets. Then, we would purchase an interest rate floor to place a floor on the floating–rate return.

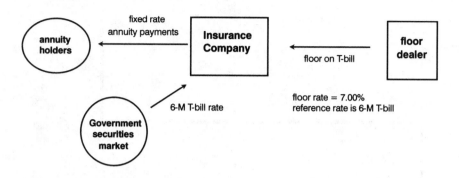

FIGURE 6.4   Using a Floor to Protect Returns

We leave it to the reader to draw the cash flow diagram corresponding to this structure.

6.5   CREATING SYNTHETIC INSTRUMENTS

Synthetic instruments, often called **synthetic securities,** are not, in and of themselves, securities at all. Rather, they are cash flow streams formed by combining or decomposing the cash flow streams from one set of instruments in order to replicate the cash flow streams of another set of instruments. Because the cash flow streams replicate or *synthesize* the cash flow streams of the real instruments, the synthesized cash flow streams can be regarded as synthetic instruments.

When properly structured and combined with appropriate cash positions, it is possible to use swaps to replicate the cash flow stream associated with virtually any financial instrument. We have already seen several examples in this book. For example, we have seen how a fixed–for–floating interest rate swap can be used to convert a floating–rate financing, such as a commercial paper rollover strategy, into fixed–rate debt. We have seen how a financial obligation denominated in one currency can be converted to an obligation in another currency. And we have seen how swaps can be used to convert a floating commodity price in one currency to a fixed price in another currency. We will use this section to explore a few other possibilities.

6.5.1   Synthesizing a Dual Currency Bond

A **dual currency bond** is a bond that is sold and redeemed in one currency

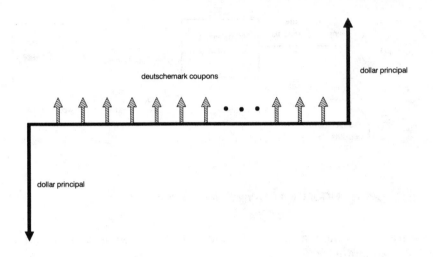

FIGURE 6.5   Dual Currency (DEM/USD) Bond

with coupon payments in another currency. The cash flows for such an instrument are depicted in Figure 6.5 using the time–line arrow method of cash flow illustration described in Chapter 2. (Arrows up indicate cash flows received, arrows down indicate cash flows paid, different arrow patterns indicate different currencies, and variable sized arrows indicate a floating rate.) The figure depicts a dual currency bond in which the principal is in dollars and the coupon payments are in deutschemarks.

Such a bond can be synthesized by taking an ordinary Treasury or corporate bond that pays both interest and principal in dollars (called here **dollar–pay bonds**) and entering an appropriately structured currency swap. To make this work, we will need a fixed–for–fixed currency swap. The swap will be amortizing (the level payment variety) and written without an initial exchange of principals. The cash flows from the ordinary dollar–pay bond are depicted in Figure 6.6 and the cash flows on the swap (interest flows only) are depicted in Figure 6.7. The combined cash flows are depicted in Figure 6.8.

It is clear that the cash flows in Figure 6.8 are identical to the cash flows in Figure 6.5. Thus, the dual currency bond has been synthesized. Whether or not it is profitable to synthesize a dual currency bond will depend on whether, by doing so, the investor in need of such a bond can earn a return greater than that on a real dual currency bond having equal risk.

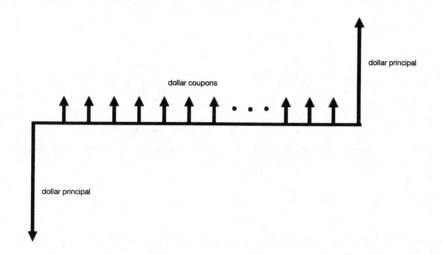

FIGURE 6.6 Cash Flows on a Conventional Dollar–Pay Bond

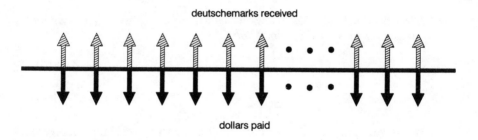

FIGURE 6.7 Level Payment Amortizing Currency Swap (*with no initial exchange of principals*)

The swap pricing issue has been ignored in this example. Clearly, swap pricing is extremely important in any decision involving a choice between a "real" instrument and a synthetic equivalent. (We consider this issue later.)

6.5.2 Synthesizing a Foreign–Pay Zero

Suppose that a Japanese investor would like to hold yen–pay zero coupon bonds. Can such a bond be synthesized from a U.S. Treasury zero? The

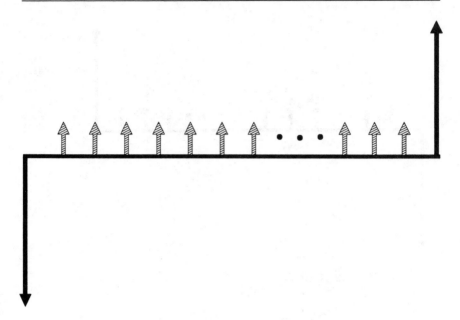

FIGURE 6.8 Combined Cash Flows on Dollar–Pay Bond and Swap (*synthetic deutschemark/dollar dual currency bond*)

answer is yes. The investor would buy the Treasury zero and then enter two separate swaps. The first swap is a zero coupon interest rate swap in which the investor is the zero coupon payer floating–rate receiver. The second swap is a JPY–to–USD zero coupon currency swap in which the investor is the zero coupon yen receiver and floating–rate dollar payer. The cash flows appear in Figure 6.9.

The net cash flows from these transactions, after the cancellation of all offsetting transactions, appear as Figure 6.10. Notice that the end result is a synthetic yen–pay zero coupon bond.

Assuming that yen–pay zeros are available to this investor as "real" instruments, the investor would compare the return offered by the real yen–pay zero and the synthetic yen–pay zero and select that which offers the better return, assuming risk levels to be equivalent. If, on the other hand, real yen–pay zeros are unavailable, then the investor in need of a yen–pay zero must synthesize one.

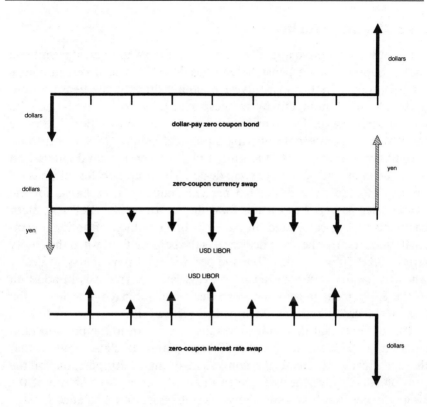

FIGURE 6.9 Components of a Synthetic Foreign–Pay Zero

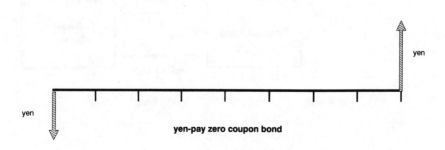

FIGURE 6.10 Net Flows: Synthetic Foreign–Pay Zero

6.5.3   Synthetic Equity

Let's consider a simple application of an equity swap to create synthetic equity. Suppose that a pension fund has $1 million to invest in equity for three years. Rather than invest in equity directly, the pension fund decides to invest indirectly by synthesizing equity from a fixed–rate note and an equity swap. The pension fund purchases a $1 million face value three–year corporate note offering an annual coupon of 9 percent and currently priced at par. At the same time, the pension fund enters into an equity swap with an equity swap dealer. The swap calls for the pension fund to pay the swap dealer 8.5 percent annually in exchange for the swap dealer paying the pension fund the return on the S&P 500. Both payments will be calculated on the basis of $1 million of notional principal. Importantly, the swap dealer pays the pension fund when the equity return (S&P 500) is *positive* but the pension fund pays the swap dealer when the equity return in *negative*. (This latter payment is in addition to the 8.5 percent it pays the swap dealer on the fixed–rate leg of the swap.) The cash flows are illustrated in Figure 6.11.

It is obvious that this strategy results in a return to the pension fund equal to the S&P 500 return plus 50 basis points. It is also obvious that the net effect is to create the equivalent of an equity position for the pension fund. Nevertheless, due to the off–balance sheet nature of the swap, the pension fund only shows its note asset on its balance sheet.

Equity swaps can also be used to construct synthetic asset allocation strategies. For example, an idea that has recently gained favor is to write equity swaps, like the one here, which pay the *higher* of the return on two different stock indexes. Such an equity swap might pay the higher

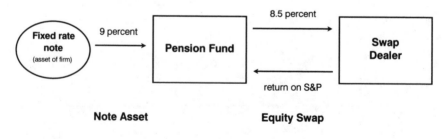

FIGURE 6.11   Components of One Form of Synthetic Equity

of the S&P 500 index (a U.S. stock index) or the Nikkei 225 index (a Japanese stock index). There are, of course, no free lunches in synthetic securities. As we would expect, an equity swap offering the higher of two different stock index returns will require a higher fixed rate on the fixed-rate leg than would an equity swap that paid on the basis of one index only. (Alternatively, the two legs of the swap could be equated by requiring the equity return receiver to pay a front-end fee in lieu of a higher fixed rate.)

6.6 ARBITRAGING MARKETS

Arbitrage is an activity with a long history. It involves two or more simultaneous transactions in different markets in order to exploit price discrepancies between the markets. As simple as this definition is, however, arbitrage is anything but a simple activity. There are many different forms of arbitrage and some of them involve the use of synthetic instruments. Arbitrage strategies involving the use of synthetic instruments are often quite complex and reach to the limits of the financial engineer's talents. Consider some simple examples.

Suppose that an arbitrager determines that near-riskless synthetic dual currency bonds can be acquired that yield 9.25 percent in pounds sterling. At the same time, the arbitrager can issue its own real dual currencies bonds having an all-in cost of 9.10 percent in pounds sterling. The arbitrager then exploits this opportunity by buying and holding the synthetic bonds and funds the purchase by issuing real bonds, thereby earning 15 basis points.

As a second case, suppose that a firm can issue real fixed-rate debt having an all-in cost of 8.875 percent. It can purchase floating-rate German assets paying DEM LIBOR and convert these floating-rate assets to fixed-rate dollar assets using a USD-to-DEM fixed-for-floating currency swap. These synthetic fixed-rate assets yield 9.05 percent. By issuing its own fixed-rate debt and using the proceeds from the debt offering to create synthetic fixed-rate assets, the firm is able to earn an arbitrage profit.

The number of ways that swaps can be used to arbitrage markets is incredible. Some of the structures are simple and straightforward, as were the two cases just described. Others are considerably more complex. In all cases, however, it is important to be aware of, and take into consideration, any qualitative differences between real instruments and synthetic instruments whether these are used in an arbitrage context or some other context.

6.7 QUALITATIVE DIFFERENCES BETWEEN SYNTHETIC AND REAL STRUCTURES

It would be inappropriate for us to discuss synthetic securities and arbitrage without considering the qualitative differences between synthetic and real securities. We defined a synthetic security as a combination of instruments or a decomposition of an instrument that produces a cash flow pattern (including both the size and the timing of cash flows), which is identical to or nearly identical to a real instrument. This is in essence a *quantitative* definition. That is, if the cash flows are equal quantitatively, then the two instruments are equivalent. This overlooks what can be important *qualitative* differences. Qualitative features include such things as the likelihood that a cash flow pattern may change on one instrument and not another, the jurisdiction for litigating an instrument in the event of a default, the difficulty of tracking the returns from the instrument, the amount and type of documentation needed to fully effect and to enforce a transaction, any lags involved in the receipt of payments, the length of time it takes to put a deal together, the accounting complexity of the structures, the tax consequences of the structures, and whether a position is *on*-balance sheet or *off*-balance sheet.

Let's consider just one such qualitative factor to make the point. Suppose that a firm wants to raise five–year fixed–rate money. The funds would be used to finance an investment opportunity expected to return an annual rate of 16 percent.

The firm is considering four alternative financing scenarios. First, it could issue a five–year fixed–rate note. If it does so, the firm can expect to pay 12 percent if it goes the public offering route. This will also involve an up-front flotation cost of 3 percent. Together with the miscellaneous fees involved, the total package has an *all–in* cost of 13.8 percent and will take three months to put together.

Alternatively, the firm's investment bank can do a private placement, but the note will carry a coupon of 13.75 percent. When the issuance and administrative costs are considered, the all–in cost of this alternative is 14.0 percent. Because the financing is a private placement, no registration with the SEC is required and the financing can be in place in just seven days.

The third alternative is to issue a floating rate note (FRN). The firm's bankers feel such a note could be issued at CP plus 100 basis points (where CP is the commercial paper rate on top grade paper). The flotation costs will be 3 percent and the issue can be distributed in about three months. With the administrative costs, the all–in cost of this alternative is CP plus 225 basis points. This FRN can be converted to a fixed–rate obligation using a fixed–for–floating interest rate swap. In such a swap, the swap dealer will pay the firm the commercial paper rate on top grade paper and the firm will pay the swap dealer 11.25 percent. The end result is that this financing alternative has an all–in cost of 13.50 percent.

Finally, the firm can issue six–month commercial paper at the commercial paper rate (top grade) plus 50 basis points. With the various administrative and issuance costs, this translates to CP plus 80 basis points. The spread over CP might change, however, should the firm's credit quality change. The financing would be given a long–term character by rolling over every six months for five years, and it would be converted to fixed rate using the same swap described above. The all–in cost of this alternative is 12.05 percent. The financing could be in place in seven days. (Importantly, with this alternative, the firm runs the risk of a serious deterioration in its creditworthiness with the possibility that it might, at some point, find the commercial paper markets completely closed to its paper.)

When all is said and done, the four financing alternatives presented here have identical cash flow patterns (except for the size). Figure 6.12 depicts the interest flows (on an all–in basis) for the four alternatives. The principal flows are not depicted. If there were no qualitative differences between the financing alternatives, the selection would be simple.

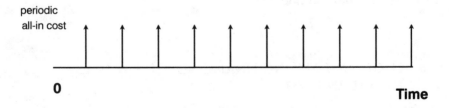

FIGURE 6.12 Interest Payments on Fixed–Rate Financing

Table 6.1   Identifying Qualitative Differences

| | | | Qualitative Considerations | |
Alternative	Description	Cost	Issue Time	Cost May Rise
1	Fixed–rate issue (public)	13.80%	3 months	No
2	Fixed–rate issue (private)	14.00%	7 days	No
3	FRN with swap	13.50%	3 months	No
4	CP with rollover with swap	12.05%	7 days	Yes

Choose the alternative that can be effected at least cost. This is, of course, the commercial paper with rollover and swap conversion strategy, which has an all–in cost of 12.05 percent. But, there *are* qualitative differences. These are summarized in Table 6.1.

We see that there are two important qualitative differences between these financing alternatives. One is the time necessary to put the financing in place and the second is the possibility of an increase in the cost of the financing. The only two strategies that can be directly compared, because the qualitative factors are the same, are Alternatives 1 and 3. Of these two, Alternative 3 has the lower cost, and so Alternative 1 can be rejected. The choice then comes down to balancing the qualitative differences with the cost savings. If speed is the ultimate criterion—perhaps the very attractive investment opportunity might be lost if it is not seized immediately—then the choice comes down to Alternatives 2 and 4. If, on the other hand, the firm's management is extremely risk averse so that they would not take the chance of any increase in their borrowing costs, then the choice might come down to Alternatives 2 and 3.

The upshot of these closing remarks is that qualitative differences between real instruments and synthetic instruments and qualitative differences among different synthetic instruments simply cannot be ignored. To ignore the qualitative differences is to open the door to unpleasant surprises that may develop later.

6.8   CHOOSING AMONG FINANCING ALTERNATIVES—THE ALL–IN COST

We have repeatedly referred to the all–in cost associated with financing opportunities. Before closing this chapter, it will be worth our while to consider the concept of all–in cost and its uses from the corporate end user's perspective.

It can be extremely difficult for a financial manager presented with multiple financing alternatives to choose among them without first having a conceptual tool with which to reduce the costs to some common denominator. There are a number of approaches that have been suggested over the years, but none has proved superior to the concept of **all–in cost**, also called **effective annual percentage cost**. The term all–in cost implies that this calculation considers *all* costs associated with a financing, not just the explicit interest costs. Other, less obvious, costs include such things as flotation costs (underwriters' fees, etc.) and miscellaneous administrative expenses.

The concept is much easier for the beginner to understand if he or she is already familiar with the concept of **internal rate of return**. An all–in cost is the cost–side equivalent of the revenue–side notion of internal rate of return. Internal rate of return, often denoted IRR, is a concept familiar to most modern financial managers. It is defined as the discount rate that equates the present value of all the future cash flows from an investment with the investment's initial cost. In equation form, the IRR is the value k, which solves Equation 6.1. In Equation 6.1, CF_t denotes the cash flow at time t, n is the number of periods of cash flow involved, and k is the discount rate:

$$\text{Cost} = \sum_{t=1}^{n} CF_t \times (1 + k)^{-t} \tag{6.1}$$

The solution to the IRR equation is found using an iterative approach. That is, we select a value for k and plug it into Equation 6.1. If the right–hand side (the sum of the present values) is greater than the left–hand side (the cost), then the discount rate was too low. If the right–hand side is less than the left–hand side, then the discount rate was too high. By successively trying different values for k, we can determine the IRR to any degree of accuracy we desire.

The only difference between an internal rate of return and an all–in cost is that in an internal rate of return, the "cost" of an investment precedes the "revenues" from the investment, whereas in an all–in cost, the "revenue" from a financing precedes the "cost" of the financing. With this understanding, the solution is simple. First, calculate the firm's initial proceeds from a financing (the revenue) and then calculate each subsequent cash outlay (cost). When all the "cash flows" have been generated, we simply reverse all the signs, that is, we treat the initial proceeds as the initial cost and we treat the subsequent cash outflows as cash inflows (revenues). Once the signs have been changed, we can compute the internal rate of return in the usual manner and call it an all–in cost. It would certainly help to consider an example.

6.8.1   All–In Cost: An Example

The Gremlin Corporation needs to raise $20 million of seven–year debt capital. The firm's financial managers would like a fixed rate of interest and they are considering two financing alternatives. Management has no strong preference for the structure of the financing. Consequently, the sole objective is to minimize the firm's cost of funds as measured by the "all–in cost."

Alternative 1:

The firm would issue a straight fixed–rate note (nonamortizing). The firm's investment bank has told the firm that the note can be sold at par if the firm is willing to pay a semiannual coupon of 12¾ percent. The investment bank would offer the note to the public at par (100) with 97½ going to the firm. The difference represents the flotation costs of the issue. The firm would also bear the administrative costs of servicing the issue. These costs amount to $41,000 every six months payable at the same time as the coupon.

Alternative 2:

The firm would issue $20 million of six–month commercial paper through a commercial paper dealer. Every six months new paper would be sold and the proceeds used to pay off the maturing paper. This strategy would involve an initial issue and then 13 rollovers (refundings). The paper dealer would charge ¹⁄₁₆ of a point for each issue to handle the distribution.[4] This would be payable at the time of issue. The firm has an excellent credit rating and would pay the going rate on investment–grade paper. For purposes of this example, we will suppose that the commercial paper rate for investment–grade paper has averaged ½ point (50 basis points) above LIBOR. To convert this floating–rate liability to a fixed–rate liability, the firm would enter a fixed–for–floating interest rate swap. The commercial paper dealer, who also makes a market in interest rate swaps, has offered a seven–year interest rate swap with the dealer as floating–rate payer. The firm would pay the dealer a semiannual rate of 12 percent and the dealer would pay the firm six–month LIBOR. Administrative costs will total $18,000 every six months payable at the time the paper is redeemed by the firm. There are no other costs.

The key to calculating the all–in costs of these two financing alternatives is to generate the full set of net cash flows. To generate the set of net cash flows, the precise amount and time of each cash inflow and each cash outflow must be determined. Once the full set of cash flows has been obtained, the all–in cost can be determined by using an internal rate of return program. There are, however, two special considerations: First, the cash flows are stated on a semiannual basis. Thus, the IRR generated will be a half–year IRR. The rate must still be annualized. Second, if we designate cash inflows as positive ($+$) values and cash outflows as negative ($-$) values, all the flows will have the opposite sign from that ordinarily used to generate an IRR. As noted earlier, this problem is solved by simply reversing the signs when entering the cash flows into the IRR program.

The first thing to do is to list all sources of "cash in" and all sources of "cash out." For alternative 1, the "cash in" includes the proceeds from the sale of the seven–year fixed rate note. The "cash out" includes the underwriting fee (paid only once), the interest coupon paid semiannually, the administrative costs paid semiannually, and the final redemption. These individual flows together with the resultant "net flows" are depicted in Table 6.2.

The flows for Alternative 2 are a bit more complex than the flows for Alternative 1. First, there is a new issue every six months and a re-

Table 6.2 Cash Flows for Alternative 1

Period	Proceeds	Underwriting Costs	Interest	Admin. Costs	Cash Flows Redemption	Cash Flows Net Flow
0	20,000,000	−500,000				19,500,000
1			−1,275,000	−41,000		−1,316,000
2			−1,275,000	−41,000		−1,316,000
3			−1,275,000	−41,000		−1,316,000
.			.	.		.
13			−1,275,000	−41,000		−1,316,000
14			−1,275,000	−41,000	−20,000,000	−21,316,000

demption every six months. Second, there are two sets of interest flows—the interest flows on the paper and the interest flows on the swap. It is important that we don't need to concern ourselves with the unknown value "LIBOR," since the firm will pay LIBOR plus ½ percent (the approximate paper rate) and receive LIBOR on one leg of its swap. The LIBORs cancel, leaving a net cost of ½ percentage point per year (25 basis points every six months). The swap coupon is 12 percent paid in two semiannual installments ($1.2 million each). The full set of cash flows are depicted in Table 6.3.

We are now ready to determine the all–in cost of the two financing alternatives. We reverse the signs of all the net cash flows above and then calculate the internal rates of return. These internal rates of return are the all–in costs. Alternative 1 is found to have a half–year all–in cost of 6.863 percent. This half–year IRR can be translated to an effective annual percentage rate using Equation 6.2. This translation yields an all–in cost of about 14.20 percent. The same procedure applied to Alternative 2 produces an annual all–in cost of 13.22 percent:

$$\text{Effective annual percentage cost} = (1 + IRR)^2 - 1 \qquad (6.2)$$

The all–in cost calculations suggest that Alternative 2 is the better financing alternative. It accomplishes the same end result as Alternative 1 but saves the firm 98 basis points a year. It is important to note that we have ignored any qualitative differences between the two alternatives. While commercial paper is, by definition, short–term debt, the strategy of rolling the paper over every six months for a period of seven years

Table 6.3   Cash Flows for Alternative 2

				Cash Flows			
Period	Proceeds	Underwriting Costs	25 bps Interest	Swap Coupon Interest	Admin. Costs	Redemption	Net Flow
0	20,000,000	−12,500					19,987,500
1	20,000,000	−12,500	−50,000	−1,200,000	−18,000	−20,000,000	−1,280,500
2	20,000,000	−12,500	−50,000	−1,200,000	−18,000	−20,000,000	−1,280,500
3	20,000,000	−12,500	−50,000	−1,200,000	−18,000	−20,000,000	−1,280,500
·	·	·	·	·	·	·	·
13	20,000,000	−12,500	−50,000	−1,200,000	−18,000	−20,000,000	−1,280,500
14			−50,000	−1,200,000	−18,000	−20,000,000	−21,268,000

coupled with an interest rate swap gives the strategy a long–term fixed–rate character, and it is therefore best viewed as long–term debt.

The all–in cost approach discussed here is particularly useful when the firm is considering capping a floating–rate liability, or placing a floor under a floating–rate asset. The reader should recall that the premiums paid to acquire interest rate caps and interest rate floors can be amortized to obtain their percentage annual cost equivalents. For example, suppose that a firm has priced a floating–rate financing and determined that the all–in cost is LIBOR plus 1.25 percent. The firm would like to place a 10 percent cap on the floating rate so it also prices a 10 percent interest rate cap. Suppose that the cap has an annual percentage cost equivalence of 0.25 percent. We can now obtain the all–in cost of the capped floating rate financing by simply adding the 0.25 percent cost of the cap to the LIBOR plus 1.25 percent cost of the financing to get an all–in cost of LIBOR plus 1.50 percent but capped at 10.25 percent (10 percent plus cost of cap). The point, once again, is that the merits of alternative forms of financing can only be intelligently compared if we reduce all costs to a common denominator.

6.9 SUMMARY

In this chapter we examined the development of financial engineering and the use of swaps by financial engineers to solve problems and to exploit financial opportunities. We have seen that, despite their simple structure, swaps can be used to solve complex problems. Sometimes this requires that different types of swaps be combined, and sometimes it requires that swaps be combined with other derivative instruments. We have seen that swaps can be used to create synthetic instruments and that these same synthetic instruments can be used to arbitrage markets. Quite often the arbitrage is between a real instrument and a synthetic instrument. Finally, we have seen that we can reduce all costs associated with a structure to one annual percentage cost called all–in cost in order to objectively evaluate and compare alternative financing opportunities. However, we must still consider the qualitative differences between different structures.

REVIEW QUESTIONS

1. Why does the term "financial engineering" accurately describe what modern financial problem solvers are doing? Describe a few activities at which you might find financial engineers working.

2. The process of financial engineering has been described by some as a "building block" approach to problem solving, and it has been described by others as a LEGO approach to problem solving. Do these descriptions make sense? Discuss.

3. Suppose that a German investor would like to hold a basket of U.S. stocks but obtain its return based on the performance of the Nikkei 225 (a Japanese stock index). Additionally, the German investor wants his return denominated in deutschemarks rather than in yen or dollars. Sketch a set of swaps and cash market transactions that could achieve the desired outcome.

4. In Section 6.3.1, it was asserted that the German firm's goal of fixing the price of oil could be accomplished using amortizing swaps rather than nonamortizing swaps and that the end results (i.e., the fixed price paid for oil in DEM) would have been identical. Demonstrate that this is indeed the case and determine the notionals on the required swaps.

5. Define the term "synthetic security." How might a synthetic security differ from a real security in a way that is nontrivial? Discuss.

6. Synthesize a dual currency (DEM/JPY) bond from a dollar–pay conventional bond and an appropriate combination of swaps. Illustrate your solution using arrow–type cash flows.

7. Synthesize a zero–coupon deutschemark bond from a diversified U.S. stock portfolio that returns the S&P 500. Illustrate with arrow–type cash flows.

8. What is "all–in cost"? Why is it important to consider each financing alternative's all–in cost before selecting from alternative structures? Discuss.

9. What do the authors mean by "qualitative differences" between financing structures? Discuss.

10. Why is it important to express all–in cost on an effective annual basis?

NOTES

1. See Finnerty (1988).
2. The first book published in the United States to incorporate the term "financial engineering" in its title was Smith and Smithson (1990), which took the form of an edited collection. This was followed shortly thereafter by the works of Marshall and Bansal (1992a, 1992b), which described the full scope of financial engineering in a textbook format.

3. The International Association of Financial Engineers was formed in 1991. This not–for–profit professional membership association quickly attracted leading figures in both the practitioner and academic communities. It also has a special student membership classification that has proven effective at helping student members enter the profession. Persons interested in membership or further information about the association should contact Dr. Vipul K. Bansal, Associate Director, IAFE, Graduate School of Business, St. John's University, Jamaica, NY 11439 or call (718) 990–6161 extension 7381.
4. The typical dealer charge for handling commercial paper issues is $1/8$ of a point per dollar per year. For a six–month issue, then, the charge is $1/16$ of a point.

REFERENCES AND SUGGESTED READING

Finnerty, J. D. "Financial Engineering in Corporate Finance: An Overview." *Financial Management*, Winter 1988.

Marshall, J. F., and V. K. Bansal. *Financial Engineering: A Complete Guide to Financial Innovation*. New York: New York Institute of Finance, 1992a.

Marshall, J. F., and V. K. Bansal. *Financial Engineering*. Boston: Allyn & Bacon, 1992b. (The second edition of this text was published in 1993 by Kolb Publishing of Miami.)

Smith, C. W., and C. W. Smithson. *The Handbook of Financial Engineering*. Grand Rapids, MI: Harper Business, 1990.

Titman, S. "Interest Rate Swaps and Corporate Financing Choices." *Journal of Finance,* 1992.

7

The Pricing of
Interest Rate Swaps

7.1 OVERVIEW

In earlier chapters we discussed how swap dealers quote swap prices. For example, in the case of U.S. dollar interest rate swaps, we noted that indicative swap-pricing schedules routinely quote swap coupons as a spread over Treasuries of the same average life. In the case of currency swaps, the dealer typically quotes a midrate and then adds or subtracts some number of basis points. These two methods of quoting prices are equivalent. That is, we can take the average of a dealer's pay rate and receive rate for a given tenor swap to obtain the dealer's midrate.

Despite our description of how swap dealers *quote* swap prices as a midrate plus or minus some number of basis points, we have not yet addressed what the key issue really is. That is, we have not yet discussed how swap midrates are determined. This is really the heart of swap pricing.

We will focus our discussion here on the pricing of interest rate swaps. This is reasonable for, as shown by Yasick (1992), there is an identity in the pricing of interest rate swaps and currency swaps. Similarly, as shown by Marshall, Sorensen, and Tucker (1992), the logic underlying the pricing of equity swaps follows directly from the logic underlying the pricing of interest rate swaps.

The pricing of interest rate swaps requires us to distinguish between short–dated interest rate swaps and long–dated interest rate swaps. In the early days of swaps, short–dated swaps were described as swaps with tenors out to a year or two. Today, however, we define short–dated interest rate swaps as any swap that can be priced off a series of successive Eurodollar futures contracts. In market parlance, a sequential series of futures contracts is called a "strip" and the strip of Eurodollar futures is often called a Eurodollar strip or a Eurostrip. The latter term, Eurostrip, could also apply to a Euroyen strip, a Eurodeutschemark (Euromark) strip, and so on. As we will use the term in this chapter, Eurostrip is always understood to refer to a Eurodollar futures strip. The maximum tenor for a swap to qualify as a short–dated swap is then defined by the most forward Eurodollar futures contract that is considered liquid. The point then is that the distinction between short–dated and long–dated interest rate swaps depends on the availability of a precise pricing vehicle, that is, Eurodollar futures.

In this chapter we will first look at the pricing of short–dated swaps. Next, we will look at the pricing of long–dated swaps. Finally, we will extend the pricing discussion to look at the pricing of forward swaps. Forward swaps are swaps in which: 1. the swap coupon is fixed at the time of contracting, but 2. the swap does not commence (i.e., begin accruing interest) until a later date. We assume throughout that we are pricing plain vanilla interest rate swaps in which the swap coupon is quoted on a semiannual bond basis against six–month LIBOR flat. We have already discussed, in earlier chapters, how the pricing would be adjusted to fit all sorts of special cases including different payment frequencies, different amortization assumptions, off–market situations, and so on. The reader is forewarned that this chapter is the most difficult in this book. Read it carefully and take the extra time to work through each example we present to be certain that you fully understand it before moving on.

A Brief Note on Eurodollar Futures

Because Eurodollar futures play such a key role in pricing interest rate swaps, it would perhaps be beneficial to say a few words about the structure of these futures. A Eurodollar futures contract is a cash–settled contract written on a "Eurodollar deposit." A Eurodollar deposit refers to dollars on deposit at a bank outside the United States. These deposits are lent between banks at an interest rate called the London Interbank Offered Rate or LIBOR. These futures contract may be regarded as contracts for the later delivery (taking the form of a cash settlement) of three-month Eurodollar deposits. The contracts are priced as "100 less three-month LIBOR." Thus, the price of a contract moves inversely with the market's expectation of the spot LIBOR that will prevail at the time the contract settles. These "expected future spot LIBORs" represent forward rates.

The point in time when a Eurodollar deposit begins accruing interest is called the **value date**. The point in time when it stops accruing interest is called the **maturity date**.

While identical contracts trade on a number of futures exchanges, the Eurodollar futures traded on the International Monetary Market (IMM) are the most widely used for pricing U.S. dollar interest rate swaps.[1] At present, these Eurodollar futures contracts are the most heavily traded of any futures contract anywhere in the world. This is, in large part, a consequence of swap dealers' transactions in these markets for purposes of synthesizing short–dated swaps to hedge unmatched swap books and/or to arbitrage between real and synthetic swaps. Kapner and Marshall (1992) document this link between the trading volume of Eurodollar futures and the size of the interest rate swap market.

7.2 SHORT–DATED SWAPS

The pricing of interest rate swaps off the Eurodollar futures strip can only work to the extent that: 1. Eurodollar futures exist, and 2. the futures are liquid. As of this writing, three–month Eurodollar futures are traded in quarterly cycles (March, June, September, and December) with delivery (final settlement) dates as far forward as five years.[2]

The pricing of short–dated interest rate swaps off the Eurodollar futures strip is predicated on two important assumptions. The first is that the forward rates that are embedded in the Eurodollar futures prices are unbiased estimates of future spot LIBORs. The second is that long–term yields are fully explained by the pure expectations theory of interest rate term structure. That is, current long–term interest rates are the geometric average of spot and forward short–term interest rates.

7.2.1   Using Eurodollar Futures to Price Swaps

The key to setting a swap midrate is to equate the present values of the
fixed–rate leg and the floating–rate leg of the swap. Eurodollar futures
contracts provide a way to do that. The prices of these contracts imply
unbiased estimates of three–month LIBOR expected to prevail at various
points in the future.[3] The fixed rate that equates the present value of the
fixed leg with the present value of the floating leg based on these unbiased
estimates of future values of LIBOR is then the dealer's midrate. The
estimation of the fair midrate is, however, complicated a bit by the facts
that: 1. the convention is to quote swap coupons for generic swaps on a
semiannual bond basis, and 2. the floating leg, if pegged to LIBOR, is
usually quoted money market basis. (Note: On very short–dated swaps
the swap coupon is often quoted on a money market basis. For consistency, however, we will assume throughout that the swap coupon is quoted
bond basis.)

The procedure by which the dealer would obtain unbiased midrates
and swap coupons involves five steps. The first step is to use the implied
three-month LIBORs from the Eurostrip to obtain terminal values for a
single dollar that earns these successive rates and reflects appropriate
compounding. The second step is to use these terminal values to obtain
implied zero coupon swap rates, stated quarterly bond basis. The third
step is to use these zero coupon rates to obtain a swap midrate, on a
quarterly bond basis, for each tenor swap. The fourth step converts these
quarterly bond basis midrates to the appropriate payment frequency,
usually semiannual. The resultant set of swap midrates constitutes the
par swap yield curve for short–dated swaps. Finally, the dealer de-
ducts/adds a few basis points to the midrates to obtain his pay/receive
rates. These are the swap coupons—which are normally restated as a
spread over Treasuries, at least for U.S. dollar interest rate swaps.

For purposes of notation, if the swap is to have a tenor of n years and
is to be priced off three–month Eurodollar futures, then pricing will require m sequential futures contracts, where $m = 4n$. The time subscript
on terminal value (TV) is measured in years. The time subscript on
LIBOR (L), however, represents the contract's position in the Eurodollar
strip. For example, the implied LIBOR for the near contract (the first in
the strip) is denoted L_1 while the implied LIBOR for the next contract
out (the second in the strip) is denoted L_2. Certain variables have double
subscripts: these are the swap midrates (M) and the zero coupon rates

(y). The first subscript, which is a, s, or q, represents the compounding assumption (annual, semiannual, and quarterly, respectively). The second subscript represents the term, measured in years, to which the rate applies. For example, $y_{a,2}$, denotes the 2-year zero coupon rate stated on an annual bond basis. Similarly, $M_{q,3}$ denotes the three-year swap midrate stated on a quarterly bond basis. Using this notation, let's now run through the five steps in detail. Importantly, the following procedure assumes that the swap will use IMM settlement dates (i.e., the same settlement dates employed by the Eurodollar futures). Necessary adjustments for pricing swaps that use dates other than IMM dates are discussed in a subsequent footnote.

Step 1: Calculate the implied value of $1 at the end of each quarter from the first quarter through the tenor of the swap, n, based on repeated reinvestments at LIBOR, as suggested by the Eurostrip. Equation 7.1 is used to obtain these terminal values.

$$TV_\tau = \left(1 + \frac{L_1 \times D_1}{360}\right)\left(1 + \frac{L_2 \times D_2}{360}\right) \cdots \left(1 + \frac{L_m \times D_m}{360}\right) \quad (7.1)$$

where τ is a time subscript measured in years such that $\tau = .25, .5, .75, \ldots, n;\ m = 4\tau$; and D_i denotes the actual number of days spanned by the i-th Eurodollar deposit.

Step 2a: Calculate implied zero coupon swap rates at quarterly intervals for terms up to the tenor of the swap. These rates are effective annual rates (i.e., annual bond basis). That is, we must solve for $y_{a,\tau}$ such that Equation 7.2a is satisfied for $\tau = .25, .5, .75, \ldots, n..$

$$(1 + y_{a,\tau})^\tau = TV_\tau \quad (7.2a)$$

implying that

$$y_{a,\tau} = TV_\tau^{1/\tau} - 1 \quad (7.2b)$$

Step 2b: Restate the effective annual zero rates on a quarterly bond basis using Equation 7.2c.

$$y_{q,\tau} = [(1 + y_{a,\tau})^{1/4} - 1] \times 4 \quad (7.2c)$$

Step 3: The zero coupon rates from Step 2b are now used to obtain the implied swap midrate on a quarterly bond basis. The annual swap midrate *per $100* of notional principal stated on a quarterly bond basis $M_{q,\tau}$ is the value that satisfies Equation 7.3a. (This valuation formula is based on the idea that the proper way to value any fixed–income instrument is to treat each cash flow it generates as a zero coupon bond, and to discount each cash flow at the appropriate zero coupon rate. For further explanation, see the discussion of bootstrapping in Chapter 8.)

$$100 = \frac{1}{4}M_{q,\tau}\left[\sum_{t=1}^{T}(1 + y_{q,t}/4)^{-t}\right] + 100(1 + y_{q,T}/4)^{-T} \qquad (7.3a)$$

where $T = 4n$, that is, the number of quarters in the tenor of the swap. This implies that the midrate is given by Equation 7.3b.

$$M_{q,\tau} = \frac{100 - 100(1 + y_{q,T}/4)^{-T}}{\sum\limits_{t=1}^{T}(1 + y_{q,t}/4)^{-t}} \times 4 \qquad (7.3b)$$

Step 4: The midrate from Step 3 must be restated on the appropriate payment frequency. This is usually semiannual but could also be annual or even monthly. In our case, which is plain vanilla, the assumption is semiannual. The simplest procedure to make this conversion is to first restate on an annual basis, and then restate the annual rate on whatever frequency is desired. The annual midrate $M_{a,\tau}$ is obtained from Equation 7.4.

$$M_{a,\tau} = (1 + M_{q,\tau}/4)^4 - 1 \qquad (7.4)$$

And, the semiannual midrate $M_{s,\tau}$ is obtained from Equation 7.5a

$$M_{s,\tau} = [(1 + M_{a,\tau})^{1/2} - 1] \times 2 \qquad (7.5a)$$

Similarly, the midrate on a monthly basis, should that be desired for any reason, is obtained from Equation 7.5b.

$$M_{m,\tau} = [(1 + M_{a,\tau})^{1/12} - 1] \times 12 \qquad (7.5b)$$

As noted elsewhere in this book, it is understood that a semiannual swap coupon is quoted against six–month LIBOR; that a monthly swap coupon is quoted against one–month LIBOR; and that an annual swap coupon is quoted against one–year LIBOR—unless we specifically state otherwise. Once again, the plain vanilla swap always assumes semiannual payments against six–month LIBOR and this will, generally, be the assumption underlying a swap dealer's indicative pricing.[4]

Step 5: The swap midrate that we have obtained is now used to obtain swap coupons S by deducting/adding a few basis points to obtain the dealer's pay–receive rates. These pay–receive rates are then restated as a spread over Treasuries of the same average life.

$$S_{pay} = M_{s,\tau} - x\ bps$$
$$S_{rec} = M_{s,\tau} + x\ bps$$

An Example

It would surely help if we run through a complete example. As we do, you should stop at various points and check out the numbers that are reported to be sure you understand how we obtained them. In order to have a set of prices and rates with which to illustrate the calculations, we will employ the Eurodollar futures prices for June 16, 1993, in Table 7.1.[5] These contracts settle on the third Wednesday of the contract month. For the June 1993 contract, this is June 16, 1993. Swaps using IMM settlement dates would take value two business days later (June 18, 1993). For this reason, we assume here that the goal is to price plain vanilla swaps that have an effective date of June 18, 1993.

We are treating three–month LIBOR for JUN 93 (L_1) as a spot rate but all the others are forward rates implied by the Eurodollar futures price.[6] Thus, the contracts imply the 3-M LIBOR expected to prevail three months forward (L_2), the 3-M LIBOR expected to prevail six months forward (L_3), and so on.

Suppose that we want to price a two–year fixed–for–floating interest rate swap against 6-M LIBOR. The fixed rate will be paid semiannually and, therefore, should be quoted semiannual bond basis.

The **first step** is to find the terminal values of a single dollar on a quarterly basis using Equation 7.1. For example, the terminal value after three months is given by:

$$TV_{.25} = \left(1 + \frac{.0331 \times 92}{360}\right) = 1.0084589$$

The terminal value after six months is given next. Note that the terminal

Table 7.1   Eurodollar Futures Prices
June 16, 1993

Contract	Price	Implied LIBOR	Contract Notation	Number of Days Covered
JUN 93	96.69	3.31	L_1	92
SEP 93	96.53	3.47	L_2	91
DEC 93	96.04	3.96	L_3	90
MAR 94	95.91	4.09	L_4	92
JUN 94	95.59	4.41	L_5	92
SEP 94	95.28	4.72	L_6	91
DEC 94	94.84	5.16	L_7	90
MAR 95	94.75	5.25	L_8	92
JUN 95	94.52	5.48	L_9	92
SEP 95	94.31	5.69	L_{10}	91
DEC 95	93.99	6.01	L_{11}	91
MAR 96	93.97	6.03	L_{12}	92
JUN 96	93.78	6.22	L_{13}	92
SEP 96	93.64	6.36	L_{14}	91
DEC 96	93.40	6.60	L_{15}	90
MAR 97	93.40	6.60	L_{16}	92
JUN 97	93.25	6.75	L_{17}	92
SEP 97	93.14	6.86	L_{18}	91
DEC 97	92.94	7.06	L_{19}	90
MAR 98	92.94	7.06	L_{20}	92

Note: Eurodollar futures contracts assume a deposit of 91 days even though any actual three-month period may have as few as 90 days and as many as 92 days. For purposes of pricing swaps, the actual number of days in a three-month period is used in lieu of the 91 days assumed by the futures. This can introduce a very small discrepancy between the performance of a real swap and the performance of a synthetic swap created from a Eurostrip.

value for one period is simply the terminal value from the previous period adjusted to reflect the interest earned during the subsequent period.

$$TV_{.5} = TV_{.25} \times \left(1 + \frac{.0347 \times 91}{360} \right)$$
$$= 1.0173045$$

This process is repeated until all the terminal values have been calculated, at quarterly intervals, out to two years (the tenor of the desired swap).

The **next step** is to find the zero coupon rates that generate these same terminal values. For example, to find the annual zero coupon rate for three months, we solve for $Y_{a,.25}$ using Equation 7.2b.

$$y_{a,.25} = 1.0084589^{1/.25} - 1$$
$$= 3.4267\%$$

This three–month zero rate is now restated on a quarterly bond basis:

$$y_{q,.25} = [1.034267^{1/4} - 1] \times 4$$
$$= 3.3836\%$$

For the six–month zero rate, the calculation is:

$$y_{a,.5} = 1.0173045^{1/.5} - 1$$
$$= 3.4908\%$$

and it is restated on a quarterly bond basis by:

$$y_{a,.5} = [1.034908^{1/4} - 1] \times 4$$
$$= 3.4461\%$$

The full set of zero rates, out to two years, are provided in Table 7.2.

Table 7.2 Implied Zero Coupon Rates (quarterly bond basis)

Term	Zero Coupon Rate
0.25 years	3.3836%
0.50	3.4461
0.75	3.6173
1.00	3.7581
1.25	3.9080
1.50	4.0519
1.75	4.2100
2.00	4.3544

The **third step** is to use the zero coupon rates to obtain the swap midrate, stated on a quarterly bond basis. This is found from Equation 7.3b, which is repeated below.

$$M_{q,\tau} = \frac{100 - 100(1 + y_{q,T}/4)^{-T}}{\sum\limits_{t=1}^{T}(1 + y_{q,t}/4)^{-t}} \times 4 \qquad (7.3b)$$

For a two–year swap, the numerator of Equation 7.3b is:

$$100 - 100 (1 + .043544/4)^{-8} = 8.2972109$$

The denominator of Equation 7.3b is:

$$\left(1 + \frac{.033836}{4}\right)^{-1} + \left(1 + \frac{.034461}{4}\right)^{-2} + \left(1 + \frac{.036173}{4}\right)^{-3} +$$
$$\left(1 + \frac{.037581}{4}\right)^{-4} + \left(1 + \frac{.039080}{4}\right)^{-5} + \left(1 + \frac{.040519}{4}\right)^{-6} +$$
$$\left(1 + \frac{.042100}{4}\right)^{-7} + \left(1 + \frac{.043544}{4}\right)^{-8} = 7.65143$$

Thus, the two–year swap midrate, stated quarterly bond basis, is:

$$M_{q,2} = \frac{8.29721}{7.65143} \times 4$$
$$= 4.3376\%$$

Note that the result may be treated as a percentage rate because the calculation was based on a par value of $100.

The **fourth step** is to restate the swap midrate on the desired payment frequency, which is semiannual in this case. We first state the rate on an annual bond basis using Equation 7.4 and then convert that rate to a semiannual bond basis using Equation 7.5a.

$$M_{a,2} = (1 + M_{q,2}/4)^4 - 1$$
$$= (1 + .043376/4)^4 - 1$$
$$= 4.4087\%$$

and

$$M_{s,2} = [(1 + M_{a,2})^{1/2} - 1] \times 2$$
$$= [(1 + .044087)^{1/2} - 1] \times 2$$
$$= 4.3611\%$$
$$\approx 4.36\%$$

The final step is to convert the midrate to a swap coupon. To do this, the dealer will deduct a few basis points to obtain its "pay rate" and add a few basis points to obtain its "receive rate." Also, the dealer will observe the current two–year T–note rate and then state the swap coupon as a spread over that rate. For example, if the dealer deducts/adds 3 basis points to get its pay–receive rates, and if the current two–year T–note rate is 4.04 percent, then the dealer would quote his two–year swap rates as:

Tenor	Dealer Pays	Dealer Receives	Current TN
2–year	TN + 29 bps	TN + 35 bps	4.04%

These quotes are against six–month LIBOR flat and assume bullet transactions.

Assuming the dealer is fixed–rate payer, the swap priced above is depicted in Figure 7.1

The full set of midrates for plain vanilla swaps obtainable from the Eurodollar strip in Table 7.1 is provided in Table 7.3. These rates are all stated semiannual bond basis and constitute the par swap yield curve out to five years. The zero coupon swap curve, stated semiannual bond basis (as opposed to the zero coupon rates in Table 7.2, which were stated quarterly bond basis), is also included in Table 7.3.

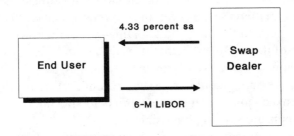

FIGURE 7.1   The Dealer Pays Fixed–Rate Swap

Table 7.3 Implied Swap Midrates for Par Swaps and Implied Zero Coupon Rates (*semiannual bond basis*)

Tenor	Par Swap Coupon	Zero Coupon Rate	Tenor	Par Swap Coupon	Zero Coupon Rate
0.25	3.3979%	3.3979%	2.75	4.7463%	4.7793%
0.50	3.4609	34609	3.00	4.8594	4.8982
0.75	3.6319	3.6337	3.25	4.9687	5.0140
1.00	3.7724	3.7758	3.50	5.0670	5.1186
1.25	3.9213	3.9271	3.75	5.1623	5.2206
1.50	4.0638	4.0725	4.00	5.2538	5.3192
1.75	4.2195	4.2322	4.25	5.3424	5.4153
2.00	4.3611	4.3781	4.50	5.4227	5.5028
2.25	4.4962	4.5181	4.75	5.5002	5.5877
2.50	4.6186	4.6454	5.00	5.5765	5.6721

The procedure just described allows a dealer to quote swap prices having tenors out to the limit of the liquidity of Eurodollar futures on any payment frequency desired and to fully hedge those swaps in the Eurostrip. The latter is accomplished by purchasing the components of the Eurostrip to hedge a dealer–pays–fixed–rate swap or selling the components of the Eurostrip to hedge a dealer–pays–floating–rate swap.

7.3 LONG-DATED SWAPS

The pricing of long–dated swaps is a more complex undertaking than the pricing of short–dated swaps because a precise pricing vehicle is lacking. However, just as the pricing of short–dated swaps hinges on arbitrage relationships, the pricing of long–dated swaps also hinges on arbitrage relationships. In this case, however, the arbitrage is between better credits and poorer credits in the fixed– and floating–rate corporate debt markets. The essence of the argument is that if swaps are in fact motivated by an effort to exploit comparative borrowing advantages, as is so often touted, then market pressures should drive the swap midrate and the borrowing costs in the fixed– and floating–rate markets to an equilibrium in which arbitrage profits are no longer possible.

While this argument seems logical, observers have long pointed out that apparent cost savings persist and, therefore, it seems that arbitrage opportunities persist. In fact, the issue is far more complex than it first appears and the measurement of the gains from swaps is not nearly as simple as we have led the reader to believe in earlier chapters. *The key to achieving equilibrium pricing for long-dated swaps is accounting for all the costs involved, not just the obvious ones that we have heretofore described.* The analysis that follows is based on the work of Bansal, Bicksler, Chen, and Marshall (1992).

Importantly, because many swaps are explained by objectives other than comparative borrowing advantages, deviations from equilibrium pricing can be expected to occur. At the very least, interest–rate expectations, the absolute level and shape of the yield curve, the volume of asset–based swaps, and numerous technical factors that affect dealers will all play a role. For example, a firm with an existing floating–rate liability which concludes that interest rates are far more likely to rise than to fall may wish to convert its floating–rate liability into a fixed–rate liability before rates rise. If this view is widely enough held, such trading can have a significant, although generally short–lived, effect on swap pricing. Similarly, a desire to convert the interest–rate character of existing assets can have the same effect. We would also note that the significant lags associated with debt issuance in the U.S. markets introduce potential for significant deviations from equilibrium pricing.[7] We begin with the conventional view and then we introduce the complications in a stepwise fashion.

7.3.1 Swap Pricing: The Conventional View

As one would expect, the key to understanding the pricing of long–dated swaps is arbitrage. The arbitrage is between corporate borrowing costs for better credits and corporate borrowing costs for poorer credits. While better credits (borrowers with a top investment grade rating) will have an absolute borrowing advantage in *both* the fixed–rate and the floating–rate markets, they tend to enjoy a comparative borrowing advantage in the fixed–rate markets. At the same time, poorer credits tend to enjoy a comparative advantage in the floating–rate market even though they are at an absolute borrowing disadvantage in both the fixed–rate market and the floating–rate market.[8] It is often noted that the comparative advantage of poorer credits in the floating–rate market is at a maximum when the floating rate is achieved by a commercial paper, denoted CP, or certificate of deposit, rollover strategy.[9] We will assume throughout that the poorer credit is a CP issuer and that the expected CP rate (CPR) can be expressed in terms of LIBOR ($CPR = $ LIBOR $+ X$ basis points (bps), where X may be positive or negative).

At any given point in time, there is a measurable cost difference between the borrowing costs of poorer credits and the borrowing costs of better credits for each debt maturity and each interest–rate character. This difference in borrowing costs is called a **quality spread.** While the quality spread varies over time, at any point in time it is a measure of the market–perceived quality of the borrower. Importantly, the quality spread differs at different maturities and for different interest–rate characters (fixed versus floating). For example, we might observe that better credits (AAA rated) can borrow for six months at LIBOR less 30 basis points (LIBOR $-$ 30 bps) and for five years at a fixed rate of 8.95 percent.[10] At the same time, we might observe that poorer credits (A rated) can borrow for six months at LIBOR plus 60 basis points (LIBOR $+$ 60 bps) and for five years at a fixed rate of 10.55 percent. In the six–month market, the quality spread is 90 basis points. In the five–year market, the quality spread is 160 basis points. From these quality spreads, a **quality spread differential** (QSD) is obtained. In this specific case, the QSD is 70 basis points. The calculations are summarized in Table 7.4. (Throughout, we state all rates and rate differentials, including LIBOR, on a bond basis in order to make different rates directly comparable.)

The quality spread differential exists because the slope of the yield curve for poorer credits is somewhat steeper than the slope of the yield curve for better credits.[11] This difference in slopes is illustrated in Figure 7.2.

It is generally argued that the QSD represents the source of the comparative advantage and it is the exploitation of this differential that is the source of the cost savings for the counterparties to a swap. Under this argument, the better credit, henceforth denoted as Counterparty 1, is the floating–rate paying counterparty on the swap and the poorer credit,

Table 7.4 Sample Calculation of a Quality Spread Differential

	A Credit		AAA Credit		Quality Spread
Five Years	10.55%	$-$	8.95%	$=$	160 bps
Six Months	LIBOR + 60 bps	$-$	(LIBOR $-$ 30 bps)	$=$	90 bps
					QSD = 70 bps

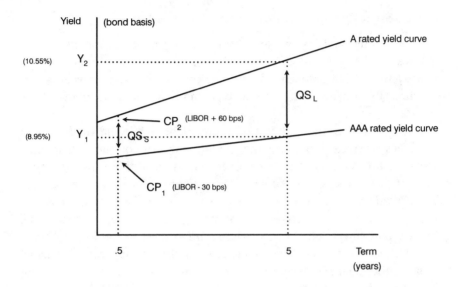

FIGURE 7.2 Explaining the Quality Spread Differential

henceforth denoted as Counterparty 2, is the fixed–rate paying counterparty on the swap. The purported savings (QSD) from a matched pair
of swaps is then given by Equation 7.6,

$$QSD = Y_2 - Y_1 - (LIBOR + X_2) + (LIBOR + X_1) \quad (7.6)$$

where Y_1 and Y_2 denote the at-par fixed-rate coupons (yields) on long–
term debt for Counterparties 1 and 2, respectively; and X_1 and X_2 denote
the premium over (if $X > 0$) or under (if $X < 0$) LIBOR for short–term
debt for Counterparties 1 and 2, respectively.

The logic of Equation 7.6 follows from the reduction in costs achieved
by the poorer credit when it creates fixed–rate debt synthetically (as
opposed to issuing fixed–rate debt directly), and the reduction in costs
achieved by the better credit when it creates floating–rate debt
synthetically (as opposed to issuing floating–rate debt directly). That is,
if we denote the gains to the poorer credit by G_2 and the gains to the
better credit by G_1, then the QSD is given by $G_1 + G_2$,

where G_1 = cost of synthetic floating − cost of real floating
and G_2 = cost of synthetic fixed − cost of real fixed

7.3.2 Swap Pricing: A More Complete Model

The preceding analysis, while a good starting point, is incomplete. It ignores: 1. the real cost of issuing debt, 2. the cost of transacting in a swap, and 3. any qualitative differences that might exist between a real (or direct) financing of the desired type and a synthetic financing of the desired type.

Let's begin with the real cost of issuing debt. While the yield on debt securities is typically stated as the yield–to–maturity on the instruments, this does not represent the *true* cost to the issuer of those instruments— even at the moment of issue when the coupon and yield are the same.[12] To ascertain the true cost, we must also consider the flotation costs of the issue, the administrative costs of managing the issue, the cost of the trustee, and so on. The *real* cost is the *all–in* cost of the issue. This is true for both the fixed–rate financing and the floating-rate financing. Clearly, the ancillary expenses associated with debt issuance and debt administration contribute positively to the all–in cost. Denote the difference between the all–in cost of a direct fixed–rate financing and the par yield by a. Similarly, denote the difference between the all–in cost of a direct floating–rate financing and the floating-rate yield by f. Thus the all–in cost of fixed–rate debt is Y plus a and the all–in cost of floating-rate debt is LIBOR plus X plus f.

Next, consider the cost of transacting in the swap. This cost consists of the dealer's pay–receive spread, any front–end fees that might be charged for special financial engineering, and miscellaneous administrative and accounting costs introduced by the greater complexity of the structure. Denote the dealer's midrate swap coupon for *best–credit* counterparties by M. Denote the dealer's spread above or below its midrate, including the amortized value of any front–end fees, by s. That is, the dealer's pay rate is M minus s, and the dealer's receive rate is M plus s. Importantly, the pay–receive rates are only indicative because they are for swaps with counterparties that are best credits. Not all counterparties will be best credits so it is necessary to subscript s to distinguish among credits. Denote the additional administrative and accounting costs associated with the greater complexity by c.

The final consideration is the qualitative differences between different financial structures. That is, even if two financing structures give rise to the same pattern of cash flows, there can be considerable qualitative differences between them. For example, in the case of a synthetic fixed–

rate financing formed by a six–month commercial paper rollover strategy coupled with a fixed–for–floating interest rate swap, the fixed rate is not fully assured because the issuer's CP rate will change if the issuer's credit quality changes. Second, the CP–LIBOR spread may change, even without a change in the issuer's credit quality, because the CP rate and LIBOR are not perfectly correlated (a manifestation of basis risk).

Finally, long–term debt issues are usually callable. This call feature, which represents an embedded option, can have considerable value to the issuer. A plain vanilla interest rate swap, on the other hand, is not callable. If we fail to consider the value of the embedded option, which is not replicated in the swap, we may overlook a significant part of the explanation for the quality spread differential. To make synthetic fixed–rate debt equivalent to real fixed–rate debt requires that the fixed–rate payer on the swap purchase a call feature. That is, the swap must be a callable swap. The call feature will add to the cost of the swap.

Although it is difficult to assess, qualitative differences have a monetary value. Let's assume that we can assign a monetary value of q, expressed as an annual percentage rate in basis points, to these qualitative differences. Thus, a counterparty that desires fixed–rate financing would require a minimum savings of q basis points to compensate for the qualitative differences on the rollover–with–swap strategy before even considering this alternative for achieving fixed–rate financing. Importantly, the value of the qualitative differences can be positive or negative depending upon whether or not the synthetic structure is preferred to the direct structure. As a general rule, q will be positive for a synthetic fixed rate and negative for a synthetic floating rate.

With these pieces in place, the conditions under which synthetic financings that produce real benefits for a better credit (seeking floating–rate financing) and a poorer credit (seeking fixed–rate financing) can be defined.

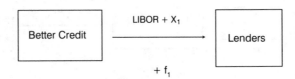

FIGURE 7.3 A Direct (Real) Floating–Rate Financing

As can be seen in Figure 7.3, if the better credit issues floating–rate debt directly, its cost is LIBOR $+ X_1 + f_1$. And, as illustrated in Figure 7.4, if it creates floating–rate debt synthetically, its cost is $Y_1 + a_1 - (M - s_1) +$ LIBOR $+ q_1 + c_1$. The necessary condition then for the better credit to enter into a swap is given by Equation 7.7a.

cost of synthetic floating $\leq$ cost of direct floating

$$Y_1 + a_1 - (M - s_1) + \text{LIBOR} + q_1 + c_1 \leq \text{LIBOR} + X_1 + f_1 \quad (7.7\text{a})$$

By the same logic, the poorer credit, in need of fixed–rate financing, will find the synthetic attractive if and only if Equation 7.8a is satisfied.

cost of synthetic fixed $\leq$ cost of direct fixed

$$\text{LIBOR} + X_2 + f_2 - \text{LIBOR} + (M + s_2) + c_2 + q_2 \leq Y_2 + a_2 \quad (7.8\text{a})$$

Canceling LIBOR, and rearranging terms, it becomes clear that the conditions for the synthetic financing to be viable are given by Equation 7.7b and 7.8b.

$$Y_1 + a_1 + s_1 + q_1 + c_1 - X_1 - f_1 \leq M \quad (7.7\text{b})$$

$$M \leq Y_2 + a_2 - X_2 - f_2 - s_2 - c_2 - q_2 \quad (7.8\text{b})$$

Since both conditions must be satisfied simultaneously in order to have a pair of matched counterparties (or, equivalently, to avoid an imbalance

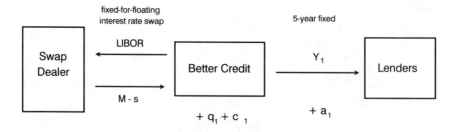

FIGURE 7.4 A Synthetic Floating–Rate Financing

in the dealer's book), the range of allowable swap coupons for sustained swap activity motivated by comparative advantage is given by Equation 7.9.

$$Y_1 + a_1 + s_1 + q_1 + c_1 - X_1 - f_1 \leq M \leq Y_2$$
$$+ a_2 - X_2 - f_2 - s_2 - c_2 - q_2 \quad (7.9)$$

7.3.3 Comparative Statics

Equation 7.9 provides a number of useful insights. First, the greater the dealer's spread s_1 or s_2, the less likely the synthetic financing will be preferred to the direct financing. Second, the greater the all-in cost of direct fixed–rate financing, relative to the yield, for the better (poorer) credit, a_1 (a_2), the less (more) likely the synthetic structure will be preferred. Third, the greater the all-in cost of a direct floating–rate financing, relative to the nominal cost, f_1 (f_2), the more (less) likely the synthetic will be preferred. Fourth, the greater the CP spread over LIBOR, X_1 (X_2), the more (less) likely that the synthetic will be preferred. Fifth, the greater the additional administrative and accounting costs induced by the complexity of the synthetic financing, c_1 and c_2, the less likely the synthetic will be preferred. Finally, the greater the qualitative benefits from a synthetic financing, q_1 (when $q_1 < 0$), and the less the qualitative costs of a synthetic financing, q_2 (when $q_2 > 0$), the more likely the synthetic will be preferred.

To condense the notation, let:

$$v_1 = a_1 + s_1 + q_1 + c_1 - f_1$$
$$\text{and } v_2 = a_2 - f_2 - s_2 - c_2 - q_2$$

Equation 7.9 then becomes Equation 7.10, which represents boundary conditions for ongoing swap activity motivated by comparative advantage.

$$Y_1 - X_1 + v_1 \leq M \leq Y_2 - X_2 + v_2 \quad (7.10)$$

7.3.4 Pressure toward an Equilibrium

Equation 7.10 suggests a number of important things. First, if $Y_1 - X_1 + v_1 \leq M > Y_2 - X_2 + v_2$, then there would be losses to the poorer credit from entering swaps but there would be gains to the better credit. Under such conditions, dealers will attract more activity to the dealer–pays–fixed–rate side of the swap book than to the dealer–receives–fixed–rate side of the swap book and the book would become badly out of balance. Similarly, if $Y_1 - X_1 + v_1 > M \leq Y_2 - X_2 + v_2$, then there would be losses to the better credit from entering swaps but there would be gains to the poorer credit. Again, the dealer's book would become badly out of balance. Clearly, the dealer has an incentive to set the coupon such that Equation 7.10 is satisfied. Second, if Equation 7.10 is satisfied, the better credits will have a greater incentive to borrow fixed—driving Y_1 ever higher as long as arbitrage profits remain. At the same time, the poorer credits will have an incentive to decrease fixed–rate borrowing—causing Y_2 to drift progressively lower as long as arbitrage profits remain. In the end, arbitrage drives the yield curves for better credits, for poorer credits, and for swaps until Equation 7.10 reduces to Equation 7.11.[13]

$$Y_1 - X_1 + v_1 = M = Y_2 - X_2 + v_2 \qquad (7.11)$$

For any given values of v_1, v_2, X_1 and X_2 then, Y_1, M, and Y_2 are jointly determined such that no arbitrage profits will remain. Importantly, Equation 7.11 is a testable condition. Those studies that have ignored the ancillary costs associated with issuing debt, servicing debt, entering a swap, accounting for debt, or failed to value the qualitative differences between direct financing of a desired type and synthetic financing of that same type, all of which are embodied in v_1 and v_2, could easily conclude that persistent large arbitrage opportunities exist when, in fact, they do not. Also, issuers of debt that fail to recognize or to incorporate these ancillary costs when making financing decisions could easily make financing choices that are not cost minimizing, even though they may appear to be.

To see that this can indeed be the case consider a hypothetical example. Suppose that the par–yield for the better credit for five–year fixed rate is 8.95 percent and that six–month CP for the better credit is LIBOR less 30 bps. Suppose further that the par–yield five–year fixed rate for the poorer credit is 10.55 percent and the six–month CP rate is LIBOR plus 60 basis points. Then, the QSD is 70 basis points and these are the perceived savings from a swap. (This is the same example employed earlier.) If the five–year swap coupon is 9.45 percent, then we would conclude that the better credit would derive a 20 basis point gain from

Table 7.5 Hypothetical Ancillary Expenses in Basis Points

	Better Credit	Poorer Credit
	$a_1 = 30\ (+)$	$a_2 = 35\ (+)$
	$s_1 = 5\ (+)$	$s_2 = 8\ (-)$
	$q_1 = -25\ (+)$	$q_2 = 35\ (-)$
	$c_1 = 25\ (+)$	$c_2 = 25\ (-)$
	$f_1 = 15\ (-)$	$f_2 = 17\ (-)$
	$v_1 = 20$	$v_2 = -50$

the swap and that the poorer credit would derive a 50 basis point gain from the swap. This accounts for the full 70 basis point gain, as represented by the QSD. It would appear that at least one of the markets is inefficient.

Now suppose that the components of v_1 and v_2, which were overlooked in the earlier example, are as given in Table 7.5. It becomes clear that the markets are efficient after all, relative to one another, and that there are no gains to be derived from arbitrage.

The point of this exercise is *not* to suggest that the values employed in the hypothetical example are realistic, or that the corporate debt markets or the swap markets are efficiently priced. Rather, the point is to illustrate the forces that should drive the markets to an equilibrium and the often overlooked ancillary costs and benefits that play a role in determining that equilibrium. Only by fully appreciating and accessing these costs can: 1. a user of the interest rate swap product determine the true benefits, if any, to be derived from a synthetic financing vis-à-vis a real financing; and 2. can the empiricist conduct a thorough analysis and assessment of market efficiency.

7.3.5 Swap Futures

In June of 1991, the Chicago Board of Trade introduced two swap futures contracts. The first was a futures contract written on a three–year constant maturity generic swap and the second was a futures contract written on a five–year constant maturity generic swap. The three–year swap was largely redundant in that it was easily replicated with existing products. Five–year swap futures were not redundant at the time they were introduced, but the recent extension of Eurodollar futures on the IMM from four years to five years has served to lessen the need for a five–year swap futures product. Nevertheless, the fact that five–year swap futures can be written as far forward as several years suggests that they are not entirely redundant. The three–year swap futures product ceased trading in early 1992 and trading volume in the five–year contract has largely disappeared. The CBOT has recently announced plans to introduce ten-year swap futures, which stand a much better chance of being accepted as a swap hedge than did either the three–year or five–year varieties because there is, currently, no way to replicate ten–year swaps in the Euorstrip.[14]

While only time will tell, it is possible that these futures contracts, and others like them, will do for long–dated swap pricing what Eurodollar futures have done for short–dated swap pricing.

7.4   IMPLIED FORWARD PRICING

Forward swaps are swaps that are transacted at one point in time but that do not commence (i.e., take value) until a later point in time. Such swaps could be one month forward, three months forward, six months forward, and so on. For example, we might enter into a two–year swap six months forward. This would describe a two–year swap that is transacted immediately but does not actually begin for six months. It terminates two years after it commences, which is why it is a two–year swap.

A forward swap would not be priced the same as a par swap of the same tenor. The reason is simple. The par swap is priced off a sequence of implied LIBORs, the first of which is effective immediately. The forward swap is priced off a sequence of implied LIBORS, but the first of these is not effective until some later date. For example, to price the two–year par swap in our earlier example, we employed the eight Eurodollar contracts starting with June 1993 and ending with March 1995. To price a two–year swap six months forward, we would use the eight Eurodollar contracts starting with December 1993 and ending with September 1995.

Other than the sequence of Eurodollar futures to employ, the procedure for pricing a forward swap is no different than that used to price a par swap. There are, however, alternative ways to do it, but we will not go into these here. The swap yield curve for six–month forward swaps derivable from the same Eurodollar futures prices used to derive the par swap coupons earlier in this chapter are depicted in Figure 7.5. The par swap yield curve also appears in Figure 7.5 for comparison.

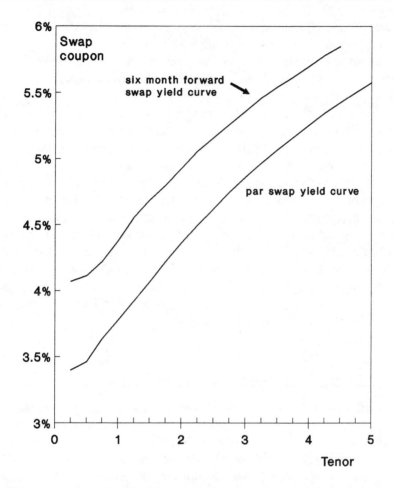

FIGURE 7.5   Par and Forward Swap Yield Curves (From data in Table 7.1)

7.5   A FINAL NOTE ON SPREADS OVER TREASURY

It should be clear from the discussion thus far that swap coupons are determined without reference, at least not direct reference, to the yields on Treasury securities. Nevertheless, once a swap coupon has been determined the coupon is reexpressed as a spread over Treasuries. For example, in an earlier case, we found the three-year swap midrate to be 4.8594 percent (Table 7.3), which we will round to 4.86 percent. Suppose that, at that time, the three-year Treasury note yield was quoted at 4.18

percent. Then, we can, and probably would, quote the three–year swap coupon midrate as three–year T–note plus 68 bps.

It seems reasonable to consider why we would bother to reexpress the swap coupon as a spread over Treasuries. The answer is simple. When a swap dealer quotes a swap coupon, the potential counterparty will usually need a little time to check around and compare other dealers' rates and/or to get back to his or her superiors to get an approval to enter the swap. Consequently, some time might elapse between the quotation of the coupon and the actual transaction, assuming that it occurs at all. In the interim, swap coupons might change in response to volatile interest rates. Suppose, for example, that over the course of a few hours, the dealer's three–year midrate swap coupon drops to 4.80 percent and three–year T–note yields drop to 4.12 percent. If the dealer had quoted a coupon of 4.86 percent with the stipulation that the quote is good for two hours, the dealer would be stuck. But, if the dealer quoted three–year T–note plus 68 basis points with the stipulation that the quote is good for two hours, it is protected. Thus, pricing as a spread over Treasuries helps to protect the dealer from interest rate risk.

7.6   PRICING CURRENCY SWAPS (AN EXTENSION)

The logic of pricing dollar interest rate swaps is equally applicable to pricing yen interest rate swaps, deutschemark interest rate swaps, and so on. Indeed, short–dated interest rate swaps in any currency can be priced off Eurocurrency futures if such futures are traded.

If we make one additional assumption, the pricing of interest rate swaps can be further extended to price currency swaps. Specifically, if we accept the interest rate parity theorem as a complete explanation of forward exchange rates, then the pricing of currency swaps follows directly from the pricing of interest rate swaps. The interest rate parity theorem, which is enforced by arbitrage and is widely accepted, states that markets equalize real returns across all currencies. The difference between nominal interest rates for two currencies is fully explained by differences in inflation rates between the two countries and this difference is reflected in forward exchange rates.

Suppose then that two–year deutschemark interest rate swaps are currently priced at DEM 6.54 percent sa against six–month DEM LIBOR. At the same time, two–year dollar interest rate swaps are priced at USD

7.32 percent sa against six–month USD LIBOR. Then, the following two–year currency swap rates are implied:

1. DEM 6.54 percent sa against six–month USD LIBOR
2. USD 7.32 percent sa against six–month DEM LIBOR
3. USD 7.32 percent sa against DEM 6.54 percent sa
4. six–month USD LIBOR against six–month DEM LIBOR

7.7 SUMMARY

This chapter has considered the current practice of pricing short–dated dollar interest rate swaps off the Eurodollar futures strip. It has been shown that the secret to pricing short–dated interest rates is to equate the values of the floating and fixed legs. This is made possible by unbiased estimates of future LIBOR rates contained in Eurodollar futures prices. The process requires us to first derive implied zero coupon swap rates and then, from these, to derive par and forward swap prices.

This chapter has also considered the many factors that are all too often overlooked in pricing long–dated interest rate swaps. It is shown that the quality spread differential, most often used to explain the gains from interest rate swaps, may seriously overstate the potential gains because the quality spread differential overlooks the true cost of issuing debt, the cost of administering debt, accounting costs, and any qualitative differences between real and synthetic structures.

Finally, this chapter has considered the recently introduced swap futures, the merits of quoting swap prices as a spread over Treasuries, and the reasonableness of pricing currency swaps as a direct extension of pricing interest rate swaps.

REVIEW QUESTIONS

1. If a three–month Eurodollar futures contract is priced at 95.42, what is the implied 3-M LIBOR rate for the Eurodollar deposit having a term that corresponds to that underlying the futures contract?
2. What is a Eurodollar futures strip? Briefly, in words, what is the fundamental logic involved in pricing a swap coupon off a Eurodollar strip?

3. Why do we distinguish between the pricing of short–dated swaps and the pricing of long–dated swaps? What is the basis for distinguishing between them?

4. What are the steps involved in pricing short–dated swaps of the Eurostrip?

5. What is a zero coupon swap rate? How does it differ from a par swap rate?

6. Suppose that the two–year swap priced in the example in Section 7.2.1 was to be priced with a monthly coupon against one-month LIBOR, instead of a semiannual swap coupon against six–month LIBOR. What would the monthly swap midrate be?

7. Use the Eurodollar futures prices in Table 7.1 to obtain a swap midrate for a one–year swap six months forward having a semi-annual coupon. This would be a swap with a tenor of twelve months that takes value in six months.

8. Summarize the factors that distort the potential gains on a matched pair of swaps relative to what the authors have called the "conventional view."

9. Why are the slopes of the yield curves for different quality credits different and, specifically, why would we expect the poorer credit to have a steeper yield curve?

10. Is it possible for a quality spread differential (QSD) to be positive and for there to still be no potential gains to either party to a swap? Why or why not?

11. Why might the swap market pricing deviate from a state of no gains from arbitrage? (In other words, what market imperfections could lead to temporary disequilibrium in swap pricing?)

NOTES

1. Technically, the contracts trade on the International Monetary Market (IMM) Division of the Chicago Mercantile Exchange (CME). Identical or nearly identical contracts trade on the Tokyo International Financial Futures Exchange, the Singapore International Monetary Exchange, and the London International Financial Futures Exchange. The Singapore contracts are linked, for purposes of offset, to the IMM contracts.

2. In addition to three–month Eurodollar futures, one–month Eurodollar futures are now also traded. These futures can be used to augment the pricing process discussed in this chapter in those cases in which the swap

will take value on a date that does not coincide with the value date of one of the three–month Eurodollar futures. This adjustment is described later in endnote 6.

3. Barring some very minor differences between forward prices and futures prices induced by the daily marking–to–market of the latter, a swap may also be viewed as a strip of forward rate agreements (FRAs). Indeed, FRAs are priced off the Eurodollar strip in the same manner that swaps are priced off the Eurodollar strip. There is one important difference, however, between single–period FRAs and multiperiod swaps. FRAs cash settle on the contract's value date (i.e., at the front end of the hypothetical Eurodollar deposit) while swaps cash settle on the maturity date for each settlement period (i.e., at the back end of the hypothetical Eurodollar deposit). For this reason, swaps are often described as a strip of in–arrears forward contracts.

4. If the swap coupon is to be stated on a money market basis rather than on a bond basis, then the midrate can be converted to a money market rate in the usual way:

$$M_s \ (mm) = M_s \times \frac{360}{365}$$

5. These prices are actually IMM settlement prices for May 18, 1993 (the latest available prices when this chapter was written). We are pretending that they are June 16 prices in order that the swap can employ IMM settlement dates.

6. Calling the implied three–month rate on the June Eurodollar contract "spot LIBOR" in June is only technically correct if we are writing a swap that will employ IMM settlement dates (called IMM swaps). At any given point in time, spot LIBOR, for any given deposit term, is the current LIBOR quote set in London at 11:00 A.M. London time and does not change until the next day. The June Eurodollar futures contract's implied three–month LIBOR is the market's consensus of the spot rate, which will prevail at the time of the futures contract's final settlement. This difference is important for non–IMM swaps. In these cases, the further the near Eurodollar contract is from its final settlement, the more poorly its implied three–month LIBOR rate approximates the current spot rate and, therefore, the greater the influence of spot LIBOR on the swap yield curve. For this reason, traders will often use the London spot rate (from the current date through the near Eurodollar futures contract), in lieu of the rate implied by the near Eurodollar futures contract, for the first observation on LIBOR. (Recently, one–month Eurodollar futures have been introduced and these can also be used for the same purpose.) An adjustment must also be made for the final period covered by the swap, since the final settlement date would fall between two Eurodollar futures settlement dates. The latter adjustment is a simple interpolation between the two implied Eurodollar yields. For example, suppose that a two–year swap with quarterly payments commences on April 10, 1993, and ter-

minates on April 10, 1995. Suppose that the next IMM date is June 16, 1993, and the last two IMM dates that are applicable to this swap (i.e., between which April 10, 1995, falls) are March 16, 1995, and June 15, 1995. The LIBOR quote from April 10, 1993, through June 16, 1993, is the London spot rate for that period. From June 16, 1993, through March 16, 1995, we use the Eurodollar futures. For the final period from March 16, 1995, through April 10, 1995, we interpolate a rate from the March 1995 and the June 1995 futures.

7. In general, public offerings having a maturity of more than 270 days must be registered with the Securities and Exchange Commission. Registration is a time-consuming and costly undertaking. To some degree, both the cost of registration and the issuance lag have been reduced by the introduction of shelf registration and the rapid development of offshore markets.

8. Comparative borrowing advantages are sometimes called relative advantages.

9. The explanation for the lower cost of the CP with rollover, as opposed to floating rate achieved with a floating rate note (FRN) issue, is explained by: 1. the lower issuance costs of short-term CP relative to long-term FRNs—the latter must be registered with the SEC while the former does not; and 2. the CP purchaser possesses an embedded put option relative to the FRN purchaser in the sense that the CP holder may elect not to accept the rollover—an option the FRN holder does not enjoy.

10. The ability of the better credit to borrow floating rate below LIBOR is often described as **sub–LIBOR financing.**

11. Lenders in the short–term debt market have the option not to renew the debt contracts. This option has relatively greater value for holders of poorer quality debt than for holders of better quality debt and, hence, the difference in the slopes of the yield curves.

12. The yield is based on the market price of the debt and the future cash flows to the holder of that debt. The all–in cost is based on the proceeds to the issuer and the issuer's costs of servicing the issue.

13. As noted earlier in the chapter, the swap coupons on dollar interest rate swaps are most often stated as a spread over Treasuries of comparable average life. If Equation 7.11 was expressed as a spread over Treasuries, it would appear as Equation 7.11b below.

$$p_1 - X_1 + v_1 = p_s = p_2 - X_2 + v_2 \qquad (7.11\text{b})$$

where $Y_1 = T + p_1$, $M = T + p_s$, $Y_2 = T + p_2$

and where T denotes the N–year Treasury yield (five years in our example). Then, p_1 denotes the better credit's risk premium over Treasuries, p_2 denotes the poorer credit's risk premium over Treasuries, and p_s denotes the spread over Treasuries for the swap coupon—defined as the difference between the indicative midrate coupon M and the Treasury yield T.

14. The CBOT's swap futures and their uses are described in Marshall and Bansal (1992).

REFERENCES AND SUGGESTED READING

Bansal, V. K., J. L. Bicksler, A. H. Chen, and J. F. Marshall. "The Pricing of Long–Dated Interest Rates Swaps," working paper, St. John's University, 1992.

Cox, J. C., S. A. Ross, and M. Rubinstein. "Option Pricing: A Simplified Approach." *Journal of Financial Economics* 7, no. 3 (1979): 229–64.

Evans, E., and G. Parente. "What Drives Interest Rate Swap Spreads." Salomon Brothers, Inc., 1987.

Kapner, K. R., and J. F. Marshall. *The Swaps Handbook.* New York: New York Institute of Finance, 1990.

Kapner, K. R., and J. F. Marshall. "1991–92 Market Update." *The Swaps Handbook: 1991–92 Supplement.* New York: New York Institute of Finance, 1992.

Liaw, T. "Interest Rate Swaps and Interest Rate Savings." In *The Swaps Handbook: 1991–92 Supplement.* New York: New York Institute of Finance, 1992.

Marshall, J. F., and V. K. Bansal. "Hedging Swaps." In *The Swaps Handbook: 1991–92 Supplement."* New York: New York Institute of Finance, 1992.

Marshall, J. F., E. H. Sorensen, and A. L. Tucker. "Equity Derivatives: The Plain Vanilla Equity Swap and Its Variants." *Journal of Financial Engineering* 1, no. 2 (September 1992): 219–41.

Smith, D. J. "Measuring the Gains from Arbitraging the Swap Market." *Financial Executive* 4, no. 2 (Mar/Apr 1988): 46–49.

Sundaresan, S. "Futures Prices on Yields, Forward Prices, and Implied Forward Prices from Term Structure." *Journal of Financial and Quantitative Analysis* 26, no. 3 (September 1991): 409–24.

Sundaresan, S. "The Pricing of Swaps." First Boston working paper series, 1990.

Yasick, R. "Swaps, Caps, and Floors: Some Parity and Price Identities." *Journal of Financial Engineering* 1, no. 1 (June 1992): 105–15.

8
Managing a Swap Portfolio

8.1 OVERVIEW

The swaps market was not very liquid until banks began to assume the role of swap dealers. As dealers, banks stand ready to enter swaps as counterparties—without regard to the timeliness with which matched swaps can be arranged. This process of making a market in swaps is often called **warehousing**. The portfolio of swaps so warehoused is often called a **swap book**. Running a swap book requires a considerable appreciation of the risks involved and the ways in which these risks can be managed.

In this chapter, we consider the management of a swap portfolio from the perspective of a swap dealer bank. We will concentrate our discussion on identifying, quantifying, and managing the various risks to which the dealer is exposed from its swap activity. We will also briefly consider two other issues in this chapter. One is the development of standard form agreements for documenting swap contracts and the other is the recently adopted capital requirements for banks that are counterparties to swaps.

8.2 RISK EXPOSURES FOR THE SWAP DEALER

Throughout this chapter it is assumed that the swap dealer is not a speculator in swaps. That is, the dealer looks to profit from its market–making activities alone. As a market maker, the dealer does not take naked positions in swaps, and it wants to be fully hedged with respect to interest rate and exchange rate risk at all times. Thus, to the extent that the dealer makes an effort to forecast interest rates and exchange rates, it does so as a service to its clients and to more accurately quantify the risks associated with its swap portfolio. In reality, however, swap dealers do use swaps to speculate (within narrow bounds set down by senior management and/or the bank's asset/liability committee) on the direction of interest rates and exchange rates.

The risks we examine in this chapter include interest rate risk, exchange rate risk, credit/default risk, mismatch risk, basis risk, spread risk, sovereign risk, and delivery risk. Because interest rate risk, exchange rate risk, and default risk are the most significant risks faced by a swap dealer, we will devote most of our discussion to the management of these forms of risk after reviewing all the forms of risk to which the dealer is exposed.

8.2.1   Interest Rate Risk and Spread Risk

The inverse relationship between debt instrument yields and the prices of fixed–rate debt instruments is the source of interest rate risk. All other things being equal, a change in the level of interest rates for debt of a given maturity will necessitate an equivalent change in the yield of all existing debt instruments of that same maturity. This yield adjustment must take the form of a change in the instrument's price because the coupon on a fixed–rate instrument is, by definition, fixed. This is, of course, also true for the swap coupon. Thus, a swap with a given tenor exposes the counterparties, who are paying or receiving at a fixed rate, to an interest rate risk. Interest rate risk is sometimes called market risk. The extent of the risk for the dealer, the focus of this discussion, will depend on the degree to which the dealer has offset the risk in other swaps or, alternatively, offset the risk in temporary hedges.

The floating–rate side of a swap will periodically adjust to the prevailing interest rate. This adjustment is called a **reset** and it occurs at discrete intervals, usually semiannually. The **reset dates** are specified in the terms of the swap agreement. Because the floating rate adjusts to prevailing market conditions, the floating–rate side of a swap is characterized by significantly less interest rate risk than the fixed–rate side. This is not to imply that there is no interest rate risk on the floating–rate side. As long as there is a lag between resets, there is some interest rate risk. The risk is small but real. However, the cost of managing the risk may exceed the value of the benefits to be derived from managing it. For this reason, we concentrate our discussion on the management of the interest rate risk associated with the fixed–rate side.

Consider a swap dealer that is approached on June 1, 1992, by a client firm in need of a swap. The client requires a three–year $25 million interest rate swap in which the client would receive a fixed rate and pay a floating rate. The dealer's current pricing for three–year swaps is in line with the rest of the market and appears below. The swap pricing is for a generic swap that pays semiannual fixed against six–month LIBOR on nonamortizing notionals and assumes the counterparty is a top credit, which, as it happens, the client firm is.

	Dealer		
	Pays	Receives	T–note
Three-Year Swap	TN + 112 bps	TN + 118 bps	8.78% sa

Based on its pricing schedule above, the dealer quotes the client a swap coupon of 9.900 percent sa against 6–M LIBOR. The swap would commence immediately and terminate in exactly three years. The client accepts these terms and the swap becomes effective. The swap is depicted in Figure 8.1 using the usual boxed cash flow approach.

Ideally, the swap dealer would like a perfectly matched swap that could be effected immediately at the dealer's current receive rate. This is depicted in Figure 8.2. But the dealer's world is not so perfect. First, there may not be a counterparty immediately available. Second, if there is an immediately available counterparty, it might not be of sufficient credit quality. Finally, even if there is an immediately available counterparty of sufficient credit quality, the counterparty's requirements may not per-

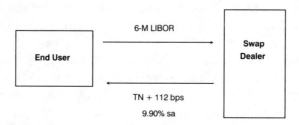

FIGURE 8.1   Dealer Pays Fixed–Rate Swap

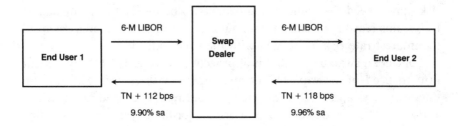

FIGURE 8.2   Dealer's Goal: A Matched Pair of Swaps

fectly match the dealer's requirements for an offsetting swap. The potential counterparty, for example, may require a five–year swap with notionals of $25 million, or a three–year swap with notionals of $10 million, or a five–year swap with notionals of $10 million, so that there are multiple mismatches, and so on.

For illustration, let's assume that there is no currently available counterparty so that the dealer has a naked position in the first swap. What risks does this expose the swap dealer to? First, the dealer runs the risk that the T–note yield will change even if the dealer's spread over Treasuries does not change. An upward shift in the Treasury yield curve would benefit the dealer, but a downward shift would be detrimental. In such a situation, hedging is prudent provided that the cost of the hedge is not prohibitive.

Let's assume that the dealer's variable cost of running a swap book amounts to 2 basis points on the notional principal for a perfectly matched pair of three–year swaps covering $25 million of notionals. Then, if a perfect match can be found for the first swap before the current price has had a chance to change, the dealer can expect to make a profit of 4 basis points on the matched pair of swaps. This translates to a profit contribution of $5,000 every six months for three years. At the dealer's current midrate of 9.93 percent sa, the swaps have a combined present value to the dealer of about $25,407. (Note, as a practical matter, swap portfolios are usually marked–to–market on a daily basis and the profits on these swaps would, therefore, be booked up front.)

It would only take an unfavorable yield curve shift of 4 basis points to completely eliminate the dealer's profit. Such a shift can occur in a few minutes in today's markets and, at times, in only a few seconds. Thus, the dealer is exposed to interest rate risk. Suppose, for example, that the T–note yield declines to 8.74 percent from the original 8.78

percent before a matched swap is found and that the dealer's pricing on the receive side is still TN plus 118 bps. The dealer's profit is completely gone. But it could be much worse. Suppose that T–note rates decline by 8 or 12 basis points before an offsetting swap can be effected. Now, not only is the profit gone, but the dealer has suffered a sizable loss on its swap activity.

There is another problem. It could easily happen that the unhedged dealer is lucky and the Treasury yield curve does not shift. But, even if the Treasury yield curve does not shift, the swap spread over Treasuries still might. Single day changes in the spread over Treasuries of 5 or more basis points are not uncommon, particularly for short–tenor swaps. Thus, suppose that the three–year T–note rate stays at 8.78 percent but market conditions dictate a revision of the pay–receive rates such that the new rates look like the following.

	Dealer		
	Pays	Receives	T–note
Three-Year Swap	TN + 104 bps	TN + 110 bps	8.78% sa

We see that, again, the dealer is a loser. Instead of making a profit of $25,407, the dealer suffers a loss of about that amount, even though there is no change in the T–note yield. This sort of risk is called **spread risk**, to distinguish it from shifts in the Treasury yield curve. In truth, however, both Treasury yield curve risk and spread risk are manifestations of interest rate risk. The distinction is actually wholly artificial and stems from the contrived convention of quoting swap rates as spreads over Treasuries. In any case, it is clear that the dealer runs a sizable financial risk as a consequence of the volatility of the swap yield curve.

The interest rate risk associated with holding a position in a fixed–rate instrument (or fixed cash flow) is most often measured by way of its **dollar value of a basis point**, or **DV01**. This measure provides the same sort of information as duration but it is more intuitive and easier to apply. An instrument's DV01 is defined as the dollar amount by which the present value of the instrument (or cash flow) will change if the yield changes by 1 basis point. DV01s are typically measured with respect to some standardized par value, usually $100. We will see an application of this concept later, but a quick example now will make the concept more intuitive.

DV01: An Example

Suppose that a seven–year $100 par value bond having a coupon of 8.50 percent is priced to yield 8.00 percent (semiannual bond basis). The present value of this bond is 102.64078. Now suppose that the yield on this bond were to rise to 8.01 percent (an increase of 1 basis point). The present value of the bond will decline to 102.58711. The difference between the original value of the bond and the new value of the bond is $0.05367. This is the bond's DV01.

8.2.2 Exchange Rate Risk

Just as there is an interest rate risk whenever there is an unhedged fixed–rate commitment, there is also an exchange rate risk whenever there is an exchange rate commitment. Consider an example: A U.S.–based swap dealer agrees to a nonamortizing five–year exchange of borrowings with a French firm. The swap dealer would provide the French firm with $25 million, and the firm would provide the dealer with 100 million French francs (FRF). The spot exchange rate at the time the swap is written is 4.000 FRF/USD. This can be stated equivalently as 0.2500 USD/FRF. We employ the latter in this example. The dealer's five–year midrate is 11.29 percent FRF. The French firm agrees to pay six–month LIBOR and the dealer agrees to pay the French firm a semiannual rate of 11.25 percent FRF. (The dealer prices the swap by deducting 4 bps from its midrate.) Now suppose that the dealer carries the swap unhedged while it looks for a matched swap.

In this particular case, there is both an exchange rate risk and an interest rate risk. To make matters worse, these risks tend to be positively correlated. All other things being equal, higher interest rates generally mean stronger currencies, and lower interest rates generally mean weaker currencies. If the value of the franc falls, vis–à–vis the dollar, it is highly likely that French interest rates will also fall relative to the dollar. Suppose that, at the time the second swap is written, the dealer's five–year semi-annual midrate is 10.46 percent FRF. The second counterparty agrees to pay the dealer 10.50 percent FRF in exchange for the dealer paying the second counterparty six–month LIBOR. Thus, the net result is that the dealer is receiving 10.50 percent FRF and paying 11.25 percent FRF. The bank has lost on both the exchange rate and the interest rate fronts.

8.2.3 Credit/Default Risk

There is some ambiguity in the way the terms **credit risk** and **default risk** are used in the context of swaps. Some dealers define credit risk as the probability of default by a counterparty and define default risk as the financial consequences of a default by a counterparty. Other dealers use the term default risk to mean the probability of default and credit risk to mean the financial consequences of a default. Still other dealers use the terms synonymously. Irrespective of usage, the terms, taken together, are intended to quantify a dealer's exposure to the risk that a counterparty will default. We will treat the two terms synonymously and we will use the term default risk.

Default risk is the risk that a counterparty to a swap will be unable to fulfill its obligations due to bankruptcy, supervening illegality, change in the tax or accounting laws relative to those applicable at the time the swap was originated, and so on. Swap dealers are independently obligated to all their counterparties. That is, even though a swap dealer may be viewed as an intermediary between end users, its obligations to each end user counterparty are independent of its obligations to the others. Thus, while the termination provisions of its swap with Counterparty A will release the dealer from its obligation to make payments to Counterparty A, should Counterparty A default on its obligation to the dealer, the termination provisions with A do not release the dealer from its obligations to Counterparty B.

Default risk is closely related to two other forms of risk: interest rate risk and mismatch risk. For the moment, we assume that a default on the part of one of the dealer's counterparties will force the dealer to seek a **replacement swap**. Ideally, a replacement swap would have terms identical to those of the defaulted swap. But, it is highly probable that market conditions will have changed since the time the defaulted swap was originated. The dealer, therefore, must seek a replacement swap that involves off–market pricing. The dealer may have to pay (or receive) a front–end fee for such a swap. Calculating the size of the monetary inducement necessary to obtain a replacement swap on the same terms as the defaulted swap is called **marking–to–market**. Dealers routinely mark their swaps to market in an effort to assess their default exposure and marking–to–market is now required as part of recently enacted bank capital adequacy rules. We will address these rules later.

8.2.4   Mismatch Risk

Swap dealers make markets in swaps by accommodating their clients' needs. If a dealer insisted on matching every provision of every pair of swaps to which it serves as an intermediary, it would have a very difficult time finding counterparties. Furthermore, even if it could induce a prospective counterparty to take a swap on its terms, the dealer would likely find that it must agree to pricing concessions.

For these reasons, swap dealers generally do not insist on exact pairing of swap provisions. Instead, the dealer running a swap portfolio will focus on the overall character of the portfolio rather than the character of the individual swaps.

Mismatches, which can include mismatches with respect to notional principal, maturity, the swap coupon, the floating index, the reset dates for the floating index, the payment frequencies, or the payment dates, expose the dealer to some additional risk—especially if a counterparty defaults. Consider the following possibility: Suppose that a dealer agrees to pay a counterparty six–month LIBOR on a notional principal of $30 million. Payment dates are 30 January and 30 July. The counterparty will pay the dealer a single annual payment at a rate of 9.80 percent. This payment is to be made each year on 30 July. When payment dates on an interest rate swap are matched, the counterparties only need pay, or receive, the interest differential. But, when the payment dates are mismatched, as they are in this example, the full interest payment must be made, at least on the unmatched dates. Suppose now that the bank pays $1.2 million in interest to the counterparty on 30 January. The counterparty is not due to make any payments to the dealer before 30 July. Now suppose that the counterparty defaults on its obligation to the dealer at the time it is to make its first payment on 30 July. The counterparty's default releases the dealer from its obligation to make its second payment to the counterparty, but, the dealer must now resort to legal channels to recover its earlier payment to the counterparty. The dealer will likely find itself in the position of a general creditor in the proceedings that follow.

As a second example of mismatch risk, consider mismatched reset dates. Suppose the initial swap is made when LIBOR is 6.5 percent. Several days elapse before a matched swap can be arranged. In the interim, LIBOR has risen to 7.20 percent. The dealer is now locked into a significant payment mismatch until at least the next reset date. Importantly, date mismatch risk is an unsystematic form of risk and a large swap portfolio is, therefore, date insensitive. That is, this risk is diversified away.

8.2.5 Basis Risk

The **basis** is the difference between two prices. In the case of interest rate swaps, the basis is the difference between two different floating–rate indexes. Basis risk is the risk that the two indexes might fluctuate relative to one another. Basis risk can arise in two ways. In the first, the counterparty requires a floating–for–floating rate swap but the two sides of the swap are pegged to different indexes. This scenario is depicted in Figure 8.3 for a floating–for–floating interest rate swap involving three-month LIBOR and six–month LIBOR. In the second, two separate counterparties do fixed–for–floating rate swaps with the dealer but the floating rates are pegged to different indexes. This is depicted in Figure 8.4 for fixed–for–floating interest rate swaps involving the six–month T–bill rate and six–month LIBOR.

Floating–for–floating mismatches, like those depicted in Figures 8.3 and 8.4, are quite common—both in the context of swaps and in other

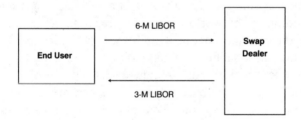

FIGURE 8.3 Basis Risk: From a Basis Swap

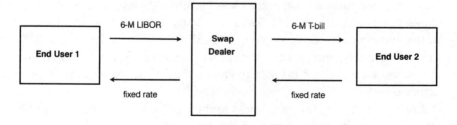

FIGURE 8.4 Basis Risk: From a Mismatched Pair of Swaps

forms of financial spreading. Indeed, many of these spreads are so common that they have been given special names. For example, the spread between the T–bill rate and LIBOR for the same maturities is called, in market parlance, the **TED spread**. The term is derived from T–bills and Eurodollars, since LIBOR is the interest rate paid on Eurodollar deposits.

Suppose that, initially, LIBOR is 9.5 percent and the T–bill rate is 8.5 percent. If the 1 percent (100 basis points) rate differential was absolutely fixed, there would be no basis risk to the dealer. But, the differential is not absolutely fixed. The rate differential between LIBOR and the T–bill rate could have been as small as 10 basis points and as large as 140 basis points in recent years. These fluctuations are the source of basis risk. In this particular case, basis risk is measured as the variance of the TED spread.

In the language of statistics, basis risk exists when the two indexes are less than **perfectly correlated**. It is for this reason that the effectiveness of a hedge is routinely measured in terms of the degree of correlation.

8.2.6   Sovereign Risk

Sovereign risk generally arises in currency swaps but will also arise in any cross–border interest rate swap. It is a reflection of a country's financial standing in the world community, and, to some degree, it is a function of the country's political stability and historic performance in meeting its international financial obligations. The greater the probability that a government may impose foreign–exchange controls, thus making it impossible for a counterparty to honor its commitments, the greater is the sovereign risk. This is one form of a condition called **supervening illegality**.

Because the existence of sovereign risk affects a counterparty's creditworthiness, many analysts simply regard it as another aspect of default risk. This is a mistake. Default risk is counterparty specific, while sovereign risk is country specific. Thus, all swaps made with counterparties in the same country share sovereign risk. Routine diversification, which can substantially reduce default risk, will do little to reduce sovereign risk unless an extra step is taken to ensure that the diversification is also across countries.

Most swap dealers set strict limits to their allowable exposure by country. These can be set in terms of the total notional principal or some other criteria. Importantly, the limits usually encompass more than just the swap exposure. They may also embody country–specific exposures to the dealer bank from its positions in other derivatives, general credit, and so on. This is important, because the bank's exposures to sovereign risk (and foreign–exchange risk) are correlated across all its positions in any one country or any one currency.

8.2.7 Delivery Risk

The final risk we discuss is **delivery risk**, also called **settlement risk**. This risk exists when payments are made between counterparties who must effect their payments to each other at different times of the day owing to different settlement hours between the capital markets of the two parties. This most often occurs when the payments are made between counterparties in two different countries. For example, the Japanese capital markets close for the day before the U.S. markets open.

Delivery risk is greatest in currency swaps at the time of the principals' exchanges. Though this risk can be considerable, it can be managed. For example, many banks place a limit on the size of the allowable daily settlement with any one party. In some cases, banks make their exchanges through a neutral third party that does not make payment to either involved party until payments have been received from both parties. When the currencies are the same, delivery risk is considerably less than it first appears because the swap agreement usually requires the counterparties to make net payments rather than gross payments. That is, only the difference in the value of the payments needs to be exchanged with the higher value–paying party making a payment to the lower value–paying party equal to the difference in the values to be exchanged. Thus, **netting** payments significantly reduces the delivery exposure of both parties to a swap. Because it is so easily managed, we do not discuss this risk any further.

8.3 QUANTIFYING AND MANAGING THE EXPOSURE

It is not enough to simply *identify* the risks to which the dealer bank is exposed when it books a swap. It is also important to *quantify* the exposure associated with swaps for at least four reasons. First, the greater the collective risks associated with booking a swap, the greater the compensation the swap dealer should require from its counterparty client.

This compensation may take the form of a front–end fee but will usually take the form of a larger coupon (if the dealer is receiving the fixed rate) or smaller coupon (if the dealer is paying the fixed rate). Second, the dealer will need to hedge the hedgeable risks (including interest rate risk, exchange rate risk, and possibly basis risk) until such times as matched swaps can be negotiated. Formulation of the optimal hedge requires a quantification of the risks that are the subject of the hedge. Third, as suggested by portfolio theory, many risks will be, at least to some degree, offsetting so that the total risk associated with the dealer's portfolio will be substantially less than the sum of the risks individually. This tendency for certain risks to be coincidentally offsetting is sometimes called a **natural hedge**. Accurate assessment of these risks requires quantification. Finally, the dealer's internal policy, as well as regulatory compliance, will likely require some objective assessment of the risks and some explicit limitation to the risks that can be taken with respect to a single counterparty or a group of related counterparties.

As a general rule, management teams set the maximum allowable risk that the dealer can bear. These risk levels have several dimensions. Risk limits are set by individual counterparties, maturities, types of exposure, and as noted earlier, by country—to mention a few. Most swap dealers assign the measurement of risk exposures to risk management specialists. These experts monitor both the absolute size of the individual exposures and the portfolio implications of the risks. They then make pricing recommendations, devise and execute hedging strategies, and formulate policies to encourage or discourage specific swaps in order to bring about a better portfolio balance.

8.3.1 Quantifying and Managing Default Risk

Default risk encompasses both credit risk and market risk. Credit risk is an objective assessment of the likelihood that a prospective counterparty will default. Market risk is a quantitative estimate of the financial injury that will be experienced should the client default.

A bank with a long history in the credit markets has considerable experience estimating the likelihood that potential clients will default on their financial obligations. All such banks have extensive training programs for credit managers. The assessment of credit risks includes an examination of the potential counterparty's financial statements, financial history, its management's track record, collateralization of the obligation, and other pertinent factors. Some banks rely heavily on point scoring systems. Others use regression and discriminant analysis.[1] Some banks take a much more subjective approach, relying heavily on their own managers' personal knowledge of the client firm and its management. Whatever the system employed, the dealer will impose a larger spread on poorer credits than on better credits.

The simplest and most widely employed way to manage credit risk is to establish a cutoff level for credit quality, below which the swap dealer will not do business. For example, this might be double A–rated firms. That is, the bank's swap traders are empowered to enter swaps with triple A and double A clients but not with single A or lower–rated clients. In addition, the swap dealer will typically have limits to the size of the bank's commitments, after netting, with any one client. For example, the dealer might be allowed to enter swaps with notionals, after netting, of $100 million with Client A but only $25 million with Client B, based on a credit evaluation by the bank's credit department.

There are other ways to manage default risk including requiring collateral on the net amount by which a swap with any one party is out–of–the–money. This is another way of describing the replacement cost of a swap and it is found by marking the swap to market. There is a complication here, however. The CFTC ruled in 1989 that swap dealers cannot use a mark–to–market margining system like that used in futures markets to guarantee performance. Such a system would render swaps too much like futures. There is some disagreement over precisely how to interpret the restrictions on margining swaps.

Perhaps the most important way to manage default risk is to include default provisions in the swap agreement that come into play upon the occurrence of certain events. All swap contracts include **termination clauses** that provide for the assessment of damages in the event that one party to a swap should default. These clauses detail the various "events of default" and "termination events" and the procedure for "measuring damages." The latter is one of the most important clauses in a swap agreement, and it is not surprising that the ISDA's code of swaps devotes more space to detailing the available options for measuring and assessing damages in the event of a default or early termination than it does to almost any other single issue.

The ISDA's 1986 code provided three basic methods for measuring and assessing damages from defaults and early terminations: **agreement value method**, **indemnification method**, and **formula method**. In the years since the 1986 code was released, the agreement value method has become nearly universal. In this method, damages are determined on the basis of "market quotations" obtained by the nondefaulting party. The market quotation is an amount (which may be negative) determined on the basis of quotations from reference swap dealers equal to the replacement cost of the swap. The party that is "out–of–the–money" then makes a close-out or termination payment to the other party.

The principal problem with close–out payments required under default and termination provisions is that this protection is likely to fail if the default is associated with a counterparty's bankruptcy. In such an event, the counterparty may not be in a position to pay the required indemnity and, indeed, may be stayed from making payment by the bankruptcy laws of its country. Furthermore, even when payment is effected, it will likely be at less than full face value. For this reason, default provisions rarely require an actual "default" in the traditional sense of the term. Rather, a default, for purposes of a swap agreement, might be defined as a downgrading of a counterparty's debt, irrespective of whether or not it has made its required swap payments.

Swap dealers often engage in multiple swaps with the same counterparties. It is common today for dealers that frequently engage in swaps with the same counterparties to employ a **master swap agreement**. Such an agreement is simply a document that governs all swaps between the parties with each new swap representing a supplement to the master agreement. Such a master agreement provides for a netting of obligations. Thus, payment flows between the parties are limited to the payment differentials. Dealers generally maintain that this **netting** of obligations reduces their exposure on their swap portfolios and, for internal risk–management purposes, swap dealers typically calculate a net exposure to each institution with which they transact. For purposes of bank regulation of credit exposures, however, it has not yet been decided, as of this writing, whether this netting of exposures under master swap agreements will affect bank capital requirements.

The final approach to the management of credit risk is to assign the swap to another party. That is, a booked swap can, theoretically, be **assigned** and the credit risk transferred in the process. This approach is difficult because it requires the approval of both counterparties to the swap. The uninvolved counterparty may be unwilling to allow its swap to be transferred, since that party derives no benefit from the transfer. A solution is to include an assignment clause at the time the swap is written, thus permitting the dealer to make such a transfer. These assignments, however, are quite complicated. As a general matter, permissive assignments are not allowed under most swap agreements. Most often assignment is a matter left to subsequent negotiation should interest in an assignment arise.

8.3.2 Managing Interest Rate Risk and Exchange Rate Risk

A number of times in this book, we considered the hedging problem of the swap dealer exposed to interest rate risk. We suggested that a swap dealer could hedge a swap in cash Treasuries, in Treasury futures, in Eurodollar futures, or in swap futures. In each of these cases, we considered a situation in which the dealer hedges one swap at a time. This approach, which was widely employed in the early days of swaps, is called **microhedging**. The near universal approach used today, however, is **macrohedging**. In a **macrohedge**, we consider the risk character of our overall book (i.e., portfolio), or some specific subset of it, without regard to the individual components. We then hedge the overall character of the book.

Macrohedging is a three–step process:

1. Derive a spot (zero coupon) swaps yield curve.
2. Determine bucket cash flows.
3. Determine the DV01 for each bucket.

The first step in macrohedging requires the derivation of a **spot swaps yield curve**. The spot swaps yield curve is the implied zero coupon yield curve for swaps. It is derived from a par swap yield curve using an iterative procedure called **bootstrapping**. We do not go into the derivation of the spot swaps yield curve here, but we assume that the swap dealer does derive such a yield curve and that the dealer has it available.[2]

The next two steps will be illustrated in the context of an example. We will focus on hedging the fixed–rate side of the dealer's swap book. (The floating-rate side of the swap book would be hedged separately in the Eurodollar futures market or, more likely, not hedged at all.) Suppose that a swap dealer, starting from scratch, enters four generic fixed–for–floating interest rate swaps in quick succession. For simplicity, each involves a semiannual fixed rate against six–month LIBOR. The four swaps are detailed next.

Swap	Dealer Is	Tenor of Swap	Coupon	Notionals
1	fixed-rate payer	5 years	8.24%	$20 million
2	fixed-rate payer	3 years	8.06%	$15 million
3	fixed-rate receiver	6 years	8.42%	$42 million
4	fixed-rate payer	2 years	7.88%	$12 million

None of these swaps is a perfect match for any of the others and, therefore, the dealer might choose to view each swap and hedge each swap independently of the others. Nevertheless, the cash flows on the swaps may still be largely offsetting so that a macrohedging approach would prove superior.

The second step in the macrohedging approach requires that we divide time into discrete intervals called **buckets**, and that we break down each swap into its cash flows (one for each bucket). In this example, we will use six–month bucket intervals.[3] We then net the cash flows to see what we are really dealing with. For the four swaps above, this netting process is detailed in Table 8.1. Note that the final cash flow for each swap

Table 8.1 Netting Cash Flows—The Macrohedge
(all values in millions)

Period	Swap 1	Swap 2	Swap 3	Swap 4	Net Flow
1	$-0.8240	$-0.6045	$1.7682	$-0.4728	$-0.1331
2	-0.8240	-0.6045	1.7682	-0.4728	-0.1331
3	-0.8240	-0.6045	1.7682	-0.4728	-0.1331
4	-0.8240	-0.6045	1.7682	-12.4728	-12.1331
5	-0.8240	-0.6045	1.7682		0.3397
6	-0.8240	-15.6045	1.7682		-14.6603
7	-0.8240		1.7682		0.9442
8	-0.8240		1.7682		0.9442
9	-0.8240		1.7682		0.9442
10	-20.8240		1.7682		-19.0558
11			1.7682		1.7682
12			43.7682		43.7682

Cash flow = $D \times S/2 \times NP$

Where D is a dummy variable that is +1 if the dealer is the fixed−rate receiver and −1 if the dealer is the fixed−rate payer. *S* is the swap coupon and *NP* is the notional principal.

includes the notional principal (as noted earlier the offsetting notional principal on the floating–rate side is hedged separately).

In the macrohedge approach, the net cash flows are often referred to as **bucket cash flows**. In the final step in the hedging process, we use the spot swaps yield curve to determine the dollar value of a basis point (DV01) for each of the cash flow periods. Recall that the spot swaps yield curve is the implied zero coupon yield curve for swaps. These zero coupon rates are usually quoted on a semiannual bond basis.

The DV01 is computed per $100 of cash flow. The computation procedure for a single future cash flow, such as that associated with a zero coupon bond, is illustrated in Equation 8.1, in which t denotes the bucket period number and y denotes the spot yield.[4]

$$DV01 = \$100 \times \left[\left(1 + \frac{y}{2} \right)^{-t} - \left(1 + \frac{y + .0001}{2} \right)^{-t} \right] \quad (8.1)$$

To continue with the example, suppose that we have derived the spot (zero coupon) yields reported in Table 8.2 from the par swaps yield curve. Suppose further that we would like to hedge in a five–year T–note or, alternatively, in five–year T–note futures. (We are treating the five–year T–note as the baseline or benchmark instrument.) We begin by computing the DV01s per $100 of par value of the bucket cash flows and the DV01 of a five–year Treasury note. We then divide each bucket DV01 by the T–note DV01 to get a hedge ratio. Finally, we multiply the face value of the bucket cash flow by the appropriate hedge ratio to get a T–note (baseline) risk equivalent.[5] As it happens, the T–note is currently priced to yield 7.32 percent (semiannual bond basis) and has a DV01 of $0.04124.

Table 8.2 makes it clear that we need a hedge in T–notes having a face value of $12.766 million. Since our swaps are risk equivalent to a long position in T–notes (because the sign on the total is positive), we would sell $12.766 million of T–notes short, or, alternatively, we would sell 128 T–note futures having a face value of $0.1 million each.[6]

There was no specific reason for using five–year T–notes or T–note futures as the baseline security to hedge the swap book in the preceding example. We could just as easily have used some other cash Treasury or Treasury futures and we could have used swap futures. We could even have used a complex strip of Eurodollar futures to hedge the bucket cash flows out to the limit of the Eurodollar futures, but the calculations would

Table 8.2 Macrohedging with the Spot Swaps Yield Curve

Period	Spot Swap Yield	DV01 of Cash Flow	DV01 T-Note	Hedge Ratio	Bucket Cash Flow (in millions)	TNote (baseline) Equivalent (in millions)
1	7.46%	$0.00465	$0.04124	0.11267	$−0.1331	−0.015
2	7.59	0.00894	0.04124	0.21683	−0.1331	−0.029
3	7.71	0.01289	0.04124	0.31263	−0.1331	−0.042
4	7.92	0.01647	0.04124	0.39933	−12.1331	−4.845
5	8.02	0.01974	0.04124	0.47876	0.3397	0.163
6	8.11	0.02271	0.04124	0.55067	−14.6603	−8.073
7	8.18	0.02539	0.04124	0.61574	0.9442	0.581
8	8.26	0.02778	0.04124	0.67371	0.9442	0.636
9	8.34	0.02990	0.04124	0.72505	0.9442	0.685
10	8.41	0.03177	0.04124	0.77049	−19.0558	−14.682
11	8.48	0.03341	0.04124	0.81005	1.7682	1.432
12	8.54	0.03483	0.04124	0.84456	43.7682	36.965
					Total	12.766

be somewhat different in the Eurodollar case. The choice of a hedging vehicle will involve, as always, a trade–off between cost, effectiveness, and flexibility.

While we have used the macro approach to hedge the interest rate risk associated with USD interest rate swaps in the preceding example, the same procedure can be used to macrohedge interest rate swaps in any currency and to hedge both the interest rate risk and the exchange rate risk associated with crosscurrency swaps. The procedure is analogous.

8.4 MISCELLANEOUS PORTFOLIO MANAGEMENT CONSIDERATIONS

There are a great many other considerations in the management of the risks associated with swaps. Many of these arise only when specialty swaps are created. For example, a dealer may have a difficult time finding a match for a putable or a callable swap. Or, it may find that such a swap can only be matched if the dealer buys the necessary provisions from a second counterparty. But different features of different specialty swaps can, sometimes, be offsetting. For example, if the dealer grants a floating–

rate payer the right to terminate a seven–year swap after four years (a putable swap), the dealer might be able to offset the risk by entering a second swap with a four–year maturity as a floating–rate payer while reserving the right to extend the life of the swap for three additional years (an extendable swap).

If the first counterparty elects to "put" its swap with the dealer, the dealer would not extend its swap with the second counterparty. If the first counterparty elects not to "put" its swap with the dealer, the dealer would extend its swap with the second counterparty.

8.5 TREATMENT OF SWAPS UNDER THE NEW INTERNATIONAL CAPITAL STANDARDS

Many of the institutions that act as dealers in swaps are commercial banks. These banks are attracted to the swaps market because swaps allow them to enhance their return on equity. This opportunity to increase profitability is possible because swaps are off–balance sheet transactions. That is, swaps do not appear on either the asset side or the liability side of a balance sheet.

There is a public interest in maintaining the soundness of the banking system. For this reason, banks are subject to a great number of regulatory controls. Despite the considerable amount of deregulation in the banking industry over the past ten years, banking remains one of the most highly regulated of all industries. One of the most important of these regulations is the requirement that banks, and bank holding companies, maintain satisfactory levels of bank capital.

Capital provides a cushion for depositors in the event that the bank suffers operating losses and/or some of the bank's assets lose value. Historically, the capital requirement was determined as a percentage of bank assets. But, because swaps provide a source of earnings for banks without increasing bank assets, swap activity did not increase capital requirements. Thus, swaps were seen as a way to enhance shareholder returns. As swaps and other off–balance sheet activity became a progressively larger portion of bank business, bank regulators became increasingly concerned about the adequacy of bank capital under the existing capital requirements. They believed that swaps exposed the banks to risks that conventional risk measures ignored.

On several occasions, bank regulators made capital adequacy proposals to correct what they perceived to be a dangerous situation. Many of the proposals were extreme. In addition, banks were concerned that the imposition of capital requirements on off–balance sheet activity would place domestic banks at a competitive disadvantage to nondomestic swap banks. The swap business would then simply move overseas—mostly to London. The banks further argued that if the United States was to remain a leader in international finance it could not afford to surrender to its foreign competition.

These arguments proved persuasive. As a first step, the Federal Reserve, together with the Bank of England, issued proposals that called for risk–based capital requirements, which were put out for public comment during 1986 and 1987. Subsequently, the Fed sent representatives to Basle, Switzerland, to work with representatives of the central banking authorities of the Group of Ten plus Luxembourg.[7] This group became known as the **Basle Supervisors' Committee**, and, in December of 1987, it agreed to a set of principles that dealt with the definition of bank capital and new risk–based capital requirements. This set of principles became known as the **Basle Accord**. The Basle Accord standardized bank capital requirements across nations and removed the argument that stiffer swap capital requirements would unfairly impact U.S. banks.

After a period of public comment, the Federal Reserve issued final guidelines on 19 January 1989. These guidelines were designed to achieve several important goals:[8]

- Establish a uniform capital framework, applicable to all federally supervised banking organizations
- Encourage international banking organizations to strengthen their capital positions
- Reduce a source of competitive inequality arising from differences in supervisory requirements among nations

The Fed's new guidelines encompass more than just swap activity. Indeed, the guidelines impose risk–adjusted capital requirements based on all off–balance sheet and on–balance sheet activities that contribute to a bank's risk exposure.

The procedure for assessing capital requirements for a swap is a four-step process. The first step is to determine the notional principal on the swap. Based on this notional principal, the swap coupon, and the prevailing level of interest rates, the swap is marked–to–market and the replacement cost of the swap is ascertained. To this replacement cost, an additional amount is added on to account for future volatility. This **add-on factor** ranges from 0 to 5 percent depending on the type of swap and the tenor of the swap. The result of these calculations is called the **credit risk equivalent**. Ascertaining this value constitutes the second step. The third step involves a risk weighting. This requires a simple multiplication of the credit risk equivalent by a fixed percentage. The percentage itself depends on the general quality of the creditor. For example, a swap with a central government within the **Organization of Economic Cooperation and Development** (OECD) involves a risk–weighting factor of 0. At the other extreme is a swap negotiated with a corporation, a nonbank financial institution, or a bank incorporated outside of the OECD. For swaps with these institutions, the risk–weighting factor is 50 percent. This multiplication yields a value called the **risk weighted asset**. The final step is to determine the capital requirement by multiplying the risk weighted asset by the **capital ratio**. The Basle Accord set this at 8 percent and this ratio was later adopted by the Federal Reserve.

Suppose a swap bank negotiates a four–year interest rate swap with a domestic corporation having a notional principal of $50 million. Because the swap has a tenor of more than one year, the add–on factor will be 0.5 percent of the notional principal. When the swap is first written, the swap is at–market and has a mark–to–market value of $0. When the "add–on factor" of $0.25 million (0.005 × $50 million) is included, the swap is found to have a credit risk equivalent of $0.25 million. The risk weight for this swap is 50 percent, so the risk weighted asset is $0.125 million. Since the capital ratio is 8 percent, the capital requirement is $10,000. Thus, the bank must keep $10,000 of capital to support this particular swap. As interest rates change, the swap will be repeatedly marked–to–market with the result that the capital requirement will continuously change. Suppose, for example that interest rates rise and the swap is found to have a replacement cost of $50,000. The bank's capital requirement for this swap would rise to $12,000. These calculations are depicted in Figure 8.5.

To the extent that it eliminated uncertainty, the Fed's guidelines have had a very positive effect on the market. The guidelines reflect the realities of swap risks to market-making banks. They also eliminate a cloud that has hung over the swap market from the outset. Since the Fed's new guidelines were announced, the rate of growth of the market has accelerated. A subtle but interesting implication of the new guidelines is that, in the future, bank analysts will, in all likelihood, judge bank performance

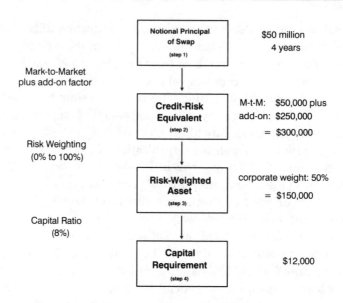

FIGURE 8.5   Sample Calculation of Capital Requirements Reflecting Off–Balance Sheet Activity

on the basis of "return on risk assets" (RORA) rather than the traditional "return on assets" (ROA).

8.6   SWAP DOCUMENTATION

Swaps are typically initiated through telephone conversations. The initial agreement usually hinges on a few key economic issues such as the swap coupon, the floating rate, the payment frequency, and the maturity. The verbal agreement is confirmed by a fax, telex, or letter (called the confirmation), usually within 24 hours. While both parties are legally bound by the initial agreement, it is still far from complete. Complete documentation, which is extensive, is exchanged later. The swap documentation must cover all terms agreed to in the initial exchange and must also cover a great many incidental issues, including many indirect economic issues and some noneconomic issues, that bear on the relationship between the counterparties. These include such things as events of default, methods of computing damages on an early termination, jurisdiction governing disputes, and so forth.

In the early days of swap finance, each swap dealer chose its own wording for all of its swap contract documentation. Variations in the phrasing of this documentation and differing definitions of certain terms necessitated careful review by each counterparty's legal counsel. This lack of standardization introduced potentially injurious delays in the approval of the contracts as well as unnecessarily large legal expenses. Lack of standardization also made it potentially difficult for swap dealers to match swaps, and it limited the swap market participants' ability to trade swaps in a well-defined secondary market and to reverse swaps with existing counterparties.

A limited amount of standardized wording began to emerge as dealers found it efficient and economical to reuse the same (or similar) clauses in swaps that had similar terms. Dealers also found it convenient to pirate one another's clauses as new features found their way into swap contracts. Despite this evolution, however, standardization remained elusive.

Most of the operatives in the swaps industry eventually came to recognize that it was in the interests of all participants to work toward standardization. As a first effort, a small group of representatives from some of the leading swap dealer banks began working on standardization of documentation in 1984. In March of 1985, this group, now expanded, organized itself as the New York–based International Swap Dealer's Association (ISDA). Then, in June of 1985, the ISDA released its first code of swaps: *The Code of Standard Wording, Assumptions and Provisions for Swaps, 1985 Edition*. The 1985 Code addressed two key issues: 1. the cash flows of a rate swap, including the specification and calculation of the fixed– and floating–rate sides; and 2. the amounts payable upon an early termination of the swap. The ISDA code proved appealing and was soon adopted, in whole or in part, by most U.S. swap dealers. During this same period, the London–based British Bankers' Association (BBA) was working on its own code of swaps; and in August of 1985 the BBA introduced its documentation guidelines—the *British Bankers' Associations Interest Rate Swaps*, or BBAIRS. This code was intended primarily as a documentation aid for interbank swaps. While the BBA's code is important, particularly for British banks, this chapter focuses on the standardization efforts of the ISDA.

The ISDA's 1985 Code was only the first step in that organization's efforts at standardizing the language and provisions of swap documentation. In 1986, the ISDA released a revised and expanded version of the code (**1986 Code**). Like the 1985 version, this version devotes considerable attention to defining the cash flows associated with rate swaps and the amounts payable upon early termination. But the 1986 Code refines these provisions to facilitate the development of integrated **master swap agreements**. The 1986 Code also addresses a number of other issues to which the 1985 Code had been silent. In particular, the 1986 Code devotes considerable attention to the subjects of "events of default" and "termination events." The 1986 Code also provides a list of representations made by the parties to a swap, a list of agreements pertaining to information to be furnished on an ongoing basis, definitions pertaining to specific entities when a swap is guaranteed or supported by an entity other than the actual counterparty, cross–border provisions, and withholding tax provisions.

In 1987, the ISDA took another giant step toward standardization of documentation by introducing standard form agreements. There are two versions of the standard form agreements. The first is a code–based form called the **Interest Rate Swap Agreement**. It is an agreement for U.S. dollar–denominated swaps and incorporates the 1986 Code by reference, with certain modifications. The second is a multicurrency form called the **Interest Rate and Currency Exchange Agreement**. This covers interest rate swaps in any currency as well as currency swaps. The Interest Rate and Currency Exchange Agreement does not reference the code directly but incorporates provisions that are virtually identical to those in the 1986 Code. Certain provisions of the code, Articles 2 through 8, which describe how fixed and floating payments are to be calculated and which provide various floating–rate options, are not included in this standard form. These issues are, instead, addressed through separate confirmations. To assist in addressing these issues, the ISDA also released in 1987 a document called the *1987 Interest Rate and Currency Exchange Definitions*. This document was revised and expanded in 1991.

In June of 1992 the ISDA published a major portion of additional swap documentation planned for 1992. Specifically, six documents were released: 1. a multicurrency, cross–border master agreement; 2. a local currency, single–jurisdiction master agreement; 3. definitions and forms of confirmation for U.S. municipal counterparties; 4. an appendix containing a schedule for transactions with U.S. municipal counterparties; 5. definitions and forms of confirmation for foreign exchange and currency option transactions; and 6. a form of confirmation for cash–settled equity index options. Additional documentation was released in late 1992.

The remainder of this chapter reviews the contents of the standard form agreements. This brief review is not, of course, a substitute for a careful examination of the actual agreements themselves.

Standard Form Agreements. While the 1985 and 1986 ISDA codes greatly enhanced the standardization of swap documentation, neither is, in and of itself, a contract. The codes simply provide standard definitions, presumptions that apply unless specifically overridden, and a menu of options for dealing with certain matters. The existence of the code does not eliminate the need for the counterparties to a swap to develop and execute contracts, although the contracts they develop should, logically, reference the ISDA code.

As already noted, the ISDA introduced two types of standard form agreements in 1987. These are structured as master swap agreements. As such, each agreement consists of a set of standard terms applicable to any swap transaction together with an accompanying schedule that allows the parties to tailor the agreement by listing terms specific to swaps between the two parties.

As master agreements, the swap documentation governs all subsequent swaps between the parties by simple reference to the master agreement. Each new swap becomes a supplement to the existing master agreement and, consequently, the swap parties can limit their negotiation on each new swap to those matters of economic importance. This minimizes the likelihood that disagreements over the terms of the swap will develop later and greatly speeds execution for parties that frequently transact swaps with one another. As previously discussed, master agreements can provide for a netting of exposures and, hence, the recording of exposures on a net basis. The agreements provide that all swap transactions governed by the master agreement are simultaneously terminated if either party defaults on any swap transaction that is governed by the master agreement. This prevents a bankruptcy trustee from selectively enforcing those swaps that have a positive mark–to–market value, while discarding those swaps with a negative mark–to–market value.

The two versions of the standard form agreements (i.e., the code–based U.S. dollar version and the multicurrency version) employ the same basic ordering of provisions and, for the most part, the same numbering of their sections. The first section provides for the identification of the parties to the swap. This is followed by sections dealing with payments, representations, agreements, events of default and termination events, early termination, transfer, multibranch provisions, notices, tax matters, credit support documentation, governing law and jurisdiction, definitions, and confirmations.

Payments.   Most payment terms are specific to the swap and, therefore, are specified in the accompanying schedule. The standard terms provide for the netting of payments on a given swap when payments between the parties are to be made on the same date and in the same currency. As an extension, the agreement provides that the parties net payments on all swaps governed by the same master agreement when those payments are to be made on the same date and in the same currency.

Representations.   This section contains representations and warranties that each party to the swap makes to the other. The representations and warranties are deemed to be repeated with each new swap that is governed by the master agreement. The **basic representations** concern corporate authority to enter into the swap agreement and the validity of the agreement. Other representations include the **absence of certain events**, such as the occurrence of an event of default or a termination event, the **absence of litigation** that might threaten the legality, validity, or enforceability of the contract, the **accuracy of financial information**, and the **accuracy of specific information** that is furnished in writing by one party to the other.

Agreements.   This section provides for supplemental agreements to furnish documents, excluding tax covenants in the code–based form, as detailed by the parties in the accompanying schedule to the master agreement. These might include such things as the periodic furnishing of financial statements or legal opinions, the provision of "credit support documentation," or other documents.

Events of Default and Termination Events.   Events of default indicate that a credit problem has arisen and entitle the nondefaulting party to terminate all swaps governed by the master agreement. Termination events are due to occurrences other than credit problems and allow for the termination of those swaps directly affected by the termination event.

The agreements provide for seven specific events of default, but the parties may specify others if they like. The specific events of default, most of which apply to both parties, are failure to pay, breach of covenant, credit support default, misrepresentation, default under specified swaps, cross default, and bankruptcy. **Failure to pay** refers to any failure by either party to pay an amount that is required under the agreement. A **breach of covenant**, as an event of default, refers to a failure to comply with any covenant of the swap agreement other than the making of a required payment, a tax–related matter, or a failure to give notice that a termination event has occurred. **Credit support default** refers to any default under an applicable credit support document. It only applies to a party if a credit support document is required by that party or on behalf of that party. **Misrepresentation** refers to a breach of any representation (other than a tax representation) made in the swap agreement or credit support documentation. **Default under specified swaps** refers to a default that results in the designation or occurrence of a termination event under another swap. **Cross default** refers to a default on some other indebtedness. This event of default can be applied to both parties, only one party, or excluded entirely from the swap agreement by so indicating in the accompanying schedule. The **bankruptcy** event of default is broadly defined to allow for significant variations in the bankruptcy and insolvency laws of the countries covered by the swap agreement.

The agreement specifies certain termination events. These are illegality, a tax event, a tax event upon merger, and a credit event upon merger. An **illegality** is deemed to have occurred if a change in law or regulation makes it impossible for either party to perform its obligations. A **tax event** occurs if a withholding tax is imposed on a swap transaction. In this event, the party required to pay the tax may opt to terminate the swap. A **tax event upon merger** occurs if a merger results in the imposition of a withholding tax on one or more swaps. Only those affected swaps may be terminated. A **credit event upon merger** occurs if a merger results in a deterioration of the creditworthiness of one of the parties. In such an event, the other party may elect to terminate all swaps governed by the master agreement.

Early Termination.   Upon the occurrence of an event of default, the nondefaulting party has the right to designate an **early termination date**. In the case of bankruptcy, the termination is automatic. With the exception of bankruptcy, the nondefaulting party must provide notice to the defaulting party as to the early termination date.

In the case of the occurrence of a terminating event, the party that is entitled to designate an early termination date varies with the nature of the terminating event. As previously mentioned, in the case of an event of default, all swaps governed by the same master agreement are terminated. In the case of a termination event, only the affected swaps are terminated.

Once a notice of early termination has become effective, each party to a terminated swap is released from its obligation to make its required payments under the swap. The parties must then calculate **termination payments**.

Transfer.   This section of the agreements provides a general prohibition against the **transfer** of rights and obligations under the agreement to other parties. Allowance is made for specifying exceptions to this general prohibition. These exceptions must be detailed in the accompanying schedule. This is the general prohibition against permissive assignment discussed earlier in this chapter.

Multibranch Provisions.   This section of the agreements allows institutions with multiple branches that operate from several locations to govern all swaps with a single master agreement.

Notices.   This section requires that addresses and telex numbers for purposes of providing required **notices** be specified in the accompanying schedule. All notices provided must be in writing and sent to the required address or telex.

Tax Matters.   The tax section of the agreements deals with three tax issues: gross up, tax representation, and tax covenants. As a general rule, counterparties are required to make their payments without any withholding or deductions for taxes. However, if a party making a payment is legally required to withhold taxes from the payment, that party is required to gross up the amount of the payment for any amount withheld on account of "indemnifiable taxes." The party is, however, released from its **tax gross up** obligation if the withholding is the result of a breach of a tax–related representation or covenant made by the other party. The parties must specify all applicable tax representations in the accompanying schedule and must agree to give notice of breaches of tax representation (tax covenants).

Credit Support Documentation. The parties should identify in the accompanying schedule all required **credit support documents**. These include guarantees, security agreements, and letters of credit.

Governing Law and Jurisdiction. The agreements require that the parties must specify in the accompanying schedule whether New York law or English law will govern the agreements.

Definitions. This section of the agreements defines a number of important terms that are used in the swap documentation.

Confirmations. The agreements require the exchange of **confirmations** that detail the terms of each new swap entered under the master agreement. In the code–based form, intended for U.S. dollar interest rate swaps only, these confirmations must specify the notional amount, the trade date, the effective date, the termination date, the fixed–rate payer, the fixed–rate payment dates, the fixed amount of each payment, the floating–rate payer, the floating–rate payment dates, the floating rate for the initial calculation period, the floating–rate option, the designated maturity, the spread (plus or minus), the floating–rate day–count fraction, the reset dates, compounding (if applicable), and certain other terms as appropriate.

In the multicurrency form, all of this same information must be provided, but other information is required as well. This includes the relevant currencies, initial exchange, final exchange, and so forth.

8.7 SUMMARY

In this chapter we have seen that swap dealers must measure and manage many different types of risk. These include interest rate risk, exchange rate risk, credit/default risk, mismatch risk, basis risk, spread risk, sovereign risk, and delivery risk. Some of these risks are systematic in nature and others are unsystematic in nature. Those that are unsystematic need not concern the dealer with a large swap book, as they are diversified away. The systematic risks, however, require much more careful management.

The most important forms of risk for swap dealers are interest rate risk, exchange rate risk, and default risk. The first two of these are managed by hedging and the latter is managed by limiting dealings to better credits, requiring collateral, and including carefully worded default provisions in the swap documentation. Interest rate risk and exchange rate risk are most often managed today using a macrohedge approach in which the swaps are decomposed into cash flow periods based on the bucket interval in which they occur. They are then netted and the net cash flows are hedged, usually in futures contracts.

We also examined the recently adopted bank capital requirements that are applicable to both on- and off-balance sheet activity. These requirements were imposed only after international agreement was reached on capital standards and requirements.

Finally, we examined the evolution of standardized swap documentation. This documentation is the consequence of concerted efforts on the part of the International Swap Dealers Association (now called the International Swap and Derivatives Association) and the British Bankers Association.

REVIEW QUESTIONS

1. Why might spread risk be regarded as a component of interest rate risk? Discuss.
2. What advantages are there for a swap dealer from quoting his or her swap pay–receive rates as a "spread over Treasuries" rather than as raw rates?
3. Why does marking–to–market result in a swap dealer booking all the profit (in a present value sense) from a swap up front?
4. What does a DV01 measure and how does it differ from a duration? Discuss.
5. Some have argued that credit risk is symmetrically distributed in the swap dealer's book, and, therefore, it should not be a significant concern for swap dealers because it is a diversifiable form of risk and the swap book is symmetric. Others have argued that the swap book is not symmetric; that is, the credit risks on one side of the swap book are greater than the credit risks on the other side of the book. Why is the latter case more likely?
6. What is meant when it is said that swap agreements are master agreements? What advantages does this have for swap dealers?
7. Why is sovereign risk more likely to have an impact on currency swaps than interest rate swaps? Discuss.

8. Calculate the DV01 of a single cash flow occurring five years from today using the method suggested by Equation 8.1. Calculate it again using the method suggested in note 4. For purposes of both calculations, assume that the cash flow is $100 and that the yield, quoted semiannual bond basis, is 7.75 percent. Why do the two results differ? Which is more precise for very small yield changes?

9. What advantages does a macrohedging approach offer over a microhedging approach? What role does the bucketing of the cash flows from different swaps play in this macrohedge approach?

10. What were the framers of the new capital standards trying to achieve in their drafting of the Basle Accord?

NOTES

1. **Regression analysis** and **discriminant analysis** are multivariate forecasting techniques that have been used to determine which financial ratios or combinations of financial ratios are most reliable at predicting business failure. As such, these tools are useful for assessing the creditworthiness of a client firm. For a more detailed discussion of these techniques and their application in measuring creditworthiness, see Foster (1986) and Altman (1983). Factor analysis has also been used for this purpose. For a discussion of this technique, see Chen and Shimerda (1981). For a discussion of the measurement of credit risk in the context of swap finance, see Cooper and Watson (1987) and Aggarwal (1990).

2. The derivation of the spot swaps yield curve from the par swaps yield curve via the bootstrapping method is fully described in Kapner and Ellis (1992) and in Bansal, Ellis, and Marshall (1992).

3. The length of each bucket, that is, one month, three months, and so on, is left to the discretion of the risk manager.

4. A more precise DV01 for a zero coupon bond can be achieved by taking the derivative of the present value function with respect to yield and then scaling the result to reflect the value of 1 basis point. The exact value of a basis point for a single cash flow, assuming that the zero coupon yields are stated semiannual bond basis, is given below:

$$PV = 100 \times (1 + y/2)^{-2n}$$
$$dPV/dy = -2n(100) \times (1 + y/2)^{-2n-1} \times 1/2$$

$$= -100n \times (1 + y/2)^{-2n-1}$$

now scale to get DV01:

$$DV01 = (dPV/dy)/(10000)$$
$$= -.01n \times (1 + y/2)^{-2n-1}$$

In this formulation, n denotes the number of years in the future when the cash flow will occur. The negative sign on the DV01 is always ignored but understood.

5. There are a number of alternative, but equivalent, versions of the DV01 hedge model. For example, some swap dealers prefer to calculate the DV01 of a bucket cash flow (BCF) on the full face value of the cash flow rather than on the basis of $100. We will call these **bucket DV01s**. The individual bucket DV01s can then be summed. The aggregate DV01 is then an accurate measure of the value change of the dealer's swap book per 1 basis point shift in the yield curve. This aggregate value may be regarded as the DV01 of the dealer's book. The conversion from our measure of the DV01 on $100 of face value (DV01$_{\$100}$) to a bucket DV01 is given below:

$$\text{Bucket DV01} = DV01_{\$100} \times BCF/\$100$$

6. Risk equivalent positions are sometimes referred to as **futures equivalents** when futures are used as the benchmark hedging instrument.
7. The Group of Ten is Belgium, Canada, France, Germany, Italy, Japan, the Netherlands, Sweden, Switzerland, and the United Kingdom.
8. See Federal Reserve Press Release dated January 19, 1989, to accompany Risk–Based Capital Guidelines.

REFERENCES AND SUGGESTED READING

Aggarwal, R. "Assessing Default Risk in Interest Rate Swaps." In *Interest Rate Swaps*, pp. 443–48. C. Beidleman, ed. Chicago: Dow Jones Books, 1990.

Altman, E. I. *Corporate Financial Distress and Bankruptcy*. 2d ed. New York: Wiley, 1993.

Bansal, V. K., M. E. Ellis, and J. F. Marshall. "The Spot Swaps Yield Curve: Derivation and Use." *Advances in Futures and Options Research*, vol. 6, 1993.

Briys, E., M. Crouchy, and R. Schobel. "The Pricing of Default–Free Interest Rate Cap, Floor, and Collar Agreements." *Journal of Finance* 46, no. 5 (1991): 1879–92.

Chen, K. H., and T. A. Shimerda. "An Empirical Analysis of Useful Financial Ratios." *Financial Management*, Spring 1981.

Chicago Board of Trade. *CBOT Swap Futures: The Reference Guide*, 1991.

Commins, K. "Risk Management: The Eight Best Hedges." *Intermarket* 4, no. 8, (August 1987): 17–23.

Cooper, D. F., and I. R. Watson. "How to Assess Credit Risks in Swaps." *Banker*, Feb. 1987, pp. 28–31.

Cunningham, D. P., and J. B. Golden. "A Practitioner's Guide to the 1986 Code of Swaps." In *Swap Finance Update*, Boris Antl, ed. London: Euromoney, 1987.

Felgran, S. D. "Interest Rate Swaps: Use, Risk, and Prices." *New England Economic Review*, Federal Reserve Bank of Boston, Nov/Dec 1987, pp. 22–32.

Foster, G. *Financial Statement Analysis*. 2d ed. Englewood Cliffs, NJ: Prentice Hall, 1986.

Gay, G. D., and R. W. Kolb "Removing Bias in Duration Based Hedging Models: A Note." *Journal of Futures Markets* 4, no. 2 (Summer 1984): 225–28.

Genova, G., and D. Thompson "A Guide to Standard Swap Documentation." *Commercial Lending Review* 3, no. 2 (Spring 1988): 44–9.

Haugen, R. A. *Modern Investment Theory*. Englewood Cliffs, NJ: Prentice Hall, 1986.

Henderson, S. K. "Termination Provisions of Swap Agreements." *International Financial Law Review (UK)*, Sept. 1983, pp. 22–7.

Hyde, J. H. "A Swap Torpedo." *United States Banker* 98, no. 10 (October 1987): 36–40.

ISDA. *1986 Code of Standard Wording, Assumptions and Provisions for Swaps*. International Swap Dealers Association, 1986.

ISDA. *1987 Interest Rate and Currency Exchange Definitions*. International Swap Dealers Association, 1987.

ISDA. *User's Guide to the Standard Form Agreements*, 1987 Edition, International Swap Dealers Association, 1987.

Kapner, K. R., and M. E. Ellis "Swap Yield Curves: Par, Spot, and Forward and the Pricing of Short–Dated Swaps." In *The Swaps Handbook: 1991–92 Supplement*, J. F. Marshall and K. R. Kapner, eds. New York: New York Institute of Finance, 1992.

Marshall, J. F. *Futures and Option Contracting*. Cincinnati: South–Western, 1989.

Marshall, J. F., and V. K. Bansal "Hedging Swaps." In *The Swaps Handbook: 1991–92 Supplement*, K. R. Kapner and J. F. Marshall, eds. New York: New York Institute of Finance, 1992.

Miller, G. "When Swaps Unwind." *Institutional Investor* 20, no. 11 (November 1986): 167–78.

Smith, D. J. "Measuring the Gains from Arbitraging the Swap Market." *Financial Executive* 4, no. 2 (Mar/Apr 1988): 46–9.

Stoakes, C. "How to Terminate a Swap." *Euromoney*, April 1985.

Stoakes, C. "Standards Make Swaps Faster." *Euromoney*, November 1985.

Winder, R. "The Art of Exposure Management." *Euromoney*, April 1986, pp. 51–4.

9

Hedging Business Cycle Risk: The Next Major Wave in Derivatives?

9.1 OVERVIEW

Financial engineers at at least one major swap dealer are busily constructing what may be the next major wave in derivatives—macroeconomic swaps and macroeconomic options. These new classes of derivatives, first proposed in early 1991 by Marshall, Bansal, Herbst, and Tucker (1992a and 1992b), would provide corporate end users with the ability to hedge business cycle risk, sometimes called macroeconomic risk, in much the same way that end users of current derivative products use those instruments to hedge interest rate risk, exchange rate risk, commodity price risk, and equity return risk. In such swaps, at least one leg is linked to a macroeconomic index.

Macroeconomic swaps and options provide, at least in theory, a vehicle to soften the impact of an economic downturn on corporate profits and government tax revenues. For macroeconomic derivatives to be viable, there must be an efficient macroeconomic index to which to peg the instruments. This requires: 1. a sufficiently high degree of correlation between the index and the end user's revenues, 2. a properly specified lag without possibility of ex-postindex revision, and 3. a vehicle in which to offset dealer risk.

This chapter reviews the macroeconomic swap (macro swap) and macroeconomic option (macro option) structures and provides empirical evidence on the usefulness of one macroeconomic index as a reference rate. We caution the reader not to confuse the term "macrohedge," as used elsewhere in this book, with the terms "macro swap" and "macroeconomic hedging" as these terms are used in this chapter.

9.2   MACROECONOMIC RISK: A FORM OF QUANTITY RISK

Most hedging is designed to offset the risk associated with a price volatility to which a producer, consumer, or investor is exposed. By engaging in a swap or other form of derivative security, a party can hedge the risk associated with fluctuations in a price on the assumption that quantity is known. However, quantity may not be known, and quantity risk has always proven to be a difficult risk to hedge.

Quantity risk is most often portrayed in the context of agricultural production. A farmer might employ a commodity swap or an agricultural futures contract, for example, to lock in a price for his product at harvest. But the farmer has done nothing to hedge the quantity risk associated with the vagaries of the weather and the like. Quantity risk also exists in the industrial sector. For instance, automobile manufacturers can employ wage contracts and commodity swaps to control the costs of input factors of production, can use currency swaps to hedge exchange rate risk, and can use interest rate swaps to hedge financial costs. But, the manufacturer can do little to hedge against a decline in unit sales (market softness) associated with a general economic slowdown. That is, the firm has a cyclical exposure, that is, business cycle risk, which can be described as a form of macroeconomic risk. Of course, it may also be viewed as a quantity risk.

To some degree, a firm can manage its quantity risk by massaging its production process (e.g., employing or laying–off evening shift assembly workers). The essence of such a strategy is to pass much of the risk on to others, principally the firm's workers and vendors. However, such a strategy may be costly (e.g., training costs). Also, a firm's ability to pass its quantity risk to others may be constrained by the nature of its contracts with its workers and vendors, and by the degree of leverage employed in its operating and financial structures. Because of these costs and constraints, the firm may have few means to control quantity risk. And, of course, profits are made more volatile by the presence of quantity risk, since profits, for any given price for the firm's product, are a function of unit sales. It is this source of profit volatility that macro swaps and options are designed to hedge.

By engaging in a swap in which the firm pays a fixed cash flow in return for a variable cash flow that is based upon changes in a macroeconomic variable to which the firm's unit sales are highly correlated, the firm can hedge its quantity risk. In soft markets, the firm can also enhance its profitability relative to its unhedged competitors.

Many, probably most, service and manufacturing industries have an exposure similar to automobile producers. These include vacation and tour operators, durable goods manufacturers, residential and commercial builders, credit card franchisers whose revenue is based on transactional card volume, and so on.

9.3 MACROECONOMIC SWAPS AND OPTIONS: THE CONCEPT

As originally proposed by Marshall and colleagues, a macro swap is a fixed–for–floating swap in which the floating–leg payment is a **function** of a macroeconomic variable or index. Alternatively, a macro swap can be designed as a floating–for–floating swap in which one leg is pegged to a macroeconomic variable and the other is pegged to a floating rate of interest. It is easily shown that the latter form can be constructed by combining the first form with a fixed–for–floating interest rate swap. For this reason we will concentrate here only on the first form.

As with any swap, the notional principal, the swap coupon (i.e., fixed rate), the payment dates, and the swap tenor (i.e., term to maturity) must be specified. Also, the macroeconomic variable or index must be specified. If a lag is employed, then that too must be specified. The end user and the macro swap dealer exchange periodic payments based on the value of the macroeconomic variable, the swap coupon, and the notional principal.

Consider now a macro swap with quarterly payments in which the macroeconomic payment on the swap is a lagged function of some macroeconomic index (MI). Call this lagged function the macroeconomic index rate or *MIR*. Specifically, for purposes of illustration, let the *t*-quarter's *MIR* be given by $MIR(t) = [100 - MI(t-s)]/100$, where *s* denotes the number of quarters of lag. The lag reflects the leading indicator nature of the index. Suppose that this lagged macroeconomic index has been shown to be positively correlated with economic activity. The notional principal is denoted *NP* and the length of the payment period, in years, is denoted *LPP*. In this case, *LPP* is 0.25. The floating- and fixed-rate payments are given by Equations 9.1a and 9.1b, respectively:

$$\text{Dealer Pays} = D \times MIR \times NP \times LPP \qquad (9.1a)$$
$$\text{End User Pays} = D \times SC \times NP \times LPP \qquad (9.1b)$$

where *D* is a dummy variable that is +1 if the dealer is the macro index payer and –1 if the dealer is the macro index receiver, and *SC* denotes the fixed-rate swap coupon. Equations 9.1a and 9.1b can be combined to reflect the end user's and the dealer's net flow. This is given by Equation 9.2.

$$\text{Dealer Pays} = D \times (MIR - SC) \times NP \times LPP \qquad (9.2)$$

If the right-hand side of Equation 9.2 is positive for any payment period, then the dealer is a net payer and the end user is a net receiver for that payment period. If the right-hand side is negative for a payment period, then the end user is a net payer and the dealer is a net receiver for that payment period. The cash flows are depicted in Figure 9.1.

Macroeconomic options are single period (calls and puts) or multi-period (caps and floors) options in which the price of the underlying

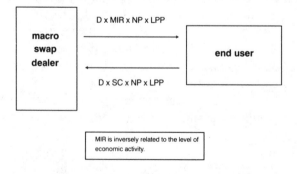

FIGURE 9.1 The Macroeconomic Swap Structure

asset, known as the reference rate, is a function of a macroeconomic index. The option has a fixed strike price, known as the contract rate (CR). For example, using the same macroeconomic index rate MIR employed earlier, we might specify the payoff function of a single–period call or multiple–period cap by Equation 9.3:

$$\text{Dealer's Payout} = D \times Max[MIR - CR, 0] \times NP \times LPP \quad (9.3)$$

If D is positive, implying that the dealer sold the contract, then the right–hand side will be either positive or zero. If positive, it implies that the dealer pays the sum on the right–hand side. If D is negative, implying that the dealer bought the contract, then the right–hand side will be either negative or zero. If negative, the dealer receives the sum on the right–hand side. The payoff function for the corresponding MIR single–period put or multiperiod floor would be given by Equation 9.4.

$$\text{Dealer's Payout} = D \times Max[CR - MIR, 0] \times NP \times LPP \quad (9.4)$$

Macro options, like other options, would ordinarily be purchased for an up–front premium. When the macro option is multiperiod, the up–front premium must be amortized to determine the per period cost of the option. It is possible, in the case of multiperiod caps and floors, to build the premium into the structure of the option—as is the case with participating caps and participating floors. In these cases, the dealer sells the option with either no up–front premium or a smaller than "fair value" up–front premium and then recoups this "fair value" in the form of a periodic payment by the option holder when the option is out–of–the–money. The size of the payment is determined by the **participation rate** (PR) and by the degree to which the option is out–of–the–money. The payoff function for a dealer that writes a macroeconomic participating cap is given by Equation 9.5.

$$\text{Dealer's Payout} = D \times \{Max[MIR - CR, 0] - (PR \\ \times Max[CR - MIR, 0])\} \times NP \times LPP \quad (9.5)$$

9.4 THE VIABILITY OF MACROECONOMIC SWAPS AND OPTIONS

The viability of macro swaps, as instruments to hedge business cycle risk, depends on a number of factors. First, the target firm's revenues must be shown to be sufficiently correlated with the macroeconomic index to achieve a satisfactory level of risk reduction. Second, the index must not be subject to revision, or, at the very least, all revisions of the index must occur prior to the periodic settlement dates of the swap. Finally, for dealers to make markets in macro swaps, there must be either: 1. an aggregate match between the dealer–pays–macroeconomic–index swaps and the dealer–receives–macroeconomic–index swaps such that the dealer's book is balanced, or 2. the dealer must have an instrument in which it can lay off the risk associated with an unmatched swap book. Macroeconomic futures (macro futures) would constitute the logical hedging instrument for the swap book and, presumably, could be used in much the same way that swap dealers use Eurodollar futures, bond futures, and swap futures to hedge unmatched interest rate swaps.

9.5   TESTING THE MACRO SWAP CONCEPT

While a macroeconomic swap can be pegged to any macroeconomic index or indicator, such as GNP, GDP, the Purchasing Managers Index, an index of consumer confidence, and so on, there is no reason to expect, a priori, that any one index is optimal for hedging all firms' business cycle risk. That is, it might easily be that one firm's business cycle risk is best hedged with a GNP swap while another's is best hedged with a consumer confidence swap. Further, the optimal lag structure for any given index will likely be different for different firms.

The first test of the viability of the macro swap concept was conducted by Bansal, Marshall, and Yuyuenyongwatana (1992). They selected the largest firm from each of ten different U.S. industries, based on 1981 sales revenue (Table 9.1). They chose to test the correlation of corporate revenues with indices of consumer confidence. Their data consisted of ten years of quarterly corporate revenues spanning the first quarter of 1981 through the final quarter of 1990 (40 quarters). They computed quarterly averages of consumer confidence using both the University of Michigan's Consumer Sentiment Index (UMI) and the Conference Board's Index of Consumer Confidence (CBI).

The test was simple and straightforward. The researchers performed a series of firm–by–firm regressions of corporate revenues on the UMI using four different lag structures (contemporaneous, 1–quarter lag, 2–quarter lag, and 3–quarter lag). They then repeated the exercise using the CBI in lieu of the UMI.

Table 9.1 Selected Industries and Firms

Industry	Dominant Firm	Ticker Symbol
Pharmaceutical	Abbott Laboratories	ABT
Insurance	Aetna Life & Casualty Co.	AET
Banking	Chase Manhattan Bank	CMB
Financial Services	American Express	AXT
Telephone	AT&T	T
Aircraft	Boeing Company	BA
Health Care	Humana, Inc.	HUM
Fast Food	McDonald Corp.	MCD
Computer	International Business Machines	IBM
Automobile	General Motors	GM

They found that two quarters of lag were optimal for eight of the ten firms and that three quarters were optimal for the other two firms. They also found that the Conference Board's Index exhibited a higher degree of correlation with corporate revenues than the University of Michigan's Index for nine of the ten firms.

The regression R^2s, with optimal lags for the regressions of corporate revenue on the Conference Board's Index, ranged from a low of 0.329 (IBM) to a high of 0.716 (GM). These R^2s provide a direct measure of the degree to which revenue volatilities are "explained" by fluctuations in consumer confidence. For example, an R^2 of 0.716 implies that 71.6 percent of the variance of GM's revenues can be explained by fluctuations in consumer confidence. Therefore, a macro swap pegged to the CBI should be able to reduce the variance of GM's revenues by 71.6 percent.[1]

The analysis, while quite limited and preliminary, suggests that some firms' revenue volatilities are largely "explained" by variations in consumer confidence and are, therefore, logical candidates for swaps pegged to an index of consumer confidence. At the same time, other firms' revenue volatilities are only moderately "explained" by variations in consumer confidence and are not good candidates for swaps pegged to such indices. Importantly, while some firms are not good candidates for macro swaps linked to consumer confidence, they may nevertheless be good candidates for swaps pegged to other macroeconomic indices.

9.6 HEDGING THE DEALER'S BOOK

The fact that most potential end users of macro swaps and options have revenue streams that parallel the business cycle suggests that, irrespective of the macroeconomic index employed, the dealer will be hard pressed to maintain a balanced book. Indeed, it is quite likely that it will be impossible to do so and still make a liquid market in macro swaps. More than any existing swap product, then, making markets in macro swaps will require a liquid futures market to offset the excess demand on the dealer–pays–macroeconomic–index. At present, no such futures contract exists.[2] On the other hand, futures exchanges are now experimenting very aggressively with new futures products, including futures on underlying assets that are neither commodities nor financial instruments in the usual sense. The Chicago Board of Trade, in particular, has been a leader in this area in recent years.

Until macro futures are developed and introduced, macro swap dealers are limited to hedging their unmatched macro swap books in a portfolio of extant futures—what Marshall (1989) has called a **composite hedge**. To hedge in extant futures, a dealer would employ sophisticated statistical techniques to identify a combination of futures that, in the properly weighted aggregate, exhibit a high degree of correlation with the pegged index. Herbst (1985) has shown how this can be done.

Alternatively, the dealer might resort to issuing debt with an inverse floating rate, where the floating rate is the MIR. For example, the coupon may be given by $FR - MIR$, where FR is a fixed rate. In the case of a consumer confidence, the interest rate would decline when consumer confidence declines and rise when consumer confidence rises. The proceeds from the debt issuance would be invested in fixed–rate Treasuries. While we have not depicted it as such, this type of hedge might logically employ a special purpose corporation to interface between the swap dealer and the capital markets. The hedge is depicted in Figure 9.2. In either the composite futures approach or the debt issuance approach, the cost of hedging will be large for the swap dealer, and this cost must be factored into the swap pricing.

9.7 SUMMARY AND CONCLUSIONS

In this, the closing chapter of the book, we have examined the recently developed concept of macroeconomic derivatives. These are swaps and options in which the floating leg is pegged to an index of macroeconomic activity. These derivatives would be used by corporations and, perhaps, governments to shield revenues from fluctuations in macroeconomic ac-

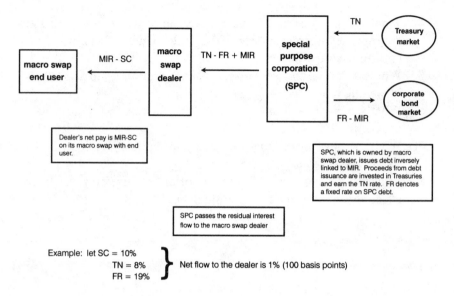

FIGURE 9.2 Hedging a Macro Swap Dealer

tivity. We have seen that the usefulness of these derivatives depends on the degree to which the end user's revenues are correlated with macroeconomic indices, the specification of an appropriate lag structure, and the ability of swap dealers to find vehicles in which to lay off the risk from making markets in these instruments.

In just over a year from the time these derivatives were first proposed by Marshall and colleagues, a major swap dealer, employing the basic model, introduced the first macroeconomic swaps. While only time will tell, it seems quite likely that macroeconomic derivatives may represent the next major frontier in financial engineering.

REVIEW QUESTIONS

1. What is business cycle risk? Discuss.
2. Is the term "macroeconomic risk" descriptive of business cycle risk? Discuss.
3. Why might business cycle risk be considered a form of quantity risk?

4. What factors must an end user of a swap consider in selecting an appropriate macroeconomic variable to which to peg a macroeconomic swap? Discuss.
5. What additional concerns does a macroeconomic swap dealer have in writing macroeconomic swaps? Discuss.
6. What is a macroeconomic option? Can you describe some specific use for these options?
7. What types of firms might be likely to employ macroeconomic swaps and options?
8. Why are the regression R^2s so important in assessing the likely effectiveness of a macroeconomic hedge?

NOTES

1. This is an oversimplified interpretation, but it does capture the gist of the implications. Marshall et al. do provide some caveats in their study that we do not consider here.
2. We would be remiss if we failed to acknowledge the difficulties associated with trading macro futures. Two, in particular, stand out. First, the observations on the "cash value" of the underlying index are discontinuous. That is, observations are made at discrete intervals. Second, the discontinuous observations on most macroeconomic indexes are themselves subject to revisions. We believe that these difficulties are surmountable, but we make no effort to offer solutions here.

REFERENCES AND SUGGESTED READING

Bansal, V. K., J. F. Marshall, and R. P. Yuyuenyongwatana. "Macroeconomic Derivatives: Consumer Confidence and Corporate Revenues," working paper, St. John's University, 1992.

Herbst, A. F. "Hedging Against Price Index Inflation with Futures Contracts." *Journal of Futures Markets*, Winter 1985, pp. 489–504.

Marshall, J. F. *Futures and Option Contracting.* Cincinnati, OH: South–Western, 1989.

Marshall, J. F., V. K. Bansal, A. F. Herbst, and A. L. Tucker. "Hedging Business Cycle Risk with Macro Swaps and Options." *Journal of Applied Corporate Finance* 4, no. 4 (1992a): 103–8.

Marshall, J. F., V. K. Bansal, A. F. Herbst, and A. L. Tucker. "Macro Swaps and Macro Options: The Next Frontier?" In *The Swaps Handbook: 1991–92 Supplement*, K. R. Kapner and J. F. Marshall, eds. New York: New York Institute of Finance, 1992b.

Schwartz, R. J., and G. Righini. "Hedging the Business Cycle." *Institutional Investor Supplement,* December 1992.

Glossary

Note: This glossary includes most terms boldfaced in the text. The exception is those legal terms boldfaced in Section 8.6 which deal with swap documentation. The reader is advised to consult ISDA literature for definitions of legal terms. The full text of the ISDA 1986 Code, with definitions, can be found in Kenneth R. Kapner and John F. Marshall, *The Swaps Handbook: Swaps and Related Risk Management Instruments*, New York: New York Institute of Finance, 1990. The chapter numbers in parentheses that follow the definitions indicate the chapters in which the terms are boldfaced.

absolute advantage   The ability of one country to produce more of a given good than another with its endowed resources. In the context of financial swaps, the ability of one party to borrow at a lower rate of interest in a given currency than another party. See also *relative advantage*. (Chapter 1)

accreting swaps   Swaps on which the notional principal increases over time, under a prespecified schedule. The opposite of amortizing swaps. (Chapter 3)

actuals   Physical commodities, securities, or real principals that are transferred in cash markets—as distinct from notionals, which exist primarily for calculating service payments in the derivative markets. (Chapter 2)

add-on factor   Part of the bank capital guidelines adopted by the Federal Reserve in 1989. In the case of swaps and other off-balance sheet positions, it is a percentage of the notional principal. (Chapter 8)

agreement value method   One of three allowable methods for determining damages upon the early termination of a swap. This method is now nearly universally employed in swap documentation. The method assesses damages based upon "market quotations" for obtaining a replacement swap. (Chapter 8)

all-in cost   Also known as the *effective annual percentage cost*. The total cost of a financing expressed as an annual percentage rate. In addition to the coupon, this will reflect flotation costs, trustee expenses, and administration expenses. It is useful for comparing the cost of several financing alternatives. (Chapter 6)

amortizing swap Any swap in which the notional principal amortizes over the tenor of the swap. Thus, interest exchanges are made on a progressively smaller notional principal. (Chapter 3)

A-Pack A software package for use on IBM-type microcomputers, published by MicroApplications (516-821-9355). Contains many useful analytical techniques with applications in finance, statistics, investment analysis, mathematical analysis, and management science. The full name of the software is *A-Pack: An Analytical Package for Business*. (Preface)

asset allocation swap An equity swap that pays the higher of the total return on two equity indexes on the equity leg of the swap. (Chapter 5)

asset-based swaps Any swap written to transform the cash flow characteristics of an asset in order to replicate the cash flows characteristics of another asset. The combination of the original asset together with the swap often constitutes a synthetic instrument. (Chapter 3)

assigned The transfer of one's rights and obligations under a contract to another party. (Chapter 8)

average life A measure of interest-rate sensitivity based on principal repayments alone. Often used to determine the maturity-equivalent Treasury note for purposes of pricing long-dated swaps. (Chapter 3)

back-to-back loans A loan arrangement involving two distinct loans between the same parties. In the first loan, Party 1 is the lender and Party 2 is the borrower. In the second loan, Party 2 is the lender and Party 1 is the borrower. (Chapter 1)

basis point One one-hundredth of 1 percentage point; that is, 0.01 percent. The term "basis points" is often abbreviated in the text as "bps." (Chapter 1)

basis risk 1. The degree to which the difference between two prices fluctuates; 2. the residual risk that remains after a hedge has been placed; 3. a swap dealer's risk from receiving one floating rate, such as LIBOR, and paying another floating rate, such as T-bill. (Chapter 4)

basis swap A floating-for-floating interest rate swap. (Chapter 3)

Basle Accord An agreement in principle reached in December 1987 by the Basle Supervisors' Committee that redefined bank capital requirements. (Chapters 1, 8)

Basle Supervisors' Committee A group of bank supervisors and regulators that met in Basle, Switzerland, to redefine bank capital and to standardize capital requirements. (Chapter 8)

bid-ask spread Also called *pay-receive spread*. The difference between the bid price and the ask price for any instrument. In dealer markets, the bid-ask spread is the dominant source of the dealer's income. (Chapters 1, 2)

blended index An equity index consisting of a weighted average of the total returns on several other equity indexes. See also *rainbow*. (Chapter 5)

bond equivalent yield Also known as the *coupon equivalent yield*. A method of calculating and stating the yield on a coupon bearing instrument. Most often assumes semiannual compounding. (Chapter 3)

booking a swap Also called *positioning a swap*. When a swap dealer enters a swap, the swap becomes part of the dealer's "book" or portfolio. (Chapter 1)

bootstrapping As the term is used in swap finance, an iterative numerical procedure to determine the implied zero coupon swap yield curve from the conventional or "par" swap yield curve. (Chapter 8)

Bretton Woods Agreement A multinational accord that established the post–World War II international monetary system for participating nations. The Agreement served as the basis for the international monetary system until it broke down in the early 1970s. (Chapter 1)

British Bankers Association A London-based trade association that deals with matters of common interest to member banks. In recent years, the BBA has dealt extensively with standardization of instrument documentation including swaps and forward rate agreements. (Chapter 1)

bucket In swap parlance, a time interval during which all cash flows that occur are aggregated. (Chapter 8)

bucket cash flow The sum of all cash flows that occur during any bucket interval. (Chapter 8)

bucket DV01 The dollar value of a basis point for a swap dealer's entire bucket cash flow. See also bucket and bucket cash flow. (Chapter 8, footnote)

bullet transaction A banking term that describes a loan in which the principal is repaid in a single transaction upon maturity of the instrument. (Chapters 1, 3)

buy down The up-front sum that will be received (paid) by a swap dealer for writing an off-market swap with itself as receiver (payer) of fixed rate when the swap requires a coupon below current market. (Chapter 3)

buy up The up-front sum that must be paid (received) by a swap dealer for writing an off-market swap with itself as receiver (payer) of fixed rate when the swap requires a coupon above current market. (Chapter 3)

call option An option that grants the holder the right to buy the underlying asset from the option writer. (Chapter 1)

callable swap A swap that may be terminated prior to its scheduled maturity at the discretion of the fixed-rate payer. (Chapter 3)

cap 1. A multiperiod option that resembles a strip of single-period call options. The most common type is an interest rate cap that pays off on each settlement date based on the market value of a reference rate and a specified contract rate. 2. A provision within a floating rate instrument that places a ceiling on the floating rate. (Chapter 1)

capital markets group A division, department, or designated group within an investment bank or commercial bank whose function is to assist clients in meeting their financing needs. The derivatives group is often a part of the capital markets group. (Chapter 4)

capital   An important tool of bank regulation and safety. Consists of long-term debt and equity and protects depositors by acting as a cushion against losses. (Chapter 8)

circus swap   A combination involving a fixed-for-floating interest rate swap and a fixed-for-floating currency swap in which the floating-rate side of both swaps are LIBOR based. Allows for the creation of a fixed-for-fixed or floating-for-floating currency swap. (Chapter 2)

clearinghouse   1. An organization that tracks, matches, and guarantees transactions in futures and options. Also known as a clearing association and, if so organized, as a clearing corporation. 2. An organization that acts as a custodian for bearer securities in international markets. (Chapter 1)

Code, 1986   The International Swap Dealers Association's Code of Standard Wording, Assumptions and Provisions for Swaps, 1986 edition. A revision and expansion of ISDA's 1985 code. (Chapter 8)

commodity price risk   The price risk associated with holding a position in commodities or an anticipated position in commodities. (Chapter 1)

commodity swaps   Swaps that are structured to convert floating prices paid (or received) for commodities to fixed prices, or vice versa. These swaps have a similar structure to interest rate swaps. (Chapter 5)

comparative advantage   A situation in which one country (or firm) can produce a good (or engage in a borrowing) at less cost than another country (or firm) in the special sense that it must sacrifice less of an alternative good to achieve production. The term is associated with the Theory of Comparative Advantage used to explain trade between nations. (Chapter 1)

cost of a hedge   The difference between the expected terminal value of an unhedged cash position and the expected terminal value of the same cash position when hedged. (Chapter 4)

counterparty   A principal to a swap or other derivative instrument, as opposed to an agent such as a broker. (Chapter 1)

creditworthiness   A reference to the likelihood that a party to a contract will default on its obligations. The greater the likelihood of default the less creditworthy the party is. (Chapter 4)

Deferred swap   See *forward swap.* (Chapter 3)

delayed rate setting swap   Also called a *deferred rate setting swap.* A fixed-for-floating interest rate swap in which the swap commences immediately but the swap coupon is not set until later. (Chapter 3)

delivery risk   Also called *settlement risk.* The risk that differences between market settlement hours may result in exchanges of interest and/or principals at different times or even on different days. The first paying party is exposed to the risk that the later paying party will default after the first paying party has made its required payment but before the later paying party has made its payment. (Chapter 8)

derivative instruments   An instrument that is defined on, and whose value is a function of, some other instrument or asset. Examples include futures, options, and swaps. (Chapter 1)

discriminant analysis   A multivariate forecasting technique often used to determine which financial ratios or combination of financial ratios are most reliable for predicting business failure. (Chapter 8 footnote)

dollar value of a basis point   The dollar value change that would result from a 1 basis point change in an instrument's yield. Often abbreviated DV01. In order to make the definition usable, the DV01 must be stated per some amount of face value. (Chapter 8)

dual currency bond   A bond on which the principal payments are made in one currency and the interest (coupon) payments are made in a different currency. (Chapter 6)

duration   A measure developed by Frederick Macaulay that allows for accurate measurement of a debt instrument's price sensitivity to yield changes. Duration is the instrument's weighted average time to maturity. (Chapter 3)

DV01   See dollar value of a basis point. (Chapter 8)

economies of scale   Any production situation, including the provision of financial services, in which the cost per unit produced decreases as the number of units produced increases. Per unit cost should not be confused with total cost. The latter will rise directly with the quantity produced irrespective of the behavior of per unit costs. (Chapter 4)

effective annual percentage cost   1. Any financial cost expressed on a percentage basis as an effective annual rate. Very useful for comparing alternative financing methods. 2. Often used to convert the onetime premium paid for multiperiod options to reexpress the cost of these options on a basis that is more easily understood. (Chapter 6)

effective date   Also known as the *value date*. The date that a swap begins to accrue interest, i.e., takes value. (Chapter 2)

end user   In the context of swaps, a counterparty, other than a swap dealer, who uses a swap for some economic purpose.

equity return risk   The price risk associated with holding a portfolio of equity securities. (Chapter 1)

equity swap   Swaps on which at least one leg is pegged to the total return on a stock index. The other leg can be fixed or floating. (Chapter 5)

Eurodollar deposit   A bank deposit in dollars held outside the United States. (Chapter 7).

Eurostrip   Also known as a *Eurodollar futures strip*. A series of successive Eurodollar futures contracts that is strung together to replicate some other instrument. (Chapter 7)

events of default   An event that is indicative of a credit problem. Occurrences that constitute events of default are specified in the swap documentation. The occurrence of such an event terminates all swaps governed by the same master agreement between the parties. (Chapter 8)

exchange of borrowings   The simplest form of a currency swap in which each counterparty to the swap obtains funds from third-party borrowings and then exchanges the funds so obtained. (Chapter 1)

exchange rate   Also called *foreign exchange rate*. The price of one unit of a currency stated in terms of units of another currency. (Chapter 1)

exchange rate risk   A form of price risk associated with volatility in exchange rates. (Chapter 1)

exotic options   Also known as *second generation options*. A general term that includes all options that are more complex than simple single-period call and put options. (Chapter 1)

expiration date   The date on which an option expires. (Chapter 1)

extendable swap   A fixed-for-floating interest rate swap in which one counterparty has the right to extend the swap beyond its scheduled maturity date. (Chapter 3)

financial engineering   In the most general sense, the work of those individuals responsible for the creation of new financial instruments, new financial processes, and new solutions to problems in finance. More narrowly, the term is often used synonymously with risk management. See International Association of Financial Engineers. (Chapter 6)

financial intermediary   A financial institution that stands between two end users of the intermediary's products. In the traditional context, one user is represented on the asset side and the other is represented on the liabilities side of the intermediary's balance sheet. In the context of swaps and related instruments, however, the products are off-balance sheet. (Chapter 1)

fixed price   A price that does not change over the life of an instrument or contract. The term is understood to include fixed rates of interest. (Chapter 2)

fixed-for-floating swaps   A swap in which one counterparty pays a floating rate of interest while the other counterparty pays a fixed rate of interest. This is the most common type of swap. (Chapters 1, 4)

floating price   The floating price paid on a fixed-for-floating or floating-for-floating swap or on a floating-price cash market transaction. In the case of an interest rate or currency swap, the term is synonymous with floating rate. (Chapter 2)

Floating rate notes   Also known as *FRNs* and as *floaters*. A promissory note paying interest on a floating rate basis. (Chapter 3)

floor   A multiperiod option that pays off on each settlement date that the reference rate is below the contract rate. It resembles a strip of single-period puts. (Chapter 1)

formula method   One of three methods for determining damages upon the early termination of a swap. No longer widely used. (Chapter 8)

forward rate agreement   Known as an *FRA*. An interest rate forward contract written on a notional principal and cash settled on the basis of the difference between the contract rate and the prevailing reference rate on the settlement date. The resultant settlement value is discounted to adjust for an up-front settlement. (Chapter 3)

forward exchange rates   Current exchange rates for currency exchanges that will take place at some point in the future. (Chapter 4)

forward swap   Also called a *deferred swap*. A fixed-for-floating interest rate swap in which the swap coupon is set at the outset but the start of the swap is delayed. (Chapter 3)

futures contract   Also known as a *futures*. Standardized contracts for deferred delivery (or cash settlement) of commodities and financial instruments. Always traded on a futures exchange and regulated by the Commodity Futures Trading Commission. (Chapter 1)

FRA   See *forward rate agreement.*

FRN   See *floating rate note.*

front months   The closest delivery months in a futures strip. (Chapter 1)

futures strip   A string of futures contracts with successive delivery (settlement) dates. Most often used to refer to a strip of interest-rate futures such as Eurodollar futures. (Chapter 1)

generic swap   Also known as *plain vanilla* and as a *basic* swap. The simplest or most standard form of a given type of swap. (Chapters 1, 2)

hedge   A position taken in order to offset the risk associated with some other position. Most often, the initial position is a cash position and the hedge position involves a risk-management instrument such as a swap or a futures contract. (Chapter 1)

indemnification method   One of three methods for assessing damages upon the early termination of a swap. No longer widely used. (Chapter 8)

indicative swap pricing schedules   Industry term used to describe the pricing schedule for the swaps in which a dealer makes a market. The term "indicative" is meant to imply that these rates are a starting point only and apply to plain vanilla swaps written at-market. Actual rates may vary depending on the creditworthiness of the client and other factors. (Chapters 1, 3)

International Association of Financial Engineers   Known by the acronym IAFE. A professional association of practitioners and academicians involved in various aspects of financial engineering. The association serves as a networking, research, and information exchange organization. The Association can be reached at 718-990-6161 ext 7381.

interbank swaps   Swaps between two swap dealers. (Chapter 3, footnote)

interest differential 1. In a swap, the difference between the amount of interest Counterparty 1 must pay Counterparty 2 and the amount Counterparty 2 must pay Counterparty 1. 2. The rate differential between the rates on two different instruments having the same maturity. In this context, the preferred term is "interest rate differential." 3. The rate differential between instruments of the same maturity but denominated in different currencies. (Chapter 1)

Interest Rate and Currency Exchange Agreement A multicurrency standard form agreement published by the ISDA in 1987. It does not reference the 1986 Code but employs virtually identical provisions. Designed to serve as a master swap agreement. (Chapter 8)

interest rate parity theorem A relationship between the nominal interest rates and the spot and forward exchange rates for two countries' currencies. Interest rate parity is a consequence of arbitrage. In brief, parity implies that the real rate of interest on equivalent risk instruments in two countries should be the same, after adjusting for spot-forward exchange rate differential. (Chapter 4)

interest rate risk 1. The risk that a future spot interest rate will deviate from its expected value; 2. the price risk associated with holding a fixed-rate debt instrument as a result of fluctuations in the instrument's yield. (Chapter 1)

interest rate swap An agreement between two parties to engage in a series of exchanges of interest payments on the same notional principal denominated in the same currency. (Chapter 8)

Interest Rate Swap Agreement A standard form swap agreement published by the ISDA in 1987 that is based on the 1986 Code and incorporates the Code by reference. It is meant exclusively for U.S. dollar interest rate swaps. Intended to serve as a master swap agreement. (Chapter 8)

internal rate of return Also known as *IRR*. The discount rate that equates the sum of the present values of the cash flows associated with an investment with the initial cost of the investment. (Chapter 6)

International Swap Dealers Association Also known as *ISDA*. A New York-based trade association that deals with matters of common interest to member swap dealers. In recent years, this organization has concentrated on standardizing documentation. In 1993 the ISDA changed its name to the International Swaps and Derivatives Association. (Chapter 1)

legs Also called *sides*. The two sides of a swap. (Chapter 1)

LIBOR An acronym for *London Interbank Offered Rate*. This interest rate is the standard rate for quoting interbank lendings of Eurodollar deposits. It is also the customary reference rate for plain vanilla interest rate swaps. (Chapters 2, 7)

LIBOR flat LIBOR quoted without any premium or discount. (Chapter 1)

listed option Any option traded on an organized exchange and having standardized terms. This is in contrast to options that trade over the counter. (Chapter 1)

London Interbank Offered Rate See LIBOR.

long-dated swaps   Any swap with a tenor too long to be priced of the Eurodollar futures strip. (Chapter 7)

macroeconomic swaps   Also known as *macro swaps*. Swaps on which at least one leg is pegged to a macroeconomic variable such as GNP growth or an index of consumer confidence. These swaps represent a recent innovation. Their purpose is to hedge business cycle risk. Macroeconomic swaps were first proposed by John F. Marshall and Vipul K. Bansal of St. John's University. (Chapter 9)

macroeconomic options   Also known as *macro options*. Options on which the reference rate is pegged to a macroeconomic variable. These options can be written as either single period or multiperiod options. Macro options represent a recent innovation. See also *macroeconomic swaps*. (Chapter 9)

macrohedge   A hedge taken to offset the risk associated with the firm as a whole or with some subset portfolio of the firm but not identified with a specific cash position. (Chapter 8)

market maker   Also known as a *dealer*. A party that makes a market in an instrument by offering to both buy and sell the instrument. The market maker profits from the difference between its bid and ask prices. (Chapter 2)

mark-to-market   In futures, the practice of periodically adjusting a margin account by adding or subtracting funds based on changes in market value. Swap dealers employ the practice to measure profits and risk exposures on their swaps portfolios. (Chapter 8)

master swap agreement   A document written in such a fashion that its terms govern all swap activity between the same counterparties. Each new swap is viewed as a supplement to the master agreement. (Chapter 8)

matched needs   When two end users have identical, but mirror image, needs and so can satisfy each other's requirements by entering into a mutually beneficial relationship. (Chapter 1)

maturity date   Also known as the *termination date*. It is the date on which a swap ceases to accrue interest, i.e., terminates. (Chapter 2)

maturity   Also known as *tenor*. The length of a swap's life. (Chapter 2)

microhedge   A hedge taken to offset the risk associated with a specifically identified cash position. (Chapter 8)

money market yield   Also known as *money market basis*. A method of calculating the yield on certain money market instruments. The method uses actual days over 360 in the yield calculation. LIBOR is stated using this yield convention. (Chapter 3)

mortgage swaps   Any of a variety of interest rate swaps on which the cash flows are structured to mimic the cash flows on a mortgage portfolio. The critical feature of such swaps is the method of notional principal amortization. (Chapter 3)

mr   An abbreviation meaning annual rate compounded monthly. (Chapter 1)

multiperiod options   Any cash-settled option that has a series of successive settlement dates. On each settlement date, the option behaves as though it were a single-period option. (Chapter 1)

natural hedge   The tendency of certain risks to be coincidentally offsetting. (Chapter 8)

netting   1. The standard practice in swap documentation requiring that only the interest differential on interest rate swaps be exchanged with the higher paying party making payment of this difference to the lower paying party. 2. The reduction of risk exposures by netting payments under a master swap agreement. (Chapter 8)

nonamortizing   A debt obligation in which the full principal is repaid in a single transaction upon maturity of the debt with no repayments of principal prior to maturity. See also *bullet transaction*. (Chapter 3)

notionals   Commodities, securities, or principals that exist primarily for purposes of calculating service payments—as distinct from actuals. (Chapters 1, 2)

notional principal   The amount of principal on which the interest is calculated on a swap or related instrument including FRAs and interest rate options. In the case of interest rate swaps, FRAs, and interest rate options, the principal is purely "notional" in that no exchange of principal ever takes place. (Chapters 1, 2)

OECD   See Organization for Economic Cooperation and Development.

off-balance sheet   A position with potential financial consequence that does not appear on either the asset side or the liabilities side of a balance sheet. (Chapter 1)

off-market swap   A swap that is written with a coupon that deviates from currently prevailing market conditions. (Chapter 3)

on the run   Those U.S. Treasury securities that are the most recent issues for their respective maturities. (Chapter 3)

OTC   See *over-the-counter*.

OTC options   Custom-designed options that trade over-the-counter. (Chapter 1)

over-the-counter   Known more commonly by the acronym *OTC*. A dealer market in which transactions take place via telephone, telex, and other electronic forms of communication as opposed to trading on the floor of an exchange. Such markets allow for great flexibility in product design. (Chapter 1)

Organization of Economic Cooperation and Development   An organization of European states for mutual economic gain. (Chapter 8)

pa   An abbreviation meaning an annual rate of interest compounded annually. (Chapter 1)

par swap   Also known as an *at-market swap*. A swap in which the swap coupon is set at current market levels. (Chapter 3)

par swaps yield curve   The current yield curve for at-market swaps. (Chapter 8)

parallel loans An arrangement in which two parent companies agree to make loans to each other's subsidiary. The parallel loan is a precursor of the modern swap and serves a similar purpose as a currency swap. The structure of parallel loans, however, is generally considered inferior to that of swaps. (Chapter 1)

payment dates The dates on which the counterparties to a swap contract exchange service payments. (Chapter 2)

pay-receive spread Also called a *bid-ask spread*. The difference between a swap dealer's receive rate and pay rate on generic swaps of a given tenor. (Chapters 1, 2)

plain vanilla Also called *generic* or *basic*. The simplest form of a financial instrument. Often associated with the first manifestation of an instrument, e.g., a "plain vanilla swap." (Chapter 1)

positioning a swap Also called *booking a swap*. The taking of a position in a swap by a swap dealer. This contrasts with a broker who acts as an agent in a swap and does not take the swap on its own books. (Chapter 1)

principle of comparative advantage A well-established theory first developed by David Ricardo in the 19th century to explain trade between nations. The concept is equally applicable in explaining trade more generally and for explaining the benefits that accrue to the counterparties to a swap. In brief, the theory holds that, assuming an appropriate exchange rate, both parties will benefit from trade if each concentrates production in that good in which it holds a comparative advantage and then trades its surplus production for the surplus production of the other. Refinements of the theory allow for transaction costs. (Chapter 1)

principle of offsetting risks This is an extension of portfolio theory, which states that risk can be reduced if two simultaneous positions are held such that manifestations of the individual risks, which take the form of deviations from expected values, are in opposite directions. (Chapter 1)

putable swap A fixed-for-floating interest rate swap in which the floating-rate payer has the right to terminate the swap prior to its scheduled maturity date. (Chapter 3)

quality spread The difference between the borrowing costs of a poorer credit firm and a better credit firm for a given type of borrowing, a given interest character, and a given term. (Chapter 7)

quality spread differential The difference between a quality spread in a fixed-rate market and a quality spread in a floating-rate market. The quality spread differential is considered a measure of the potential gains from engaging in financial swaps. This may, however, overstate the gains. (Chapter 2, footnote, Chapter 7)

rainbow A blended index of equity returns for indexing the reference rate on an equity swap. See also *blended index*. (Chapter 5)

rate-capped swap A fixed-for-floating interest rate swap in which the floating-rate side is capped. Such structures can be created as a single unit or by combining an interest rate swap with a separate interest rate cap. (Chapter 3)

reference rate   A rate (such as six-month LIBOR or three-month T-bill) designated as such on any cash-settled interest-rate contract including swaps, forward rate agreements, and interest-rate options. The reference rate is the rate that is observed on the calculation or settlement date for purposes of determining the amount of any cash settlement. (Chapters 2, 7)

regression analysis   Statistical procedures used to fit lines to data. The most widely used form is linear regression, which fits a straight line to data. This line is the "best" fit in the sense that it minimizes the sum of squared errors. (Chapter 8, footnote)

reinvestment risk   The risk that the general level of interest rates will have changed from some initial level by the time the cash flows from an investment are due to be reinvested. (Chapter 3)

relative advantage   A synonym for *comparative advantage*. The notion that one party may have a borrowing advantage in one market relative to another party even if the first party is at an absolute borrowing disadvantage. (Chapter 2)

replacement swap   A swap that is entered to replace a swap that is terminated prematurely. This most often becomes necessary when one of a pair of matched swaps is terminated early. (Chapter 8)

repurchase agreement   Also known as a *repo* and an *RP*. A method of borrowing that involves the sale of a security with the simultaneous agreement to buy it back at a specific later date and at a specific price. These agreements are widely used in the securities industry as a means of obtaining relatively inexpensive short-term financing. (Chapter 3)

reset   An adjustment to a floating rate of interest that sets the rate to that prevailing in the market. (Chapter 2)

reset dates   The scheduled dates for the resets of the floating rate of interest on swaps and other floating rate instruments. (Chapters 2, 8)

reverse repurchase agreement   Also known as a *reverse*, as a *reverse repo reverse,* as a *reverse repo,* and as a resale. The opposite of a repurchase agreement. The purchase of a security with the simultaneous agreement to sell it back at a specific later date and at a specific price. (Chapter 3)

reversible swap   A swap that provides for the fixed-rate payer and the floating-rate payer to reverse roles at some time during the life of the swap. (Chapter 3)

rights of assignment   The right to transfer one's interest in a contractual relationship without seeking permission of the other party to the contract. (Chapter 1)

risk averse   A dislike of risk. The risk averse individual suffers a loss of utility (called disutility) from the presence of risk. The greater the risk the greater the loss of utility. Risk aversion as a component of rational behavior is a tenet of almost all financial theory. (Chapter 4)

risk weighted asset Part of the bank capital guidelines adopted by the Federal Reserve in January of 1989. Obtained by multiplying the credit risk equivalent by a risk weighting factor. (Chapter 8)

roller coaster swap Any swap in which the notional principal increases for a time and then amortizes to zero over the remainder of its tenor. (Chapter 3)

rollover The issuance of new short-term money market securities to fund the retirement of an existing issue. (Chapter 1)

sa Abbreviation meaning an annual rate of interest compounded semiannually. (Chapter 1)

search costs The costs, both direct and indirect, of finding a party having matched needs. (Chapter 1)

seasonal swaps Swaps structured to generate cash flows that offset the seasonality of the end user's operating cash flows. (Chapter 3)

second generation options Also called *exotic options*. See *exotic options*.

secondary market The market in which a security or other instrument trades after its initial issue. (Chapter 1)

semiannual rate An annual rate of interest that is paid in two semiannual installments. Not to be confused with a "half-year rate," which is a rate of interest stated on a six-month basis. (Chapter 3)

service payments A generic term to describe the periodic interest payments (or other interim payments) on a swap. (Chapter 2)

Settlement risk See *delivery risk*.

short-dated swaps Swaps with tenors short enough that they can be priced off the Eurostrip. (Chapter 7)

sides Also called *legs*. The two sides of a swap. (Chapter 1)

spot exchange rate The exchange rate applicable on immediate exchanges of currencies. (Chapter 4)

strike price The price at which an option may be exercised. Analogous to the contract rate on a multiperiod option. (Chapter 1)

strip A string of successive contracts of a particular type and the accompanying price structure. The most important is the IMM strip. This is the set of Eurodollar futures traded on the IMM and often used to price swaps and forward rate agreements. (Chapter 7)

sovereign risk The risk that an issuer may be barred by its government from making interest and principal payments on its debt. In the context of swaps, the risk that a counterparty will be barred by its government from fulfilling its swap obligations. (Chapter 8)

sub-LIBOR financing The ability of some parties to borrow money on a floating-rate basis at rates below LIBOR. (Chapter 7)

supervening illegality   A change in applicable law, the imposition of foreign-exchange controls, or similar condition that makes it impossible for a counterparty to a swap to fulfill its obligations. (Chapter 8)

swap book   A swap dealer's portfolio of swaps. (Chapters 1, 8)

swap broker   An agent, acting on behalf of one or more principals, that finds parties with matching swap needs in exchange for a commission. (Chapter 1)

swap coupon   The fixed rate of interest on the fixed-rate side of a swap. (Chapters 1, 2, 7)

swap dealer   Also known as a *swap bank* and as a *market maker*. A financial intermediary that makes a market in swaps and that profits from its bid-ask spread. Unlike a swap broker, the swap dealer becomes a counterparty to each swap. (Chapters 1, 2)

swap driven   A term loosely used to describe pricing behaviors in nonswap instruments that are brought about through a linkage to the swap market. Examples include price movements in the futures and forward markets. (Chapter 1)

swaption   An option on a swap. The swaption purchaser has the right to enter a specific swap for a defined period of time. (Chapter 3)

synthetic equity   A reference to the conversion of the cash flows on a debt portfolio into equitylike cash flows by way of an equity swap. (Chapter 5)

synthetic instruments   Also known as *synthetic securities*. Cash flow streams structured to mimic the cash flow stream of some target security. Such streams can be engineered by an appropriate combination or decomposition of other instruments. (Chapter 6)

TED spread   The difference between the interest rate on Treasury bills and the interest rate on Eurodollar deposits of similar maturities. The definition applies to both cash instruments and futures contracts. (Chapter 8)

tenor   The length of the life (term to maturity) of a multiperiod derivative instrument such as a rate cap, a rate floor, or a swap. (Chapter 2)

termination clauses   Provisions in a swap agreement that provide for the assessment of damages in the event of early termination due to the occurrence of an event of default or a terminating event. (Chapter 8)

termination date   Also known as *maturity date*. The date on which a swap terminates. (Chapter 2)

termination events   Any event other than those indicative of credit problems that results in automatic termination of a swap contract. Unlike an event of default, a termination event only results in termination of the affected swaps. (Chapter 8)

transaction costs   The costs associated with engaging in a financial transaction. These include such explicit costs as commissions and front-end fees and indirect costs such as a bid-ask spread. (Chapter 1)

transfer pricing rate   The cost to a department within a bank of intrabank borrowings of funds or securities. Also sometimes called the *cost of carry* although the latter term has other uses as well. (Chapter 3)

value date   The date a swap commences in the sense that it begins to accrue interest. (Chapter 2)

warehousing   Also called *running a book*. Refers to the act of managing a portfolio of some specific type of instrument. Warehousing swaps, for example, means holding a portfolio of swaps. (Chapters 1, 8)

yield curve   A graphic portrayal of the relationship between the yields to maturity of instruments of a given class and the terms to maturity of those instruments. (Chapter 3)

yield curve swaps   Similar to a basis swap in that both legs are floating. However, one leg is tied to a short-term rate, such as 3-M LIBOR, and the other is tied to a long-term rate such as the Treasury's long bond. (Chapter 3)

zero coupon swaps   A variant of the fixed-for-floating interest rate swap in which the fixed-rate paying party pays all interest upon the termination of the swap. (Chapter 3)

zero coupon yield curve   A derived-yield curve for zero coupon instruments. Such curves are derived from the par yield curve using an iterative procedure called bootstrapping. (Chapter 8)

Answers to
Review Questions

Prepared by
Robert P. Yuyuenyongwatana

CHAPTER 1

1. Swaps evolved from back-to-back and parallel loans, which themselves were developed as a mechanism for circumventing controls on the flow of capital into and out of Great Britain. These arrangements, in essence, represented "paired" loans that enabled the parties involved to obtain required currencies without transacting in the foreign exchange markets. Back-to-back loans are similar to modern swaps, but they involved a serious "rights of set-off" problem, which became an issue if one of the parties involved defaulted on its obligation to the other. Swaps solved this problem by folding both loans into a single contractual agreement.

2. Trade, whether international or intranational, rests on the theory of comparative advantage, which states that whenever two parties have production advantages relative to one another, that is, in a comparative cost sense, then each party can, potentially, benefit by specializing in the production of that commodity in which it has a comparative advantage and trading for the commodity in which the other party has a comparative production advantage. Whether gains are actually realized from trade will depend on the exchange rate

for the two commodities and the costs of transacting. The same principle can explain swaps. If one party has a comparative borrowing advantage in one currency and another has a comparative borrowing advantage in another currency, then a currency swap can potentially be used to reduce the cost of borrowing for both parties if both parties require financing in the currencies in which they do not have comparative advantage. For benefits to be realized, however, the swap coupon must be appropriate and the transaction costs must not be too high. An identical argument can be made to motivate an interest rate swap if one party has a comparative advantage in the floating-rate market and the other has a comparative advantage in the fixed-rate market.

3. In the simplest scenario, we can imagine a corporate balance sheet in which the firm has floating-rate assets (liabilities) and fixed-rate liabilities (assets). Similarly, we can imagine a corporate balance sheet in which the assets are denominated in one currency and the liabilities are denominated in another. The former scenario gives rise to interest-rate risk, due to the mismatch in the character of the interest rates on the assets and liabilities sides of the balance sheet. In the latter scenario, the mismatch in the currency denominations of the assets and the liabilities gives rise to exchange-rate risk. These exposures can be eliminated with swaps as depicted in Figures 1.3A and 1.3B.

4. Treasury securities are very liquid, sufficiently homogeneous, and available in a near continuum of maturities such that a dealer may relatively easily replicate an offsetting swap until such time as

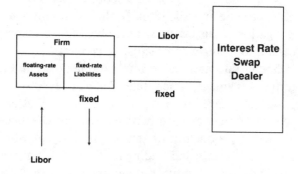

FIGURE 1.3A

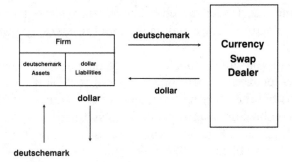

FIGURE 1.3B

matched swaps can be found. In addition, many of the early swap dealers were also government securities dealers and thus had ready access to the Treasury market. Because swaps can be replicated in cash Treasuries and because Treasuries represent the starting point for quoting yields on other instruments (such as mortgage-backed products), it makes sense to quote swap coupons as a spread over Treasuries. Additionally, this quotation method allows a dealer to quote a swap coupon and honor that quote for several hours, irrespective of what happens to interest rates in the interim.

5. The notional principals on interest rate swaps are not exchanged because they are, by definition, of the same amount and in the same currency. Thus, the notionals are a wash and an actual exchange would be pointless. In a currency swap, the notional principals are not the same and, if the counterparty to the swap dealer is in need of the other currency, an exchange of principals is called for.

6. Traditional bank businesses, such as loan making, are on-balance sheet activities. Such on-balance sheet activities require banks to maintain capital reserves as a cushion against loan losses. These capital requirements are stated as a percentage of assets. The capital requirement places a limit on the return to equity that can be earned because it limits the bank's use of leverage in the loan-making process. As off-balance sheet activity, swap transactions created a source of returns that did not, in the early days, impact capital requirements. As such, swaps made it possible to increase the return to equity. Of course, if swap activity has the potential to result in losses to the bank, then such activity exposes the depositors of the bank

to some risk. Under recently enacted rules, banks that are engaged in swap activity must maintain capital reserves against their swap portfolios.

7. The rights of set-off problem refers to the possibility that, in a back-to-back or parallel loan, one party might default on its loan obligations but the other party would still be required to fulfill its contractual obligations, thus resulting in substantial injury to the nondefaulting party. Separate rights of set-off agreements can, in theory, solve this problem but they have problems of their own. In a swap contract, the reciprocating obligations of the counterparties and the rights of set-off are embedded in the same contact, thus resolving any potential legal conflicts.

8. Amortizing debt is debt in which the principal amount is repaid gradually over the life of the loan (or swap). Nonamortizing debt is debt in which the principal amount is repaid in a lump sum at maturity.

9. The solution requires a comparison of the cost of obtaining fixed rate under both methods. We already know the cost of borrowing fixed rate directly. It is 11.75 percent. To borrow fixed rate synthetically, we would pay LIBOR plus 1.8 percent and then enter into a swap in which we receive LIBOR and pay 9.80 percent. Since the LIBORs paid and received cancel, the net cost is 11.60 percent (9.80% + 1.8%). (Importantly, this comparison ignores noncoupon costs and does not adjust for the difference between bond basis and money market basis—discussed in later chapters). Thus, the firm should borrow floating rate and swap into fixed. This is illustrated in Figure 1.9.

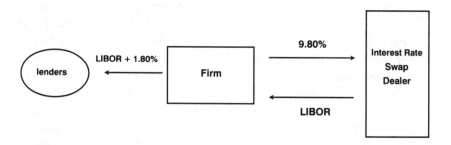

FIGURE 1.9

10. It is difficult to trade a nonstandardized contract in any sort of secondary market: The terminology employed in such contracts means different things to different people, the contract provisions are difficult to decipher and require legal opinions, and so on. Standardizing swap contract documentation does not, by itself, create a secondary market, but it creates an environment more conducive to the creation of a secondary market.

CHAPTER 2

1. *Floating price (or rate)*: A price, including an interest rate, that is periodically reset to reflect changes in market conditions.

Fixed-price (or rate): A price, including an interest rate, that does not change over the period of time spanned by the requirements of the parties.

LIBOR: An acronym for London Interbank Offered Rate. The rate of interest, set once a day in London, for an interbank lending of short-term deposits between banks. The rate can be for dollar lendings, USD LIBOR; for deutschemark lendings, DEM LIBOR; and so on. If no currency is indicated, the rate is usually assumed to apply to dollar lendings. To be complete, LIBOR must also state the term of the lending, that is, one month, three months, and so on.

Swap coupon: The fixed rate of interest on an interest rate swap. The swap coupon is usually stated bond basis.

2. *Reset dates*: specified dates on which the floating leg of a swap is set to a new level.

Effective date: the date the contract commences (takes value for interest accrual purposes).

Termination date: Also called a maturity date. The date on which a swap ceases to accrue interest.

Payment dates: the dates on which payments are exchanged between swap counterparties.

3. *Tenor*: The length of a swap term, also known as its maturity.

Notionals: The underlying principals, or other underlying assets, on a swap. These are understood to be hypothetical and are stated for purposes of calculating interest payments or service payments on the swap.

Actuals: real assets, as opposed to purely notional assets, that are traded in cash markets.

Reference rate: The rate, or price, to which the floating leg of a swap is pegged for purposes of periodic resetting.

4. The quality spread differential is the difference between: 1. the quality spread for a long-term fixed-rate financing for a poorer credit firm and a better credit firm, and 2. the quality spread for a short-term or floating-rate financing for a poorer credit and a better credit. The quality spread differential represents the maximum amount of gain that can be achieved by the counterparties to a swap because it represents the total gain that can be reaped by the counterparties from exploiting their comparative borrowing advantages.

5. There are several reasons that a domestic firm will tend to have a comparative borrowing advantage over a nondomestic firm. First, investors will tend to be more comfortable with domestic entities for legal and jurisdictional reasons. It is much clearer where and how to file a claim against a domestic issuer, relative to a foreign issuer. Second, domestic issuers tend, as a general rule, to have better name recognition in their domestic markets. Third, certain investors are barred, by regulation or policy, from investing in the issues of nondomestic issuers.

6. Bond yields and swap coupons are ordinarily quoted bond basis, which assumes either a 30/360 day-count convention, or an actual/ 365 day-count convention. Money market basis, which is the usual method for quoting LIBOR, employs an actual/360 day count convention. Thus, rates quoted by bond basis and money market basis are not directly comparable. Failure to adjust these rates to make them equivalent is like trying to compare apples and oranges. One could, quite easily, make a faulty decision with respect to which financing alternative is really most attractive if one fails to properly adjust the rate quotes.

7. The term "synthetic" is meant to imply that the strategy is itself not a real fixed rate instrument but that, when taking in its totality, it behaves like a fixed-rate instrument.

8. The plain vanilla swap is only suitable for an end user whose needs precisely match the terms applicable to a plain vanilla swap. If the end user's coupon payment frequencies, amortization requirements, preferred reference rate, or any other requirement, differs from those assumed in the plain vanilla structure, the plain vanilla structure is not suitable and a variant is called for. An end user who required

quarterly payments to meet quarterly obligations to a bank, or an end user who needed amortizing notionals to offset amortizing assets (such as a conventional mortgage portfolio) would be examples where a variant is indicated.

9. The boxed cash flow type of illustration makes it very clear who is receiving what from whom and it allows multiple and very complex cash flows to be represented at one time. The arrow cash flow diagrams are better to illustrate the timing of cash flows in and out for a single firm, but less useful for understanding the flows between firms.

10. Even though all interest rates are quoted over the span of one year, that is, as annual rates, there are nevertheless compounding assumptions that are embedded in rate quotations. These assumptions need to be made explicit, or at least to be very clear if they are implicit, to avoid confusion. For example, a three-month LIBOR rate of 7 percent is not the same as a six-month LIBOR rate of 7 percent even though both rates are stated as annual rates. The three-month LIBOR quote assumes quarterly compounding and the six-month LIBOR quote assumes semiannual compounding.

CHAPTER 3

1. Typically, a savings and loan has an interest-rate risk problem. Traditionally, S&Ls have held portfolios of conventional fixed-rate mortgages that are funded by floating rate, mostly CD, liabilities. To eliminate this risk either: 1. the fixed-rate assets must be converted to floating-rate assets (to match the interest-rate character of the liabilities) or 2. the floating-rate liabilities must be converted to fixed-rate liabilities (to match the interest-rate character of the assets). In truth, these two strategies are identical because they each result in the same interest margin. The cash flows, employing a fixed-for-floating interest rate swap to convert the fixed-rate assets to floating-rate assets is depicted in Figure 3.1. There are two special problems for the S&L. First, mortgages are amortizing instruments and, hence, the notional principals on the interest rate swap must be structured to amortize over the life of the swap. Second, the mortgagors have the right to prepay the mortgages, in whole or in part, and they often choose to avail themselves of this right. This is called

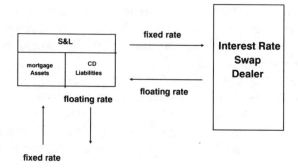

FIGURE 3.1

prepayment and it significantly complicates the amortization process. Special provisions can be included in a swap contract to deal
with this problem.

2. A callable swap is a swap in which the fixed-rate payer has the right
   to terminate the swap prior to maturity. A putable swap is a swap
   in which the floating-rate payer has the right to terminate the swap
   prior to maturity.

3. A rate-capped swap is a swap in which the floating rate is capped
   so that it cannot rise above a preset level, called the cap rate. Such
   swaps can be structured by embedding the cap into the swap or by
   purchasing a cap separately from a cap dealer.

4. A swaption is simply an option to enter into a swap at a later date.
   When the swaption is purchased, the owner is buying the right to
   enter into a later swap at a fixed swap coupon rate, which, in essence,
   represents the swaption's strike price. All other swap terms: reference
   rate, payment frequency, notionals, currencies, tenor, and so on, are
   included in the swaption contract.

5. The residual risk is that the dealer has LIBOR in and the T-bill rate
   out. Thus, the dealer has a residual interest rate risk often described
   as a form of basis risk. If LIBOR and the T-bill rate moved in perfect
   synch with one another—basis point for basis point—then this difference in interest rates would not matter. But, they do not move
   in perfect synch. The dealer can eliminate this risk by either: 1.
   entering into two other swaps with offsetting risks, 2. hedging the
   risks in T-bill and Eurodollar futures, or 3. entering into a floating-
   for-floating interest rate swap (called a basis swap) in which the

dealer is paying LIBOR and receiving the T-bill rate. The latter swap would likely be an interest rate swap with another interest rate swap dealer having the opposite exposure. Such swaps are called interbank swaps.

6. The cost of hedging refers to the cost of entering into a hedge contract, such as a futures contract or a swap. There are transactions costs, in the form of bid-ask spreads and, in the case of futures, commissions to be paid. Additionally, there are good theoretical reasons to believe that futures prices, and potentially swap prices as well, may embody a risk premium so that hedging results in small but real transfers of wealth from hedgers to other market participants.

   However, since hedging reduces risk, hedgers are usually perceived as better credits than nonhedgers and, thus, may enjoy lower financing costs. Additionally, hedgers, by controlling normal business risks can often operate on a much larger scale than can nonhedgers. These benefits accrue to the hedger and offset, to some degree, the cost of hedging.

7. Assuming the same payment frequencies, the conversion is straightforward. Money market basis is quoted actual/360 and bond basis is quoted 30/360 *or* actual/365. In either case, the conversion is:

$$\text{Bond Basis} = 9.50 \text{ percent} \times 365/360$$
$$= 9.63 \text{ percent}$$

8. Using the formula for average life presented in the text, the average life calculation is:

Principal Repaid		Year		Product
0	×	1	=	0
0	×	2	=	0
1,000,000	×	3	=	3,000,000
1,000,000	×	4	=	4,000,000
1,000,000	×	5	=	5,000,000
1,000,000	×	6	=	6,000,000
1,000,000	×	7	=	7,000,000
		Total	=	25,000,000

$$\text{Average Life} = \text{sum of products} / \text{initial principal}$$
$$= \$25,000,000/\$5,000,000$$
$$= 5 \text{ years}$$

9. For zero coupon bonds, and only zero coupon bonds, the maturity, average life, and duration are identical.

10. The quarterly rate that is equivalent to a semiannual rate of 10.32 percent is found as follows:

$$r_{qr} = (1 + r_{sa}/2)^{2/4} - 1] \times 4$$
$$= 10.19\%$$

11. Let's first calculate the buy up. What we need to do is find the present value that is equivalent to the difference between the desired coupon and the current market coupon. Since neither the tenor of the swap nor the notional principal are given, we can only represent the solution:

$$BU = \frac{1}{2}(.1148 - .1032) \times \left[\frac{(1-(1 + \frac{1}{2}(.1032))^{-2n})}{\frac{1}{2}(.1032)} \right] \times NP$$

where BU = dollar amount of buy up
       NP = notional principal on the contract

The first term denotes the coupon differential required. Notice that it is divided in half because the coupon is paid semiannually. The second term is the present value annuity factor. The third term is the notional principal.

The alternative to a buy up is to adjust the floating rate side. To adjust the floating rate, we must find the money market differential that is equal to the bond basis differential. The calculation is:

MMB differential = (11.48%–10.32%) × 360/365
                 = 1.144%

Thus, the floating-rate payer would pay six-month LIBOR plus 1.144 percent.

CHAPTER 4

1. The notional principals on an interest rate swap are in the same currency and in the same amount. Therefore, any exchange of notionals would be superfluous. In addition, it could, potentially, expose the counterparties to a settlement risk—if one party makes payment before the other and the second party defaults. Also, since swap payments are routinely exchanged on a "net" basis and the "net" is zero if the currencies and amounts are the same, dispensing

with the exchanges is consistent with the way other payments are treated. On a currency swap, the currencies are not the same and, likely, the parties to the swap will need the other currency. In such cases the exchange is useful. Additionally, since the reexchange of principals takes place at the spot exchange rate prevailing at swap initiation, and since this rate will likely have changed by swap termination, the reexchange also serves an exchange-rate risk hedging function.

2. The early currency swaps could be viewed, and many still can be viewed, as consisting of an initial borrowing in the cash markets by each counterparty followed by a swap in which these two borrowings are exchanged—so that each counterparty may be viewed as servicing the other party's debt. This is illustrated in Figure 4.1.

3. British firm's cost $= 10.45\%$ USD $+ 9.50\%$ GBP $- 9.75\%$ GBP
$$= 10.45\% \text{ USD} - 0.25\% \text{ GBP}$$
$$\approx 10.20\%$$

Gains from Swap $\approx 11.50\% - 10.20\% = 1.30\%$

American firm's cost $= 9.80\%$ GBP $+ 11.75\%$ USD $- 11.50\%$ USD
$$= 9.80\% \text{ GBP} + 0.25\% \text{ USD}$$
$$\approx 10.05\%$$

Gains from swap $\approx 10.25\% - 10.05\% = 0.20\%$

4. A midrate is simply the average of the dealer's bid and ask swap coupons (also knows as the receive and pay rates). Thus the midrate is found as:

$$\text{Midrate} = \tfrac{1}{2}(\text{pay rate} + \text{receive rate})$$

5. The buy up is nothing more than the present value of the difference between the payments that the counterparty would receive under the desired off-market swap coupon and the payments it would receive under the at-market coupon. The present value is calculated with respect to the at-market midrate. Since the present value of

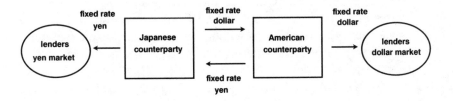

FIGURE 4.1

the rate differential in DEM has already been calculated (by step 2) as 17.332 (which represents a percentage), the present value is simply this percentage times the notionals involved:

Present value $= 17.332\% \times$ DEM 18 million

$= $ DEM 3.11976 million

6. Since the chapter deals with currency swaps, it is implied that the swap involved is a currency swap. Any time the counterparty has an *existing* liability (or asset) that needs to be denominated in a different currency, it is likely that an initial exchange of notionals will not be required. This is in contrast to a situation in which a new liability is being created and funding is required in the counterparty's currency.

7. A fixed-for-fixed currency swap can be created by a counterparty by entering into a fixed-for-floating interest rate swap as fixed-rate payer/floating-rate receiver and then entering into a fixed-for-floating currency swap as fixed-rate receiver/floating-rate payer in which the floating rate received on the interest rate swap and the floating rate paid on the currency swap employ the same reference rate. A circus swap is the combination described above. Importantly, to be a circus swap, the reference rates must be LIBOR.

8. No one would willingly enter into a swap (or any other contract for that matter) unless they believed that the value they were "getting" was at least as great as the value they were "giving." Since the only way that this can be true for both counterparties to a swap is for the values of the two legs (interest paid and interest received) to be the same. Value, as used here and everywhere in finance, means present value. Hence, swap pricing, which means setting the swap coupon, has to be done in such a way as to equate the present value of the fixed-rate leg to the present value of the floating-rate leg.

9. The cost of hedging, as defined above, ignores the ancillary monetary benefits associated with hedging. Hedged firms are generally perceived as better credit risks in the market and this should mean lower financing costs. Also, hedged firms can operate on a larger scale than unhedged firms without greater risk. Larger scale production and operation often result in lower per unit costs due to economies of scale.

10. Swaps, by enabling firms to hedge their price risks, allow firms to conduct business on a much larger scale. Most businesses enjoy certain per unit cost reductions when operating on a large scale,

relative to a small scale. These benefits are called "economies of scale." The source of economies of scale include greater production efficiency, greater bargaining power with vendors and customers, and better name recognition in the marketplace. Swaps, particularly currency swaps, can make it possible to enter markets that would otherwise be closed to the firm by allowing the firm to issue debt in one currency and then swap this obligation into the currency of the market that was closed to it.

CHAPTER 5

1. The firm entered the long-term contract at a fixed price probably to assure itself of steady supplies. If the firm enters into a fixed-for-floating commodity swap in which it receives a fixed price and pays a floating price, the net effect is to alter the nature of its long-term contract to floating price. This is illustrated in Figure 5.1.
2. The solution requires a combination of two commodity swaps. First, the country produces oil and sells this oil in the spot market at a floating (spot) price. It then enters into a fixed-for-floating commodity swap to convert this sale to fixed price. It now knows that it will receive a fixed number of monetary units (let's say dollars). Next it purchases rice in the spot market for rice paying a floating (spot) price. It then enters into a rice swap in which it pays a fixed price and receives a floating price. The swaps are sized so that the number of dollars paid on the rice swap is exactly equal to the number of dollars received on the oil swap. The end result is that

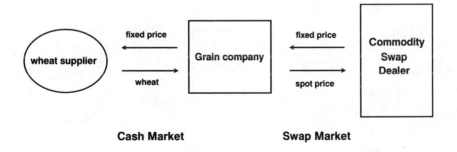

FIGURE 5.1

oil pays for rice (almost a form of barter). This is depicted in Figure 5.2.

3. The commodity swap dealer does not, ordinarily, need to be involved in physical commodity in any way. Its role is limited to monetary transfers based on what happens in the spot markets for the commodities. Nevertheless, because the value of its transactions are based on the prices in the commodity markets, it is a player in those markets.

4. This is depicted in Figure 5.4.

5. A quantro swap can be used by a pension fund, or other institutional investor, that wants to engage in asset allocation strategies. Let's suppose that a pension fund which owns a U.S. stock portfolio that generates the S&P return decides it is time to switch to a Japanese

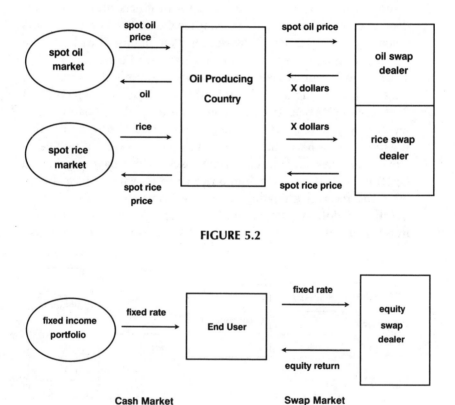

FIGURE 5.2

FIGURE 5.4

stock portfolio. But, the transaction (and other) costs associated with selling its U.S. stock portfolio and buying a Japanese stock portfolio are prohibitive. Instead, it enters into a quantro swap in which it pays total S&P return and receives total Nikkei return. For all practical purposes, the firm owns a Japanese stock portfolio. This is depicted in Figure 5.5.

6. This is analogous to the circus swap used to create fixed-for-fixed currency swaps. It is depicted in Figure 5.6.

7. A cap on an equity swap could be used to either place an upper limit on the payout of the equity-index leg or to place an upper limit on the LIBOR-leg (if the nonequity leg is floating-rate LIBOR based).

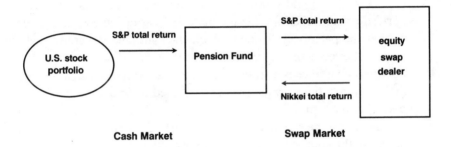

FIGURE 5.5

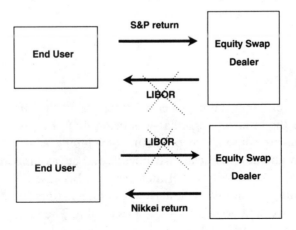

FIGURE 5.6

8. A rainbow is merely a mixture of equity index returns, for example, part Nikkei, part S&P, part DAC, and so on. An equity swap dealer could hedge such a swap with: 1. another rainbow swap, 2. a mix of simple equity swaps that collectively perform like the rainbow, 3. a mix of stock index futures contracts (if they are available), or 4. a mix of simple equity swaps and futures.

9. A number of factors, representing market imperfections, were cited in the text. Examples include: lower transaction costs, avoidance of withholding and transfer taxes, avoidance of custodial fees, and so on.

   The principal counterargument is the notion of market efficiency. If markets are truly efficient, relative to one another, then such opportunities should not exist. Also, the swap alternative to a real portfolio might overlook the creditworthiness of the counterparties so that the perceived "benefit" from the synthetic structure might be nothing more than a reward for bearing credit risk.

10. Portfolio insurance is a strategy in which derivative securities (originally futures, but now also swaps) are used to transform an equity portfolio into an effective "risk-free" portfolio. Such a portfolio should return the risk-free rate. In the early days, futures alone were used for this purpose. The investor would hold a stock portfolio and then sell stock-index futures against it. The equity risks offset each other and the investor earned the risk-free (T-bill) rate. Swaps can be used in exactly the same way. The investor would pay the equity rate and receive a fixed rate.

CHAPTER 6

1. The term "financial engineering" emerged in the late 1980s to describe the kind of work that was being done by people who were structuring solutions to problems, developing new financial technology and new financial instruments, and developing sophisticated strategies to exploit market inefficiencies. Because these people are "building" solutions, their activity is quite distinct from most other finance-related occupations that preceded it. The term also conveys the idea that financial engineering is a rigorously analytical activity

making use of cutting-edge technology. You would find financial engineers developing new forms of debt and equity, new derivative securities, designing new uses for derivatives, developing arbitrage, hedging, and speculative trading strategies, developing tax reduction or tax arbitrage strategies, and so on.

2. Yes, they do. The idea that financial engineers "build structures" by assembling them from components such as bonds, commodities, equities, swaps, caps, and so on, very much describes a "building block" approach to problem solving.

3. One possible solution is depicted in Figure 6.3.

4. The complex structure depicted in Figure 6.1 can be compressed such that the interest rate swap and the currency swap are combined into a single fixed-for-fixed rate currency swap. Since real exchanges of principal only take place on currency swaps, this consolidation is necessary. Our goal is to structure the currency swap such that

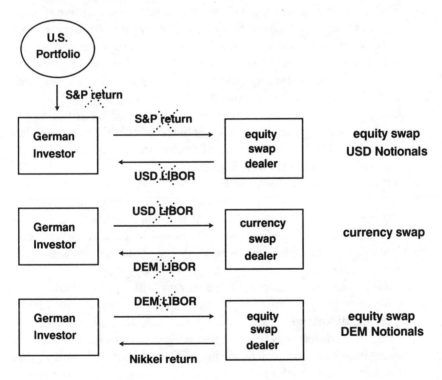

FIGURE 6.3

the swap is amortizing and gives rise to a periodic payment of $3,825,000 in exchange for a periodic payment of DEM 5,382,599.

Since we already know that the present value of the annuity payments on the dollar side is $76,365,699, an amortizing swap having notionals of this amount and a 10 percent qr swap coupon, will give rise to quarterly payments of $3,825,000.

Similarly, notionals of DEM 114,548,550 will, at an 8 percent qr swap coupon, amortize to result in a periodic exchange of DEM 5,382,599. Thus, an amortizing swap having dollar notionals of $76,365,699 and deutschemark notionals of DEM 114,548,550 will generate the appropriate cash flows. Importantly, by structuring the swap as a fixed-for-fixed amortizing currency swap, in lieu of two fixed-for-floating nonamortizing swaps, the required notionals are greatly reduced. This can have favorable consequences for bank capital requirements.

5. The term "synthetic security" refers to a structure (combination of instruments) that behaves, in terms of the size and the timing of its net cash flows, in exactly the same fashion as would a "real" security. While a synthetic security is quantitatively identical to a real security, it is not necessarily qualitatively the same. For example, one typically has to deal with multiple parties with a synthetic security and only one party with a real security. The real security and the synthetic security may have different likelihoods of default and different expected values in the event of a credit rating change, and so on.

6. The solution is depicted in Figure 6.6.

7. The solution is illustrated in Figure 6.7.

8. All-in cost is the cost side equivalent of the revenue side notion of "internal rate of return." That is, it is a single measure, expressed as a percentage of the funds actually raised in a financing, that embodies all costs including coupon interest, flotation costs, and administrative fees.

Unless all costs are considered in reviewing and evaluating different financing alternatives, one can easily select a suboptimal financing alternative.

9. Qualitative differences between financing structures refer to the nonquantitative aspects such as credit risks, complexity, accounting and tax treatments, likelihood of cash flow revisions or terminations, embedded options, and anything else that might alter either the size or timing of the planned cash flows.

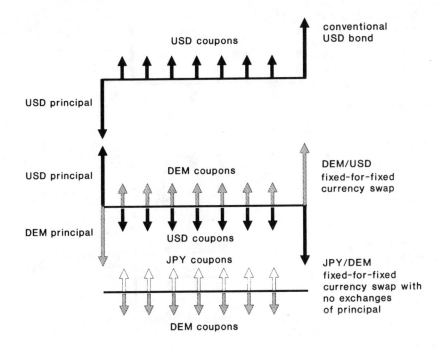

FIGURE 6.6

10. Unless we adopt a standard for objective comparison, it is difficult, if not impossible, to compare the costs of alternative financing structures. It is not actually necessary to state costs on an effective basis, provided that the method chosen is consistent for all financing structures that are compared. The advantage of the effective annual rate is that it is the easiest and clearest number to understand.

CHAPTER 7

1. The term of the Eurodollar deposit underlying the futures contract is 91 days or three months. It is found by deducting the futures price from 100 with the result understood to be a percentage. Therefore:

$$\text{implied 3-month LIBOR} = 100.00 - 95.42$$
$$= 4.58\%$$

2. A Eurodollar strip is a series of successively maturing Eurodollar futures contracts. The logic in pricing a swap contract (i.e., setting

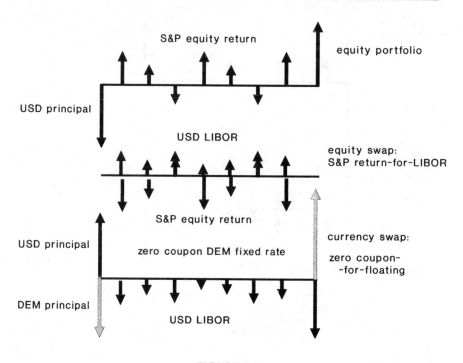

FIGURE 6.7

the fixed-rate swap coupon) off the Eurodollar futures strip rests on the assumptions that the implied three-month LIBORs are unbiased estimates of actual future three-month spot LIBOR and that long-term interest rates are the geometric average of successive short-term spot and forward rates. The long-term rates computed in this way are zero coupon rates. These zero rates can be used to derive a fixed-rate swap coupon having the same present value as the floating-rate from which the fixed rate was derived.

3. We distinguish between short-dated and long-dated interest rate swaps on the basis of how far forward Eurodollar futures are actively traded. We do so because, to the degree that forward Eurodollar futures are actively traded, we can price the fixed-rate side (i.e., the swap coupon) off these futures. Beyond the most forward Eurodollar futures, this method of pricing cannot be used and other methods become necessary.

4.   There are five steps:
      1. From the observable Eurodollar futures prices, extract the im-
          plied three-month LIBORs and use these to derive terminal val-
          ues for a single dollar that reflect appropriate compounding.
      2. From the terminal values, derive the annual bond basis zero
          coupon rates and then restate these on a quarterly bond basis.
      3. Use the quarterly bond basis zero coupon rates to derive quarterly
          swap midrates, stated on a quarterly bond basis.
      4. Restate the swap midrates on the payment frequency desired
          (usually semiannual).
      5. Price the dealer's pay/receive rates by deducting/adding an ap-
          propriate number of basis points to the dealer's midrate.

5.   A zero coupon rate is the rate of discount applicable to a single cash
      flow to be received at a single distinct point in time. A par swap
      rate is a fixed rate which, if used to discount all the cash flows
      associated with a swap, has the same present value as the floating
      leg of the swap.

6.   The 2-year swap priced in Section 7.2.1 had an annual swap coupon
      midrate of 4.4087 percent and a semiannual midrate of 4.3611 per-
      cent. The annual rate can be converted to a monthly rate using
      Equation 7.5b. That is
      $$M_{m,\tau} = [(1 + M_{a,\tau})^{1/12} - 1] \times 12$$
      $$= [(1.044087)^{1/12} - 1] \times 12$$
      $$= 4.3220 \text{ percent (monthly bond basis)}$$

7.   The first step is to treat the December 1993 Eurodollar futures con-
      tract as the spot contract (rather than the June 1993 contract). That
      is, we start the valuation process using the December 1993 contract
      (i.e., six months forward) in lieu of the June contract and then
      proceed sequentially from there. We first get the terminal values,
      then the zero coupon rates, and, finally, the swap midrate on an
      annual bond basis. The zero rates (quarterly bond basis), and the
      midrate (quarterly bond basis) are:

                    All values are six months forward
             Term   Zero coupon rates (qbb)
             0.25   4.0480%
             0.50   4.0917
             0.75   4.1978
             1.00   4.3545
             midrate = 4.3510% (qbb)

The quarterly bond basis midrate is now converted to an annual rate:

$$M_a = (1 + .043510/4)^4 - 1$$
$$= 4.4225 \text{ percent (abb)}$$

Finally, the annual bond basis midrate is converted to a semiannual rate:

$$M_s = [(1 + .044225)^{1/2} - 1] \times 2$$
$$= 4.3746 \text{ percent (sbb)}$$

8. The conventional view ignores a number of significant factors that play a role in determining the swap coupon equilibrium. Among these are: 1. the true cost of issuing and servicing debt (called the all-in cost) which reflects such things as the flotation costs and the administrative costs, 2. the cost of transacting in the swap, and 3. the qualitative differences between the real and the synthetic structure. The latter includes such things as accounting complexity and associated costs of the more complex structure, any embedded options that are involved, residual risks associated with changing spreads and credit ratings, and so on.

9. Short-term debt, relative to long-term debt, may be viewed as containing an embedded put option. That is, the investor in short-term debt retains the right to "put" the instrument back to the issuer by not accepting a rollover at the time the instrument matures. This option recurs at each rollover period. The owners of long-term debt have no such option (at least in the short run). The poorer the credit issuing the debt, the more valuable this option is. Hence, the poorer the credit, the higher the yield differential on longer-term debt necessary to induce an investor to part with the option. Thus, the yield curve is steeper for poorer credits than better credits.

10. The conventional view regards the quality spread differential (QSD) as equivalent to the total gains that can be reaped from a matched pair of swaps. However, as argued in the chapter, this overlooks a number of very important factors including the difference between all-in cost and yield, the cost of transacting in the swap, and the qualitative differences between different financing structures. These values, some of which are very difficult to quantify, can be such that they reduce the potential gains from a swap, as represented by the QSD. Indeed, it is quite possible for the QSD to be positive and for there to be no potential gains from swaps.

11. Arbitrage pressure can be expected to drive swap coupons in the direction of no gains from arbitrage. Nevertheless, there are a number of market imperfections that can cause significant and prolonged deviations from a no-gains-from-arbitrage state. Among these are swaps motivated by objectives other than the exploitation of comparative advantages—such as swaps motivated by a desire to convert the character of an existing asset or liability; expectations about future interest rates and the shape of the yield curve; and the length of time it takes to register securities with the SEC before they can be issued.

CHAPTER 8

1. Spread risk is the risk that the portion of the swap coupon that represents a "spread over Treasuries" changes in an unexpected way. This poses a risk to a swap dealer both between the time it quotes a swap coupon and actual transaction in the swap, and from holding an unmatched, but hedged, swap book if the hedging is done in the Treasury bond cash or futures markets. Since the swap coupon consists of both the Treasury rate and the spread, they are simply two components of the swap interest rate and therefore any risk associated with the spread is a form of interest rate risk.

2. The main advantage in quoting the swap coupon as a spread over Treasuries is that it allows a dealer to quote a rate and honor that rate for a period of time long enough for the potential counterparty to obtain quotes from other dealers and to make a reasoned decision. Should the Treasury yield change, the implied swap coupon also changes but the quote is unaffected. This reduces the interest rate risk for the dealer to spread risk, which is only a very small part of overall interest rate risk. Additionally, quoting rates as a spread over Treasuries is consistent with the way many other rates, such as mortgage-backed rates, are quoted.

3. Mark-to-market accounting revalues all swaps, and any other marked-to-market positions, to their values as of that point in time. Any changes in values from the previous mark-to-market then represent either a profit or a loss. Thus, if a swap dealer enters into a swap, which has a zero present value at the midrate but a positive present value at the pay or receive rate, the profit is realized im-

mediately if the dealer employs mark-to-market accounting. Mark-to-market accounting is also advantageous if it is applied to all positions including hedges. If both the swap book and the hedges are both mark-to-market, the volatility of accounting profits is greatly reduced.

4. The DV01, which stands for the dollar value of a basis point, is a measure of the dollar amount by which the market value of a standardized par value of a fixed-income instrument will change if the instrument's yield changes by 1 basis point. It is similar in concept, but less abstract, than duration. Durations measure percentage changes in value while DV01s measure absolute dollar value changes. If used properly, and with certain adjustments, duration and DV01 convey the same information and generate the same hedge ratios—when used for that purpose.

5. In the comparative advantage argument for justifying the existence of the swaps market, poorer credits benefit by borrowing short-term at floating rates and then swapping into fixed rates. Better credits do the opposite. Given this tendency for poorer credits to be fixed-rate payers/floating-rate receivers and for better credits to be fixed-rate receivers/floating-rate payers, it stands to reason that the dealer-receives-fixed-rate side of the swap book has more credit risk than the dealer-pays-fixed-rate side of the swap book.

6. Master swap agreements are agreements that govern all swaps between the same counterparties. That is, each new swap is treated as an addendum to the same swap agreement. This structure allows the netting of the swap payments and provides a better handle on managing a default should a default occur. It may also allow the parties to net the notionals and, thus, reduce the dealer's capital requirements.

7. Sovereign risk is the risk that a counterparty to a swap will be precluded from making its required payments to a swap dealer by an action of its government. Sovereign risk is clearly more likely to arise in currency swaps where the principals are often more than just notional and where currencies may cross borders. Additionally, sovereign risk will, generally, affect all swaps with counterparties in the same country and it is not, therefore, specific to individual counterparties. This suggests that dealers should limit the size of their positions based on the countries in which the counterparties are located.

8. Equation 8.1:
   DV01 = $100 × [(1 + .0775/2)^{-10} − (1 + .0776/2)^{-10}]$
         = 0.03290
   Footnote 4:
   DV01 = $-0.01 × 5 × (1 + .0775/2)^{-11}$
         = 0.03291
   (Note that the negative sign that should precede the DV01 is understood but usually not shown.)

   The difference between the DV01s measured above is due to the discrete nature of the first calculation and the continuous nature of the second. The continuous measure is a more precise measure of slope and, therefore, more accurate. For small changes, however, the difference is small.

9. The macrohedging approach has the advantage of describing the risk character of the overall swap book, as opposed to each swap individually. This has advantages in achieving a better understanding of the degree to which the risks associated with the various components of the swap book (and other nonswap positions as well) offset one another. This eliminates the need to make unnecessary hedge transactions and reduces transaction costs. It does, however, create accounting problems unless the firm adopts an across the board mark-to-market approach in accounting for profits and losses—now standard in the industry. By bucketing the cash flows, each net cash flow can be treated as an individual zero coupon bond. This allows swaps with different tenors to be combined in a rational manner.

10. Among other things, the framers of the Basle Accord were trying to standardize capital requirements, and related regulations, as they pertain to banks in the major economic powers—who are, to a growing degree, in direct competition with one another. Additionally, the framers were trying to extend the definition of capital to include off-balance sheet positions, to which capital requirements did not previously apply.

CHAPTER 9

1. Business cycle risk is the potential for corporate profits or cash flows to vary as a consequences of variations in the level of macroecon-

omic activity. This might be economic activity very generally or economic activity within the industry of which the firm is a part. Any entity with cycle-sensitive revenues has an exposure to business cycle risk. This includes corporations, national governments, and local governments.

2. Yes it is. Macroeconomic risk refers to firm-specific profit volatility associated with changes in a macroeconomic variable. Since such variables are used as indicators of general economic activity, the variations in which are ordinarily referred to as the business cycle, this terminology seems appropriately descriptive.

3. Since demand in cyclically sensitive industries varies with the business cycle, the number of product units sold will also vary with the state of the business cycle. Thus, cyclically sensitive firms may be viewed as exposed to a quantity risk on the demand size, much the same as farmers are exposed to quantity risk on the supply side.

4. First, the end user must consider which macroeconomic index is the best for purposes of pegging his or her swap. This generally means finding the index with the highest degree of correlation with its performance measure (e.g., revenue, profits, cash flow, etc.). Second, the end user must consider the lag structure between the index chosen and the performance measure. Finally, the end user must be concerned with revisions in the index used.

5. There are a number. First, the market is largely one sided. Thus, it will be very difficult, if not impossible, to run a matched book. Second, at present there is very limited ability to hedge a mismatched macro swap book with futures or other instruments. Consequently, the dealer must be somewhat innovative in developing a viable hedging program. The authors have suggested some possible solutions, but none is, as yet, ideal.

6. A macroeconomic option is a multiperiod option in which the reference rate is pegged to a macroeconomic index. These options could be structured to be macroeconomic caps or macroeconomic floors. They would be used to hedge against an adverse turn in the business cycle. Like all option hedging, they would preserve the holder's potential to benefit from a favorable turn.

7. Any cyclically sensitive firm would be a potential user. This would certainly include the home construction industry, the automobile industry, the durable goods industries, and so on. The single biggest potential user, however, is the U.S. Treasury. Since tax revenues

usually decline precipitously, the Treasury is a cyclically sensitive entity. So too are state and municipal governments, particularly those located in industrial sections of the country.

8. R^2s measure the degree of correlation (actually they are the square of the correlation coefficient, called the coefficient of determination) between two variables in the sense that they tell how much (i.e., what percentage) of the variation in the first variable is "explained" by the variation in the second variable. Since the goal in hedging is to hedge in an instrument that will perfectly offset the risk exposure, it stands to reason that the higher the R^2, the more effective the hedge will be.

Index